Jeremiah
An Archaeological Companion

Also by Philip J. King

American Archaeology in the Mideast

Amos, Hosea, Micah–An Archaeological Commentary

Jeremiah
An Archaeological
Companion

Philip J. King

Westminster/John Knox Press
Louisville, Kentucky

Book design by Christine Schueler

First edition

Published by Westminster/John Knox Press
Louisville, Kentucky

This book is printed on acid-free paper that meets the American National Stan-dards Institute Z39.48 standard. ∞

PRINTED IN THE UNITED STATES OF AMERICA

9 8 7 6 5 4 3 2 1

Library of Congress Cataloging-in-Publication Data

King, Philip J.
    Jeremiah : an archaeological companion / Philip J. King.—1st ed.
       p.   cm.
    Includes bibliographical references and indexes.
    ISBN 0-664-21920-9 (alk. paper)
    1. Bible. O.T. Jeremiah—Criticism, interpretation, etc.   2. Bible. O.T. Jeremiah—Antiquities.   3. Bible. O.T. Jeremiah—History of contemporary events.   I. Title.
BS1525.2.K56   1993
224'.2093—dc20   93-17180

To

Leon Levy

and

Shelby White

whose abiding friendship

has greatly enriched

my life

Contents

List of Illustrations

List of Maps

CHRONOLOGICAL CHART

B.C.E.	EGYPT	JUDAH	ASSYRIA	BABYLONIA
750		Ahaz 735–715	Tiglath-pileser III 744–727 Shalmaneser V 726–722	
725		Hezekiah 715–687	Sargon II 721–705 Sennacherib 705–681	
700		Manasseh 687–642	Esarhaddon 680–669	
675	Psammetichus I 663–609		Ashurbanipal 668–627	
650		Amon 642–640 Josiah 640–609		Nabopolassar 626–605
625	Neco II 609–595	Jehoahaz II 609 Jehoiakim 609–598		Nebuchadrezzar II 605–562
600	Psammetichus II 595–589 Apries 589–570	Jehoiachin 597 Zedekiah 597–586		
575	Amasis II 570–526 Psammetichus III 526–525			

ARCHAEOLOGICAL PERIODS*

Neolithic	8500 — 4300 B.C.E.
Chalcolithic	4300 — 3500 B.C.E.
Early Bronze I	3500 — 3050 B.C.E.
Early Bronze II–III	3050 — 2300 B.C.E.
Early Bronze IV/Middle Bronze I	2300 — 2000 B.C.E.
Middle Bronze II	2000 — 1550 B.C.E.
Late Bronze	1550 — 1200 B.C.E.
Iron I	1200 — 1000 B.C.E.
Iron II A**	1000 — 925 B.C.E.
Iron II B–C	925 — 586 B.C.E.
Persian	539 — 332 B.C.E.
Hellenistic	332 — 63 B.C.E.
Roman	63 B.C.E. — 324 C.E.
Byzantine	324 — 635 C.E.
Early Arab	635 — 1099 C.E.

* With respect to the chronology of the Ancient Near East, scholars are not unanimous. In the light of new archaeological evidence, chronology is constantly undergoing revision and refinement. For the most part, dates stated in this book are to be understood as only approximate.

** Iron Age II may be more simply divided as Iron II A (tenth century B.C.E.); Iron II B (ninth century B.C.E.); Iron II C (eighth century B.C.E.); Iron II D (seventh century B.C.E.).

LIST OF ABBREVIATIONS

AASOR	Annual of the American Schools of Oriental Research
ASOR	American Schools of Oriental Research
BA	*Biblical Archaeologist*
BAR	*Biblical Archaeology Review*
BASOR	*Bulletin of the American Schools of Oriental Research*
CBQ	*Catholic Biblical Quarterly*
HTR	*Harvard Theological Review*
HUCA	*Hebrew Union College Annual*
IDB	*Interpreter's Dictionary of the Bible*
IEJ	*Israel Exploration Journal*
IES	Israel Exploration Society
JANESCU	*Journal of the Ancient Near Eastern Society of Columbia University*
JAOS	*Journal of the American Oriental Society*
JBL	*Journal of Biblical Literature*
JSOT	*Journal for the Study of the Old Testament*
KAI	*Kanaanäische und aramäische Inschriften.* H. Donner and W. Röllig. 3 vols. Wiesbaden: Harrassowitz, 1962–1964
PEF	Palestine Exploration Fund
PEQ	*Palestine Exploration Quarterly*
TA	*Tel Aviv*
UF	*Ugarit-Forschungen*
VT	*Vetus Testamentum*
ZDPV	*Zeitschrift des deutschen Palästina-Vereins*

BOOKS OF THE BIBLE

OLD TESTAMENT

Book	Abbrev.
Genesis	Gen
Exodus	Ex
Leviticus	Lev
Numbers	Num
Deuteronomy	Deut
Joshua	Josh
Judges	Judg
Ruth	Ruth
1 Samuel	1 Sam
2 Samuel	2 Sam
1 Kings	1 Kings
2 Kings	2 Kings
1 Chronicles	1 Chr
2 Chronicles	2 Chr
Ezra	Ezra
Nehemiah	Neh
Esther	Esth
Job	Job
Psalms	Ps
Proverbs	Prov
Ecclesiastes	Eccl
Song of Solomon	Song
Isaiah	Isa
Jeremiah	Jer
Lamentations	Lam
Ezekiel	Ezek
Daniel	Dan
Hosea	Hos
Joel	Joel
Amos	Am
Obadiah	Ob
Jonah	Jon
Micah	Mic
Nahum	Nah
Habakkuk	Hab
Zephaniah	Zeph
Haggai	Hag
Zechariah	Zech
Malachi	Mal

NEW TESTAMENT

Book	Abbrev.
Matthew	Mt
Mark	Mk
Luke	Lk
John	Jn
Acts of the Apostles	Acts
Romans	Rom
1 Corinthians	1 Cor
2 Corinthians	2 Cor
Galatians	Gal
Ephesians	Eph
Philippians	Phil
Colossians	Col
1 Thessalonians	1 Thess
2 Thessalonians	2 Thess
1 Timothy	1 Tim
2 Timothy	2 Tim
Titus	Titus
Philemon	Philem
Hebrews	Heb
James	Jas
1 Peter	1 Pet
2 Peter	2 Pet
1 John	1 Jn
2 John	2 Jn
3 John	3 Jn
Jude	Jude
Revelation	Rev

APOCRYPHA/ DEUTEROCANONICAL BOOKS

Book	Abbrev.
Wisdom	Wis
Sirach	Sir
1 Maccabees	1 Macc
2 Maccabees	2 Macc

Preface

The late seventh century B.C.E. was a prosperous but tragic era. Biblical studies and archaeology together are revealing so much about this period as to make it one of the best known in ancient history. This was the time of Jeremiah, whose acknowledged humanness makes him an especially appealing prophet and whose political acumen makes him an especially relevant figure for the contemporary world.

In 1986, three major critical commentaries on Jeremiah appeared. Their authors are distinguished biblical scholars: Robert Carroll, William Holladay, and William McKane. I hereby express my admiration and appreciation for this trilogy, on which I have depended greatly and from which I have learned much. Holladay's focus on the historical Jeremiah, his person, life, and ministry, made his exhaustive commentary especially useful. This approach is obviously congenial to the particular interests of the present volume. These three commentators have spared me from addressing firsthand the knotty historical problems associated with the book of Jeremiah. It is well known that this book's history of formation is unusually complicated.

Intensive archaeological field work, including both excavations and surveys, is responsible for making the late seventh and early sixth centuries B.C.E. so well known. As this book was going to press, for example, the director of the Ashkelon excavations, Lawrence Stager, informed me that he and his team were in the process of uncovering the remains of the city's destruction wrought by Nebuchadrezzar in 604 B.C.E. As a consequence, the problem confronting the author of *Jeremiah: An Archaeological Companion* was not in finding pertinent archaeological data but in determining when to stop.

Archaeology has produced artifactual and inscriptional evidence touching on almost every aspect of the daily life of Judah in Jeremiah's time. As a result, cities long dead, such as Jerusalem and Lachish, have come back to life.

Viewed as a political commentary, the book of Jeremiah helps to illuminate the late seventh and early sixth centuries B.C.E. Therefore, in the context of the social and economic environment of the seventh to sixth centuries B.C.E., I have tried to deal, to a limited degree, with political, religious, social, and economic issues.

As the Notes and the Selected Bibliography attest, the scholars to whom I am indebted are too numerous to be thanked individually. Some, however, must be mentioned by name, especially Michael Coogan, James Sauer, and Lawrence Stager, who read the manuscript in whole or in part and offered valuable suggestions; also, Cynthia Thompson for her editorial skills, Catherine Alexander for the graphics, and Joseph Greene for the maps.

In addition, several archaeologists, whose excavations figure prominently in this book, generously provided photographs and graphics. I hope I have done them justice in crediting the illustrations. I am greatly honored by the friendship of so many archaeologists and biblical scholars.

The translation used in this book is that of the New Revised Standard Version which adds significantly to the clarity of the text.

Introduction
Archaeology and Biblical Studies

In a reconstruction of biblical history, dialogue between ancient Near Eastern texts, principally the Bible, and archaeological evidence has much to contribute. This is especially true today when both biblical and archaeological studies are evolving at such a rapid pace. The social sciences, with perspectives from modern sociology and anthropology, are having an important impact on both archaeology and biblical studies.

Whereas textual and artifactual data together are illuminating the ancient culture, at the same time both biblical studies and archaeology have inherent limitations and consequently must be subjected to critical analysis. From the methodological point of view, dissecting an ancient text and excavating a tell are quite similar enterprises.

The Bible

Frequently the biblical text is very complex because it may have been poorly preserved, or is ambiguous, or even tendentious. The Philistines, who are included in Jeremiah's oracles against the nations (Jer 47:1–7), are a classic example of biased biblical reporting. These most famous of the Sea Peoples lived in Canaan for six hundred years, until their demise at the end of the seventh century B.C.E. But the biblical writers fail to acknowledge the Philistines' contribution to the material culture of Canaanite civilization in the realm of technological advances, architecture, and pottery styles. Incidentally, modern-day dictionaries only perpetuate this prejudice by defining "philistine" pejoratively.

A biblical text must be interpreted by literary-critical analysis, which includes the following interrelated methods. Form criticism, focusing on the various types of oral tradition, deals with the text's preliterary state. Tradition criticism (tradition history) studies the history of oral traditions during the period of their transmission. Textual criticism attempts to establish the original wording of the text. Historical criticism seeks to understand the text in the context of time and place of authorship and transmission. Redaction criticism determines how a text was edited.

The book of Jeremiah, with its problems and uncertainties, mirrors the historical and textual difficulties inherent in biblical texts. The book contains a variety of literary forms, including poetic oracles, prose sermons, and first- and third-person narratives. The text of Jeremiah manifests substantial differences between the Hebrew and Greek versions. The complicated process of redaction reflects the Deuteronomic influence on Jeremiah.

By the definition of canon (list of religious writings deemed authoritative), the Bible as a source of historical inquiry is closed. At the same time, archaeology is a cumulative discipline, expanding almost daily by the addition of new materials.

Archaeology

Archaeology, the study of ancient cultures through the recovery and analysis of their material remains, reconstructs the past from all available data. It deals with realia defined as "the concrete, tangible objects ranging from fortresses and city walls to domestic objects, clothing, and coins. The remains of flora and fauna, including human remains, also belong to it."[1] The realia, it is said, sharpen the image that the biblical text projects, while the text illuminates the artifacts recovered in excavations. Archaeology casts light on the social, religious, and economic setting in which the political events took place.

A dialogue between archaeology and biblical studies may help to resolve some long-standing questions in biblical history. For example, understanding the complex process of Israelite emergence in the central hill country of Canaan has been a problem because the biblical record presents an ambiguous, if not contradictory, account of the "conquest" of Canaan. The literary narrative of Joshua (chs. 1–11) describes the Israelite settlement as a blitzkrieg (lightning war), whereas Judges portrays it as a gradual infiltration.

By correlating the biblical and archaeological evidence, scholars have proposed three basic models to solve the problem of settlement: conquest, peaceful infiltration into the unoccupied hill country, and internal social revolution. Although questions remain, archaeologists are able to verify the factual data surrounding the settlement and to describe traits of the inhabitants, including the nature of villages, settlement distribution, material culture, and architecture.

Archaeology has its own innate limitations, since artifacts are most often mute (uninscribed), and evidence is sometimes equivocal. As a result, archaeologists may be tempted to impose unwarranted interpretations on the realia.

Biblical Scholars and Archaeologists

Biblical exegetes (interpreters) and archaeologists must be cautious when dealing with the data of one another. With regard to biblical and archaeological evidence, the terms of one discipline cannot dictate the terms of the other. Biblical scholars who interpret the text exclusively in the light of an excavated site commit a methodological error. Similarly, excavators who allow themselves to be influenced unduly by the biblical text commit the same error.

Archaeology and Jeremiah

Archaeology is furnishing many new insights into Iron Age II, which is the era of Jeremiah. In his "judgment on the Philistines" (Jer 47:1-7), for example, Jeremiah describes the forthcoming destruction of Ashkelon and Gaza. He includes therein a prophecy against the Phoenician seaports of Tyre and Sidon, which seems strange in the Philistine context. However, during the 1992 season at Ashkelon the archaeologists, while uncovering the Babylonian destruction of 604 B.C.E., found Phoenician artifacts which suggest that the Phoenicians were allies of the Philistines.

Prophesying the destruction of Jerusalem, Jeremiah states:

> And the houses of Jerusalem and the houses of the kings of Judah shall be defiled like the place of Topheth—all the houses upon whose roofs offerings have been made (*qiṭṭeru* [burning of incense]) to the whole host of heaven, and libations have been poured out to other gods. (Jer 19:13; also 32:29)

The excavators at Ashkelon have clarified the somewhat puzzling practice of sacrificing on the roofs of houses. In the 1992 season they discovered the remnants of incense burners that had been located on the roofs of houses.

All this evidence, derived from the cooperation of biblical scholars and archaeologists, provides the subject matter of the present book.

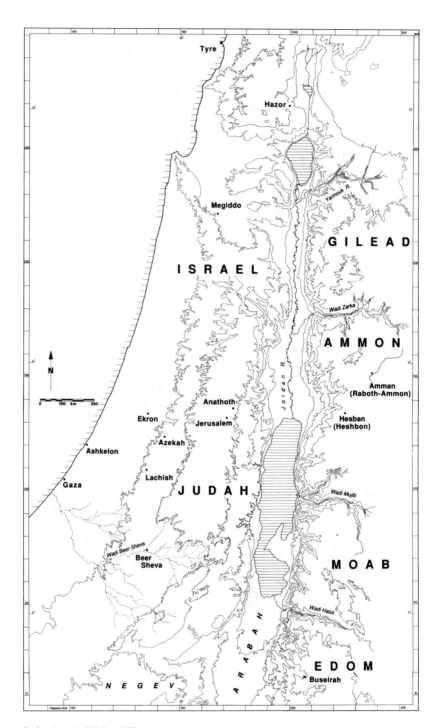

Palestine in Biblical Times

1

Jeremiah: The Prophet and the Book

Life and Ministry

Despite the fact that more is known about Jeremiah than any of the other prophets, many details of his life remain uncertain. On the basis of the biblical texts transmitted by the believing communities, which represents the final stage of the tradition, the following picture of Jeremiah emerges.

According to the common scholarly opinion, the year 627 B.C.E. marks the beginning of Jeremiah's prophetic career.[1] Jeremiah's life can be understood only in the context of the unsettled period in which he lived. He fulfilled his prophetic ministry, which spanned more than forty-five years (ca. 627–580 B.C.E.), during one of the most turbulent and tragic periods in the history of Israel.

Jeremiah (*yirmeyahu* in Hebrew) was born in the village of Anathoth, a name derived from that of the Canaanite goddess Anat and preserved in the name of the modern village of Anata, situated about two miles northeast of Jerusalem. Excavations at Anata cast doubt on its identity as the hometown of Jeremiah because evidence of pottery from the Israelite period (1000–586 B.C.E.) was lacking. Later, geographers proposed the rocky promontory of Ras el-Kharrubeh, in the vicinity of Anata, as the location of Anathoth. However, the small quantity of Iron Age pottery at this site again raised serious questions. More recently Avraham Biran proposed Deir es-Sid, situated near Ras el-Kharrubeh, as the site of Anathoth. With evidence that it was a large city in the time of Jeremiah, Deir es-Sid is a convincing location for the Anathoth of Jeremiah.

In addition to other biblical references, the book of Jeremiah mentions Anathoth several times, starting with the first verse which identifies it as the prophet's birthplace. Jeremiah's support for the reform of Josiah caused his

own family and the townspeople of Anathoth to plot against him, and even
to make an attempt on his life:

> Therefore thus says the LORD concerning the people of Anathoth,
> who seek your life, and say, "You shall not prophesy in the name of the
> LORD, or you will die by our hand"—therefore thus says the LORD of
> hosts: I am going to punish them; the young men shall die by the
> sword; their sons and their daughters shall die by famine; and not even
> a remnant shall be left of them. For I will bring disaster upon the peo-
> ple of Anathoth, the year of their punishment. (Jer 11:21–23)

As the descendants of Abiathar, the chief priest whom Solomon banished
to Anathoth for political reasons (1 Kings 2:26–27), the priests of Anathoth
may have felt even more excluded when the reformer-king Josiah decreed
the centralization of Israelite worship in Jerusalem. It meant the closing of
the local sanctuary in Anathoth where Jeremiah's priestly family served. The
prophet's support of the reform would have made the people of Anathoth
even more hostile toward him.

Remains of a house at Deir es-Sid. Pillars characterize this seventh-century
B.C.E. stone structure. Deir es-Sid may possibly be identified with Anathoth,
Jeremiah's birthplace. *Courtesy of Hebrew Union College–Jewish Institute of
Religion, Jerusalem.*

Wall of house at Deir es-Sid. Note the two niches in the western wall of the house. *Courtesy of the Hebrew Union College–Jewish Institute of Religion, Jerusalem.*

In accordance with the traditional dating, Jeremiah was born during the reign of Josiah (640–609 B.C.E.) and was called to be a prophet in the thirteenth year (627 B.C.E.) of Josiah:

> Now the word of the LORD came to me saying, "Before I formed you in the womb I knew you, and before you were born I consecrated you; I appointed you a prophet to the nations." Then I said, "Ah, Lord GOD! Truly I do not know how to speak, for I am only a boy (*na'ar*)." But the LORD said to me, "Do not say, 'I am only a boy'; for you shall go to all to whom I send you, and you shall speak whatever I command you. Do not be afraid of them, for I am with you to deliver you, says the LORD." (Jer 1:4–8)

Jeremiah's call and commission as "a prophet to the nations" took the form of a dialogue between the Lord and the young prophet. The Hebrew *na'ar* has a wide range of meanings. It may designate an unmarried male without independent status, and not yet a head of a household, as Lawrence Stager[2] points out. This title, according to Nahman Avigad, appears often on Iron Age II (1000–586 B.C.E.) seals, indicating that "there existed in the Israelite society a class of private officials who were in the service of wealthy or prominent persons."[3]

Jeremiah was not eager to embrace the prophetic vocation to which he had been predestined before birth. Prompted by personal misgivings, he protested that he was not eloquent as well as being too young. His objections echo Moses' response when commissioned to lead the Israelites out of Egypt (Ex 4:10–13). To overcome their fears, both Moses and Jeremiah were assured that the Lord's abiding presence would sustain them.[4]

Jeremiah's father, Hilkiah, was a priest, who may have been a descendant of Abiathar. Although born into a priestly family, Jeremiah appears not to have functioned as a priest. In fact, he was often in conflict with the priests of his own family as well as with the Jerusalem priesthood. He contended also with the prophets and the people:

> The priests and the prophets and all the people heard Jeremiah speaking these words in the house of the LORD. And when Jeremiah had finished speaking all that the LORD had commanded him to speak to all the people, then the priests and the prophets and all the people laid hold of him, saying, "You shall die! Why have you prophesied in the name of the LORD, saying, 'This house shall be like Shiloh [religious center destroyed by the Philistines], and this city [Jerusalem] shall be desolate, without inhabitant'?" And all the people gathered around Jeremiah in the house of the LORD. (Jer 26:7–9)

Jeremiah was prohibited from marrying and having children, factors that contributed to his loneliness. His imposed celibacy was to be a sign that all families were doomed:

> The word of the LORD came to me: You shall not take a wife, nor shall you have sons or daughters in this place. For thus says the LORD concerning the sons and daughters who are born in this place, and concerning the mothers who bear them and the fathers who beget them in this land: They shall die of deadly diseases. (Jer 16:1–4)

To soothe his loneliness Jeremiah did have some good friends, among them the Shaphan family. Ahikam, son of Shaphan, protected Jeremiah from death under King Jehoiakim:

> But the hand of Ahikam son of Shaphan was with Jeremiah so that he was not given over into the hands of the people to be put to death. (Jer 26:24; also 29:3; 36:10–12; 39:14; 40:5)

While detained in prison, Jeremiah purchased a field in his ancestral town of Anathoth as a way of keeping the property right within his own family. Those with less faith than Jeremiah thought him mad, since the property he intended to purchase was already in the territory of the enemy. But the prophet's act of purchase was a sign of his confidence that after the Babylonian exile the people of Judah would return to their homeland:

> Then my cousin Hanamel came to me in the court of the guard, in accordance with the word of the LORD, and said to me, "Buy my field that is at Anathoth in the land of Benjamin, for the right of possession and redemption is yours; buy it for yourself." Then I knew that this was the word of the LORD. And I bought the field at Anathoth from my cousin Hanamel, and weighed out the money to him, seventeen shekels of silver. . . . For thus says the LORD of hosts, the God of Israel: Houses and fields and vineyards shall again be bought in this land. (Jer 32:8–9, 15)

En route to his ancestral home in Anathoth, Jeremiah was detained, accused of desertion, and confined to prison:

> Now when the Chaldean [Babylonian] army had withdrawn from Jerusalem at the approach of Pharaoh's army, Jeremiah set out from Jerusalem to go to the land of Benjamin to receive his share of property among the people there. When he reached the Benjamin Gate, a sentinel there named Irijah . . . arrested the prophet Jeremiah saying, "You are deserting to the Chaldeans." And Jeremiah said, "That is a lie; I am not deserting to the Chaldeans." But Irijah would not listen to him, and arrested Jeremiah and brought him to the officials. The officials were enraged at Jeremiah, and they beat him and imprisoned him in the house of the secretary Jonathan, for it had been made a prison. Thus Jeremiah was put in the cistern house, in the cells, and remained there many days. (Jer 37:11–16)

After his confinement in the underground dungeon, Jeremiah was thrown into a cistern. He would have died there had Ebed-melech ("a servant of the king"), an Ethiopian palace servant, not rescued him (Jer 38:6–13).

Following the Babylonian siege of Jerusalem in 586 B.C.E., Judah became a province of the Babylonian empire. Jeremiah had the option of living in Babylon under the patronage of King Nebuchadrezzar II[5] but he declined. Instead, he remained in provincial Judah under the protection of the Babylonian-appointed governor Gedaliah, son of Ahikam:

> King Nebuchadrezzar of Babylon gave command concerning Jeremiah through Nebuzaradan, the captain of the guard, saying, "Take him, look after him well and do him no harm, but deal with him as he may ask you." So Nebuzaradan . . . and all the chief officers of the king of Babylon sent and took Jeremiah from the court of the guard. They entrusted him to Gedaliah son of Ahikam son of Shaphan to be brought home. So he stayed with his own people. (Jer 39:11–14)

After the assassination of Gedaliah, Jeremiah was taken to Egypt, against his will, along with the scribe Baruch. There is no evidence that they suffered violent death in Egypt, despite later legend.

In sum, the prophetic ministry of Jeremiah may be divided as follows: (a) from Jeremiah's call and commissioning to the reform of King Josiah (627–621 B.C.E.); (b) from the discovery of the Book of the Law in the Temple to the death of Josiah (621–609 B.C.E.); (c) from the accession of King Jehoiakim to the decisive battle of Carchemish (609–605 B.C.E.); (d) from the Babylonian victory over Egypt at Carchemish to the first deportation of Judahites to Babylon (605–597 B.C.E.); (e) from the accession of Zedekiah to the Babylonian siege of Jerusalem (597–586 B.C.E.); and (f) from the fall of Jerusalem to Jeremiah's sojourn in Egypt (586–580 B.C.E.).

Jeremiah the Man

The book of Jeremiah contains a series of candid laments, or so-called confessions, in which this most sensitive of the prophets speaks in his own name. Unique in prophetic literature, these personal prayers reveal the prophet's inner feelings, including anguish, self-doubt, bitterness, and resentment, as well as his struggles with God in the face of persecution, hatred, and ostracization. That these confessions may reflect literary convention does not detract from their poignancy. The closest verbal parallels in the Bible are the powerful laments in the book of Psalms and some of Job's speeches.

Too extensive to be quoted in full, the contents of these confessions overlap to some degree. The main features are the following. When the people of Anathoth devised a plot against Jeremiah's life, the prophet complained to God and asked why the wicked prosper (Jer 11:18–12:6). He accused God of deception, comparing God with a "deceitful brook (*'akzab*), like waters that fail." Lamenting the very day he was born, Jeremiah was filled with anger and despair (Jer 15:10–21). He called for vengeance against his persecutors who mocked him (Jer 17:14–18). Jeremiah's animosity was occasioned by religious leaders who plotted against his life (Jer 18:18–23). His bitterest words were a soliloquy in which he complained that God had deceptively coerced him into becoming a prophet, at the same time causing him to suffer ridicule (Jer 20:7–18).

Those who may be shocked by the disarming frankness of these confessions should bear in mind these words:

> God does not make his call to his servants conditional upon their purging themselves of weakness. . . . It is precisely in their weakness and frailty—even in their rebellion—that God calls his servants. So it was with Jeremiah; so it is through all the pages of Scripture; and so it is today.[6]

Jeremiah was completely dependent on God. These confessions reflect the depth of his faith, a faith that underwent lifelong trials as the prophet struggled with doubt and despair. When Jeremiah heard the call to be a prophet, he already knew it would be very costly.

Jeremiah's most appealing attribute is his humanness, a quality with which every modern reader can identify. No self-assured leader, Jeremiah was timid, reluctant, rebellious, sensitive, and introspective. He did not enjoy being misjudged, persecuted, and cursed; nor did he relish being condemned as a collaborationist and traitor for urging Judah to surrender to Babylonia as a way of averting a worse fate.

The remarkable parallels between Jeremiah and Jesus did not escape the evangelist Matthew:

> Now when Jesus came into the district of Caesarea Philippi, he asked his disciples, "Who do people say that the Son of Man is?" And they said, "Some say John the Baptist, but others Elijah, and still others *Jeremiah* or one of the prophets." (Mt 16:13–14)

Both Jeremiah and Jesus came from small towns, both suffered bitterly, both identified with the "little people" of society, both incurred the wrath of Jerusalem's civil and religious establishment, both foretold the destruction of Jerusalem and the Temple.[7]

With respect to the Temple, another parallel exists between Jeremiah and Jesus:

> The word that came to Jeremiah from the LORD: Stand in the gate of the LORD's house, and proclaim there this word. . . . Has this house, which is called by my name, become a den of robbers in your sight? (Jer 7:1–2, 11)

The contemporaries of Jeremiah looked upon the Temple as a guarantee of security, so they did not strive to reform their personal lives.

The New Testament parallel appears in the accounts of Jesus' purging Herod's Temple from profanation by merchants:

> Then Jesus entered the temple and drove out all who were selling and buying in the temple, and he overturned the tables of the money changers and the seats of those who sold doves. He said to them, "It is written, 'My house shall be called a house of prayer'; but you are making it a den of robbers." (Mt 21:12–13; also Mk 11:15–17; Lk 19:45–46)

Baruch the Scribe

Baruch[8] is a major source of information about Jeremiah, especially if the extensive biography in the book of Jeremiah (chs. 26–45) is to be ascribed to him. The fragmentary references to Baruch in the book do not provide much detail about this devoted friend and faithful secretary (*soper*) of the prophet. Baruch, the son of Neriah and the brother of Seraiah, who was King Zedekiah's minister, belonged to a distinguished family in Judah. The fact that he had access to the chamber (*liškah*) of Gemariah son of Shaphan the scribe indicates his prominence in official government circles:

> Then, in the hearing of all the people, Baruch read the words of Jeremiah from the scroll, in the house of the LORD, in the chamber of Gemariah son of Shaphan the secretary, which was in the upper court, at the entry of the New Gate of the LORD's house. (Jer 36:10)

Scribes, members of a professional class, were prominent in Judah during the late seventh and early sixth centuries B.C.E. In the period of the monarchy (1020–586 B.C.E.) the office of scribe did not carry with it any religious significance. The title was held by high royal officials. When Baruch read Jeremiah's scroll in the presence of the king's councillors, the scribes were numbered among their members (Jer 36:11–15). Besides those scribes attached to the palace, some served as secretaries transcribing documents for the general public.

On at least three occasions, according to the book of Jeremiah, Baruch was associated with the prophet. In 605/604 B.C.E. he wrote a scroll at Jeremiah's dictation and then read its menacing contents publicly in the Temple (Jer 36:1–26). Scholars have tried to reconstruct the contents of that scroll which King Jehoiakim shredded and burned, but to no avail.

Jeremiah's oracle of comfort to Baruch (Jeremiah 45) is to be read in connection with the preceding event. Baruch, agonizing over the threatening words he had been asked to read, was fearful for his life. However, the Lord assured him that his life would be spared:

> The word that the prophet Jeremiah spoke to Baruch son of Neriah, when he wrote these words in a scroll at the dictation of Jeremiah, in the fourth year of King Jehoiakim son of Josiah of Judah: Thus says the LORD, the God of Israel, to you, O Baruch: You said, "Woe is me! The LORD has added sorrow to my pain; I am weary with my groaning, and I find no rest." Thus you shall say to him, "Thus says the LORD: . . . And you, do you seek great things for yourself? Do not seek them; for I am going to bring disaster upon all flesh, says the LORD; but I will give you your life (*napšeka*) as a prize of war in every place to which you may go." (Jeremiah 45)

Baruch witnessed Jeremiah's purchase of the field of his cousin Hanamel and then deposited the deeds in an earthenware jar (Jer 32:9–15).

Baruch and Jeremiah were forced to go to Egypt following the death of Gedaliah the governor, but only after Baruch had been accused of inciting Jeremiah against the leaders of the Jewish forces (Jer 43:2–7).

Nature of the Book

Commentators distinguish three types of material in the book of Jeremiah: oracles from the prophet himself; stories about Jeremiah from Baruch; materials from the Jeremiah school of tradition.

Long, difficult, and complex are the adjectives most frequently used to describe the book of Jeremiah. The history of its formation is complicated. The book is not arranged in chronological order, and it is composite. Like the other prophetic books, Jeremiah is an anthology of oracles (an anthology of anthologies, some would say). Often, biblical books are not eyewitness accounts of the words and deeds of the persons and events they portray. Working over an extended period of time, the compilers of Jeremiah produced a book subjected to a complicated editorial process before achieving final form. In the long process of transmission, the materials in Jeremiah were revised and reinterpreted to adapt them to the religious and political situation that prevailed after the fall of Jerusalem in 586 B.C.E. This accounts for the difficulty in dating the oracles and events in Jeremiah.

Besides the problems inherent in all prophetic literature, the book of Jeremiah has its own difficulties. The differences between the Greek version (Septuagint) and the Hebrew text of Jeremiah are substantial. Not only are the content and arrangement different in each but the Greek is at least one-eighth shorter than the Hebrew.

The book of Jeremiah encompasses a variety of literary forms, including poetry, prose, and biography. Also, literary devices including puns, assonance (recurrence of similar vowel sounds), and double entendres (language that lends itself to more than one interpretation) account for some of the ambiguities in Jeremiah. In the case of double entendres, the prophet often intended both meanings.

Concerning the historical value of the book of Jeremiah, William Holladay attributes a solid historical nucleus to the prophet and maintains that the book is historically reliable. Robert Carroll, on the other hand, ascribes most of the book to the reconstruction of the Deuteronomic theologians (the compilers of Deuteronomy), who wanted to relate Jeremiah to a new situation in the exilic period. Distinguishing between authentic sayings and later interpolations is partly subjective.

These observations are not to suggest that the historical Jeremiah cannot be reconstructed; rather, they are intended to be guides. Even a casual reader would detect the lack of clear organization, logical development, and chronological order in the text of Jeremiah.

The New Testament provides an analogy with respect to the historical Jesus. The experience of the early Christian community helped to shape the figure of Jesus as portrayed in the Gospels. This Jesus is identified as the Christ of faith. In the same way, the book of Jeremiah portrays the Jeremiah of the believing community, not simply the historical Jeremiah. In the process, Jeremiah and Jesus are not diminished; they become more relevant for later generations. In other words, the Bible presents portraits, not photographs, of Jeremiah and Jesus.

Message of the Book

The book of Jeremiah, principally a collection of oracles against Judah and Jerusalem, is not a systematic theology in the modern sense, nor does it have an organizing principle. Nonetheless it is easy enough to describe its dominant theological themes.

Jeremiah was deeply conscious of the covenant ratified at Mount Sinai between God and Israel and succinctly summarized in the formula, "I will be your God, and you shall be my people" (Jer 7:23; 11:4; 24:7). Painfully aware that Israel and Judah had broken that covenant, Jeremiah looked forward to a new covenant that would mark the restoration of Israel to divine favor.

Jeremiah's optimistic description of the "new covenant" is a theological landmark in the Hebrew Bible. This vision of a new covenant, the source of the name "New Testament" (or New Covenant), is cited or alluded to several times by New Testament writers (Heb 8:8–12; 10:16–17). At the institution of the Lord's Supper, Jesus remembered the words of Jeremiah when he said to his disciples, "This cup is the new covenant in my blood" (1 Cor 11:25). The "new covenant" forms part of Jeremiah's Book of Consolation (Jeremiah 30–33), so called because of the hopeful words contained therein:

> The days are surely coming, says the LORD, when I will make a new covenant (*berit hadašah*) with the house of Israel and the house of Judah. It will not be like the covenant that I made with their ancestors when I took them by the hand to bring them out of the land of Egypt —a covenant that they broke, though I was their husband, says the LORD. But this is the covenant that I will make with the house of Israel after those days, says the LORD: I will put my law within them, and I will write it on their hearts; and I will be their God, and they shall be my people. No longer shall they teach one another, or say to each other, "Know the LORD," for they shall all know me, from the least of them to the greatest, says the LORD; for I will forgive their iniquity, and remember their sin no more. (Jer 31:31–34; also 32:38–41)

Only a prophet of boundless hope could have envisioned the restoration of Israel and Judah at the very moment the people of Judah were tottering at the edge of disaster. This new covenant, emphasizing the inwardness of personal religion as well as individual responsibility, was founded on the initiative and forgiveness of the Lord.

Jeremiah's theology, reflecting the influence of the eighth-century prophets, has much in common with Amos, Hosea, Micah, and Isaiah. Like

Amos, he denounced (although not so vehemently) the social injustice of his own people and at the same time indicted the neighboring nations for their sins. Attacking the sacrificial system, Jeremiah was vitally aware of the inescapable connection between Temple worship and social justice—the inseparableness of the holy place from the marketplace. He shared Amos's threatening view of the "day of the LORD" as a time of reckoning, not vindication.

Hosea made a deep impression on Jeremiah. No doubt the teaching of Hosea on the renewal and extension of the covenant (Hos 2:18–23) was the inspiration for Jeremiah's "new covenant." Like Hosea, Jeremiah described the relationship between God and people in family metaphors of father-son and husband-wife. Identifying infidelity to the God of Israel as harlotry and adultery, he denounced fertility cults and other abuses of the sacrificial system. Borrowing from Hosea, Jeremiah idealized the wilderness (*midbar*) as the only environment in which Israel was faithful to the Lord:

> The word of the LORD came to me [Jeremiah], saying: Go and proclaim in the hearing of Jerusalem, Thus says the LORD: I remember the devotion of your youth, your love as a bride, how you followed me in the wilderness (*midbar*), in a land not sown. (Jer 2:1–2)

The influence of Isaiah on Jeremiah, although not so pronounced, is evident. Jeremiah's oracles against foreign nations reflect Isaiah. Also, the theme of Israel as a vine is drawn from Isaiah's famous vineyard song (Isa 5:1–7):

> Yet I [the LORD] planted you as a choice vine, from the purest stock. How then did you turn degenerate and become a wild vine? (Jer 2:21)

Like Micah, Jeremiah foretold the destruction of the Temple and the city of Jerusalem in his famous "Temple sermon" indicting the people of Judah. Just as Shiloh, the original place of worship, had been destroyed by the Philistines, so too Jerusalem:

> And now, because you have done all these things [steal, murder, commit adultery, swear falsely, etc.], says the LORD, . . . therefore I will do to the house that is called by my name, in which you trust, and to the place that I gave to you and to your ancestors, just what I did to Shiloh. And I will cast you out of my sight. (Jer 7:13–15)

For Micah and Jeremiah, social justice was more important even than the survival of the Temple and Jerusalem.

An impassioned appeal by Jeremiah's supporters to the precedent set by Micah in prophesying the destruction of the Temple and the city of Jerusalem saved the life of Jeremiah, according to Baruch's version of the incident, when the prophet was accused of blasphemy:

> Then the officials and all the people said to the priests and the prophets, "This man [Jeremiah] does not deserve the sentence of death, for he has spoken to us in the name of the LORD our God." And some of the elders of the land arose and said to all the assembled people, "Micah of Moresheth, who prophesied during the days of King Hezekiah of Judah, said to all the people of Judah: 'Thus says the LORD of hosts, Zion [Jerusalem] shall be plowed as a field; Jerusalem shall become a heap of ruins, and the mountain of the house [the Temple] a wooded height.' Did King Hezekiah of Judah and all Judah actually put him to death? Did he not fear the LORD and entreat the favor of the LORD, and did not the LORD change his mind about the disaster that he had pronounced against them? But we are about to bring great disaster on ourselves!" (Jer 26:16–19)

Concerning the religious reform of Josiah, Jeremiah appeared to support it initially with enthusiasm. Then disillusionment set in when the reform failed to inspire personal repentance. It dealt more with the externals of religion—form without substance. But, then, the prophet knew that zeal can never be legislated.

No prophet had more to say about repentance than Jeremiah. The Hebrew word most often used by Jeremiah for repentance is *šub*, usually translated "return" or "turn." It is a key word in Jeremiah, who interpreted repentance as a reorientation of one's life, that is, a turning away from sin and a simultaneous turning to God. Without doubt, Hosea's frequent use of *šub* had a strong influence on Jeremiah:

> Go, and proclaim these words toward the north, and say: Return (*šubah mešubah*), faithless Israel, says the LORD. I will not look on you in anger, for I am merciful, says the LORD; I will not be angry forever. Only acknowledge your guilt, that you have rebelled against the LORD your God, and scattered your favors among strangers under every green tree [fertility rites], and have not obeyed my voice, says the LORD. (Jer 3:12–13; also 3:22; 4:1–2)

Outline of Contents

2

Historical Background

Sources

Most of the late seventh century B.C.E. was a period of independence and prosperity for Judah, although politically unsettled and a time of great tragedy. It is an especially well known era of biblical history. A wealth of archaeological remains and extant texts, both biblical and nonbiblical, makes it possible to reconstruct the historical and political background of the late seventh century B.C.E. Archaeological discoveries from excavations and surveys conducted since 1970 are providing fresh data. Several sites with seventh-century artifacts, including Lachish, Beer-sheba, Arad, and En-gedi, have already been excavated. During the seventh century B.C.E., new towns, including Tel 'Ira, Tel 'Aroer, Tel Masos, and Tel Malḥata, flourished in the Negev.

Paramount among the biblical sources is the book of Jeremiah which may be described as a personal account of the momentous events between 627 and 580 B.C.E. This book, rich in biographical and historical detail, reflects the prophet's involvement in both the political and religious realms. The books of Zephaniah, Habakkuk, and Ezekiel also cast light on this period. Other pertinent biblical texts are 2 Kings 21–25, and parallels in 2 Chronicles 33–36, dealing with the reigns of the last kings of Judah from Manasseh to Zedekiah.

Among the nonbiblical texts are the Assyrian Annals, the Babylonian Chronicle, Egyptian historical texts, and *The Antiquities of the Jews* (twenty volumes) by the Jewish historian Flavius Josephus. The Babylonian Chronicle, a contemporary and reliable collection of tablets preserved in the British Museum, is of great importance for supplementing biblical data on the final years of Judah. Despite some gaps, the Chronicle provides precise dates for events pertaining to the Neo-Babylonian empire (625–539 B.C.E.). Donald

Wiseman has made an invaluable contribution to biblical history by deciphering and translating several of these Babylonian texts.

Other contemporary written materials consist of bullae (seal impressions) from Jerusalem and elsewhere as well as ostraca (inscribed potsherds) from the fortified town of Lachish and the border fortress of Arad. These inscriptions illuminate the political, social, economic, and religious situation in Judah in the late seventh and early sixth centuries B.C.E.

Imperial Rivals

In the seventh century B.C.E., the Southern Kingdom of Judah had to cope with three principal international superpowers: Neo-Assyria, Egypt, and Neo-Babylonia (Chaldea), which were fierce rivals. Assyria had contended with Egypt, but by the reign of Judah's King Josiah (640–609 B.C.E.), Assyria and Egypt were no longer rivals but allies. The Egyptian king was a de facto Assyrian vassal. The traditional rivalry between Assyria and Egypt was transformed, ironically, into an alliance of the two superpowers between 622 and 617 B.C.E., when Egypt supported waning Assyria against rising Babylonia and its ally Media. Following Assyria's collapse in 612 B.C.E., caused by overly ambitious expansionism, another imperial power struggle developed. This time Egypt and Babylonia contended for control of the land between the Euphrates River and the Sinai, formerly ruled by Assyria. As a result, Judah found itself entrapped between Egypt and Babylonia. Later, these two imperial powers became allies against their common enemy Media.

Neo-Assyria

Tiglath-pileser III, one of the greatest conquerors among the Assyrian kings, revitalized the Neo-Assyrian empire in the second half of the eighth century B.C.E., after a fifty-year decline. Assyria became the dominant force in the Near East from 744 to 627 B.C.E., an era encompassing the reigns of Tiglath-pileser III, Shalmaneser V, Sargon II, Sennacherib, Esar-haddon, and Ashurbanipal, the last great ruler of Assyria. Tiglath-pileser reduced the Southern Kingdom of Judah to vassal status in 734 B.C.E. Sargon II conquered the Northern Kingdom of Israel in 721 B.C.E. Esar-haddon invaded Egypt in 671 B.C.E. and captured Memphis. Ashurbanipal conquered Thebes in Upper (southern) Egypt in 667–664 B.C.E., thus completing the conquest of Egypt. Until 640 B.C.E., Assyria was actively involved in the rule of the Syro-Palestinian region. After the death of Ashurbanipal in 627 B.C.E., the Assyrian empire disintegrated rapidly. By 620 B.C.E., Assyria retreated from Palestine. Then Egypt made its presence felt in the region by replacing Assyria as the imperial power. Assyria exchanged its territories with Egypt for military aid. The political situation is reflected in Jeremiah's rebuke of the people of Jerusalem, who had abandoned the LORD, their source of living water:

> What then do you gain by going to Egypt, to drink the waters of the Nile? Or what do you gain by going to Assyria, to drink the waters of the Euphrates? (Jer 2:18)

Judah Between Egypt and Babylonia

With the collapse of the Assyrian empire by 608 B.C.E., a new international struggle arose over the land that lay between the Euphrates River and the Sinai Peninsula. This time, Egypt and Babylonia were the imperial contenders; once again Judah was caught in the middle.

In Egyptian history the Third Intermediate Period (1100–650 B.C.E.), beginning with the Twenty-first Dynasty, was for the most part an era of decline. The Twenty-sixth (Saite) Dynasty (656–525 B.C.E.), inaugurating the Late Period in Egyptian history, was a time of resurgence. This dynasty ruled until the Persians under Cambyses invaded Egypt in 525 B.C.E. Psammetichus I (Psamtik I, 663–609 B.C.E.), uniting all Egypt under his rule in 656 B.C.E., established the Twenty-sixth Dynasty at Sais in the west central Delta and brought prosperity to the country. Among the international rivals he chose to ally Egypt with Assyria against Babylonia. The succeeding pharaohs of the Saite dynasty were Neco II (609–595 B.C.E.), Psammetichus II (595–589 B.C.E.), Apries (Hophra, 589–570 B.C.E.), Amasis II (570–526 B.C.E.), and Psammetichus III (526–525 B.C.E.).

Neo-Babylonia (Chaldea)

Neo-Babylonia eventually took the place of Assyria and Egypt. The Hebrew word *kasdim* meaning Chaldea, used seventy-seven times in Jeremiah, is the biblical term for Neo-Babylonia. Chaldea, synonym for Babylonia, designates the land of southern Babylonia (modern southern Iraq). Chaldea also refers to the last dynasty of Babylonia (625–539 B.C.E.), inaugurated by Nabopolassar (626–605 B.C.E.), and includes the celebrated Nebuchadrezzar II (605–562 B.C.E.). The Neo-Babylonian empire continued in existence until its defeat by Cyrus the Great of Persia in 539 B.C.E.

Babylon ("gate of God") was the Mesopotamian capital from the time of Hammurabi (1792–1750 B.C.E.) through the Neo-Babylonian period. Encompassing 2,100 acres, Babylon's fortifications included a double gateway, known as the Ishtar (one of the principal deities of Babylon) gate, and also many temples. The famous Ishtar gate, now reconstructed and standing at the modern entrance to ancient Babylon, was flanked with towers of blue-enameled brick decorated with bulls and dragons. The capital city lies about

Reconstruction of ancient Babylon. Artist's reconstruction of an elevated view of Babylon: the processional avenue and the approach to the city walls through the Ishtar gate, with the Hanging Gardens (one of the Seven Wonders of the Ancient World) in the upper right. Beyond the Hanging Gardens is the ziggurat, Etemenanki, popularly known as the Tower of Babel, which Nebuchadrezzar II rebuilt. *Reconstruction painting in oils by Maurice Bardin, 1936, after a watercolor by Herbert Anger. Courtesy of the Oriental Institute, University of Chicago.*

sixty miles due south of modern Baghdad. It was Nabopolassar's intention to make Babylon the center of culture in the ancient Near East.

Archaeologists under the leadership of Robert Koldewey worked at the ancient ruins of Babylon from 1899 to 1917. In the course of several excavations the fortifications, palaces, and temples were discovered. Before the Persian Gulf War in 1991, the Iraqi government was engaged in elaborate restoration of Babylon. Preservation of ancient sites in Iraq is especially difficult for two reasons: the original constructions were mudbrick and the water table is continually rising.

By the end of Ashurbanipal's reign in 627 B.C.E., when the vast Assyrian kingdom began to unravel, satellite nations took advantage of its weakness. In that turbulent period Nabopolassar revolted against Assyria, asserted his independence, and chose Babylon as his capital.

Nabopolassar entered into an alliance with the Medes who were leaders of the anti-Assyrian coalition. Media designates the region of northwest Iran, southwest of the Caspian Sea and north of the Zagros Mountains. Assur on the Tigris River in northern Mesopotamia (modern Iraq), the first capital of Assyria, was destroyed in 614 B.C.E. by a coalition of Babylonians and Medes. The same coalition destroyed Nineveh, the last capital of the Assyrian empire, in 612 B.C.E. Situated on the east bank of the Tigris opposite modern Mosul, Nineveh was one of the greatest and largest cities of Mesopotamia. The textual and artifactual remains unearthed at Nineveh have cast more light on the history of Mesopotamia than any other ancient site. A Babylonian-led coalition plundered Harran in 610 B.C.E. Harran ("Haran" in the Bible) in northern Mesopotamia (modern Turkey) was an important commercial center, located on the main route from Nineveh on the east to Aleppo on the west.

Judah

King Manasseh (687–642 B.C.E.), a loyal Assyrian vassal, reigned longer than any king in the Davidic dynasty. He ruled during a period of peace and prosperity. His long reign bridged the chronological gap between the eighth-century prophets (Amos, Hosea, Micah, Isaiah) and their seventh-century counterparts (Jeremiah, Zephaniah, Nahum, Habakkuk). It is remarkable that Manasseh experienced no contemporary prophetic opposition, although the author of the books of Kings strongly condemns him. Among his achievements, he built a new outer wall to strengthen the defenses of the City of David. Jeremiah remembered him negatively for reversing the religious reform measures instituted by his father Hezekiah:

> I [the LORD] will make them [people of Judah] a horror to all the kingdoms of the earth because of what King Manasseh son of Hezekiah of Judah did in Jerusalem. (Jer 15:4)

The last five kings of Judah reigned during the lifetime of Jeremiah: Josiah (640–609 B.C.E.), Jehoahaz (Shallum, 609 B.C.E.), Jehoiakim (Eliakim, 609–598 B.C.E.), Jehoiachin (597 B.C.E.), and Zedekiah (Mattaniah, 597–586 B.C.E.). They vacillated in their loyalty between Egypt and Babylonia. Although the Kingdom of Judah was formally under the control of Egypt, it did enjoy limited independence. Abraham Malamat's extensive analysis of the last days of Judah is sharply perceptive.[1]

Among these Judahite kings, the anti-Egyptian Josiah was by far the most distinguished. Josiah enjoyed a prolonged period of peace during his reign. Nonetheless his kingdom could not compare in strength with the Judahite kingdom of the previous century. During the first half of his kingship he was vassal of Assyria; then he became vassal of Egypt. As the Egyptian king Neco II was an ally of Assyria, King Josiah was an ally of Babylonia. The *'am ha'ares* ("people of the land"), a strong anti-Egyptian faction, supported Josiah's position. Despite his short life (he died at the age of thirty-nine), Josiah's achievements were historic. He has often been compared to King David, beginning with the Deuteronomic historian. Two significant events in his reign were the rise of the Neo-Babylonian empire in 625 B.C.E. and the call and commission of the prophet Jeremiah.

Josiah, like King Hezekiah before him, enacted religious and political reform measures in Judah (2 Kings 22–23; 2 Chronicles 34–35). Josiah's reform, some suggest, was a way of expressing independence from political influence of the neighboring powers by the eradication of foreign cults.[2] This reform, inspired by the book of Deuteronomy (chs. 12–26), also known as the Deuteronomic Code, mandated purification of worship and its centralization in the Temple of Jerusalem, thus making the Temple the only legitimate sanctuary in Judah. In 622 B.C.E., while the Temple was undergoing repair, a manuscript, identified as Deuteronomy, was discovered therein and precipitated the reform. At first, Jeremiah was enthusiastic about the reform, but his interest waned when it proved ineffective.

It is often stated that under Josiah's rule Judah enjoyed political freedom, allowing the king to expand control northward to the Assyrian province of Samaria (the former Northern Kingdom of Israel), westward to the coastal plain adjacent to the East Mediterranean, and eastward to En-gedi, an oasis on the western shore of the Dead Sea. Nadav Na'aman,[3] who has made a fresh study of the Kingdom of Judah under Josiah, agrees that Josiah could have expanded into the Samarian hill country, although evidence is not that clear. Na'aman insists, however, that Josiah did not annex the region of Samaria. Because the Bible relates that Josiah removed the shrines of the high places in Samaria (2 Kings 23:19) and Galilee (2 Chr 34:6), commentators argue this would not have been possible unless Josiah had political control over the northern country. Na'aman maintains there is no basis for asserting that either Galilee or the Jezreel Valley were included within the boundaries of Josiah's kingdom. Egypt would not have tolerated such territorial expansion.

Na'aman gives reasons why Josiah was unable to expand westward. In the first place, Egypt with a special interest in the Philistine coast would not have tolerated it. Also, Ekron was a geopolitical boundary that functioned as a buffer between Judah and the Mediterranean coast. Ekron (Tel Miqne), a sixty-three-acre city in the seventh century B.C.E., was situated on the frontier between Philistia and Judah. It was also the largest olive oil production center in the ancient Near East. Trude Dothan and Seymour Gitin, excavators of Ekron, have uncovered more than a hundred olive oil presses there.

With regard to the eastward expansion of Judah under Josiah, the Hebrew University excavations in the 1960s at Tel Goren in the En-gedi oasis unearthed the earliest settlement at the site. It extended from the time of Josiah (about 630 B.C.E.) until the complete destruction of the site, apparently by Nebuchadrezzar, in 582 B.C.E.

Concerning the circumstances of Josiah's death near Megiddo (in northwestern Palestine) at the hands of Pharaoh Neco II of Egypt in 609 B.C.E., the Bible makes only a few cryptic comments (2 Kings 23:29–30; 2 Chr 35:20–24), and these two accounts do not agree.[4] It is generally assumed that Josiah lost his life in battle as he tried to prevent the Egyptians from advancing northward to bolster the Assyrians in their struggle for Harran against the Babylonians. Asshur-uballit II, the last king of Assyria, was being besieged by the Babylonians and the Medes.

Na'aman makes a more convincing case. As he indicates, Neco's trek would have been shorter and less exhausting had he proceeded by sea to the Lebanese coast, and only then overland. Also, Josiah would have been foolhardy to engage the Egyptian army on the open battlefield. In reality, Neco came to Palestine, according to Na'aman, to administer the oath of fealty. When Josiah reported to the Egyptian ruler at Megiddo to swear the oath, Neco suspected him of disloyalty and killed him. Josiah's death put an end to Judah's prosperity. Palestine and Syria then came under the direct rule of Egypt.

Jeremiah paid Josiah a great tribute, while at the same time drawing an invidious comparison between him and his son Jehoiakim. Addressing Jehoiakim, the prophet said of Josiah:

> Did not your father [Josiah] eat and drink and do justice and righteousness? Then it was well with him. He judged the cause of the poor and needy; then it was well. Is not this to know me? says the LORD. (Jer 22:15–16)

Jehoahaz (Shallum) was proclaimed king upon the death of his father Josiah. After only three months, Neco deported him to Egypt, where he died. Jeremiah prophesied concerning Jehoahaz:

> For thus says the LORD concerning Shallum [Jehoahaz] son of King Josiah of Judah, who succeeded his father Josiah, and who went away from this place [Jerusalem]: He shall return here no more, but in the place [Egypt] where they have carried him captive he shall die, and he shall never see this land again. (Jer 22:11–12)

Pharaoh Neco designated the pro-Egyptian Jehoiakim (Eliakim), a son of Josiah, to succeed Jehoahaz. This puppet of Neco acted as a vassal of Egypt for four years. With the decisive Babylonian victory over Egypt in 605 B.C.E. at Carchemish, Jehoiakim then became a vassal of Babylonia for the next three years. In 601 B.C.E., contrary to Jeremiah's counsel, Jehoiakim rebelled against Babylon in favor of Egypt on the occasion of a conflict between Egypt and Babylon, hoping thereby to receive Egyptian aid. This military contest, most likely on the Egyptian border, between the two opposing imperial powers was indecisive. In fact, Nebuchadrezzar was almost defeated by the Egyptians, with both sides sustaining serious losses.

Judah's independence ceased at the end of Jehoiakim's reign in 598 B.C.E., when Babylon forced Jerusalem to surrender.

Jehoiakim had been a failure as ruler on both domestic and international fronts. Self-indulgent and luxury-loving, he was cast in the mold of Solomon. Describing the building of Jehoiakim's palace, Jeremiah delivered an invective against Jehoiakim who, by enlisting forced labor and then refusing to compensate the builders of his lavish palace, sinned against social justice:

> Woe to him who builds his house by unrighteousness, and his upper rooms by injustice; who makes his neighbors work for nothing, and does not give them their wages. . . . But your eyes and heart are only on your dishonest gain, for shedding innocent blood, and for practicing oppression and violence. (Jer 22:13, 17)

Apparently Jeremiah and Jehoiakim detested each other. Jehoiakim, furious at Jeremiah's prediction of the king's defeat by the Babylonians, defiantly burned the prophet's scroll and then sought to arrest Jeremiah and Baruch. Jeremiah, speaking for the Lord, made two dire predictions about the king's demise:

> With the burial of a donkey he [Jehoiakim] shall be buried—dragged off and thrown out beyond the gates of Jerusalem. (Jer 22:19)

> He [Jehoiakim] shall have no one to sit upon the throne of David, and his dead body shall be cast out to the heat by day and the frost by night. (Jer 36:30)

In ancient society, denial of proper burial was a great curse, especially in the case of a king.

Nebuchadrezzar II

The most powerful figure in this era was Nebuchadrezzar II (605–562 B.C.E.), the oldest son and successor of Nabopolassar. The original Akkadian royal name means "O Nabu, protect my offspring." Best known for his military exploits and his expansionist policies, Nebuchadrezzar undertook impressive building activities at the city of Babylon and elsewhere in Babylonia, including palaces, temples, canals, and ziggurats, as archaeological remains and extant building inscriptions attest. The fabled Hanging Gardens of Babylon, one of the Seven Wonders of the Ancient World, are attributed to Nebuchadrezzar. The term Hanging Gardens probably describes roof gardens planted on a series of terraces, although archaeologists have not found any such remains.

In 605 B.C.E., Neco, who had spent most of his reign fighting Babylon unsuccessfully, suffered a stunning defeat at the hands of Nebuchadrezzar, crown prince of Babylon, at Carchemish on the west bank of the Euphrates River. This marked Nebuchadrezzar's first great military victory. Carchemish (modern Jerablus), the principal Egyptian base on the Euphrates, northeast of Aleppo, is situated today just inside Turkey, across the Syrian border. Under Sargon II of Assyria (721–705 B.C.E.), Carchemish was the capital of an Assyrian province. The battle of Carchemish was decisive for the Babylonians; after 605 B.C.E. they experienced their greatest prosperity. Charles Woolley, excavating at the site in 1912–1914, unearthed the remains of weapons that indicated a fierce struggle. The battle of Carchemish is well documented in the Babylonian Chronicle:

> He [Nebuchadrezzar] crossed the river [Euphrates] (to go) against the Egyptian army which was situated in Carchemish and . . . they fought with each other and the Egyptian army withdrew before him. He defeated them (smashing) them out of existence. As for the remnant of the Egyptian army which had escaped from the defeat so (hastily) that no weapon had touched them, the Babylonian army overtook and defeated them in the district of Hamath, so that not a single man [escaped] to his own country. (British Museum Tablet No. 21946)[5]

As a result of this decisive Babylonian victory over the Egyptians that gave the Babylonians control over the Assyrian empire (including Syria and Palestine), Jeremiah advocated Judah's voluntary submission to the Babylonians, the new imperial power. The Lord, according to Jeremiah, was using the Babylonians to punish the people of Judah:

> Therefore thus says the LORD of hosts: Because you have not obeyed my words, I am going to send for all the tribes of the north, says the LORD, even for King Nebuchadrezzar of Babylon, my servant, and I will bring them against this land and its inhabitants, and against all

these nations around; I will utterly destroy them, and make them an object of horror and of hissing, and an everlasting disgrace. (Jer 25:8–9)

In Jeremiah's messages addressed to the nations, he commemorated the defeat of Neco at Carchemish:

Concerning Egypt, about the army of Pharaoh Neco, king of Egypt, which was by the river Euphrates at Carchemish and which King Nebuchadrezzar of Babylon defeated in the fourth year [605 B.C.E.] of King Jehoiakim son of Josiah of Judah. (Jer 46:2)

In 604 B.C.E., Nebuchadrezzar destroyed the Philistine city-state of Ashkelon on the East Mediterranean coast, twelve miles north of Gaza. Jeremiah included the Philistine city-states of Gaza and Ashkelon in his judgment on the Philistines:

Baldness has come upon Gaza, Ashkelon is silenced. O remnant of their power! How long will you gash yourselves? Ah, sword of the LORD! How long until you are quiet? Put yourself into your scabbard, rest and be still! How can it be quiet, when the LORD has given it an order? Against Ashkelon and against the seashore—there he has appointed it. (Jer 47:5–7)

In 1992, Lawrence Stager uncovered at Ashkelon the archaeological evidence for this Babylonian destruction which Jeremiah described.

For biblical history, a far more devastating event took place in 597 B.C.E. when Nebuchadrezzar laid siege to Jerusalem, capturing the city and imposing tribute. The Babylonian Chronicle furnishes details about this attack that resulted in the fall of the city on March 16:

In the seventh year, in the month of Kislev [December], the Babylonian king [Nebuchadrezzar] mustered his troops, and, having marched to the land of Hatti [Syria and Palestine], besieged the city of Judah [Jerusalem], and on the second day of the month of Adar [March] took the city and captured the king [Jehoiachin]. He appointed therein a king of his own choice [Zedekiah], received its heavy tribute and sent (them) to Babylon. (British Museum Tablet No. 21946)[6]

Jehoiachin (Jeconiah, Coniah), who succeeded Jehoiakim in 597 B.C.E., reigned only three months. Having resisted Babylonia, he surrendered on March 16, 597 B.C.E. He, family members, retinue, and prominent citizens, were exiled to Babylon. The deportation of the elite inevitably destabilized Judah. Had Jehoiachin not surrendered to Babylonia, Judah would have been annihilated.

Jeremiah prophesied the redemption of these deportees from Babylonian captivity:

I [the LORD] will set my eyes upon them for good, and I will bring them back to this land [Judah]. I will build them up, and not tear them down; I will plant them, and not pluck them up. I will give them a heart to know that I am the LORD; and they shall be my people and I will be their God, for they shall return to me with their whole heart. (Jer 24:6–7)

Zedekiah (Mattaniah), the last king of Judah, ruled as a Babylonian puppet during the final decade of Judah's existence. He was a tragic figure. Jeremiah, always the realist, counseled him not to revolt against Babylonia but to surrender, if Judah was to survive:

I [Jeremiah] spoke to King Zedekiah of Judah in the same way: Bring your necks under the yoke of the king of Babylon [Nebuchadrezzar], and serve him and his people, and live. Why should you and your people die by the sword, by famine, and by pestilence, as the LORD has spoken concerning any nation that will not serve the king of Babylon? Do not listen to the words of the prophets who are telling you not to serve the king of Babylon, for they are prophesying a lie to you. (Jer 27:12–14)

Zedekiah, a benevolent ruler well disposed toward Jeremiah, was eager to heed his advice. But Zedekiah's ambivalence and indecision prevented him from doing so, pulled as he was in opposite directions by the pro-Egyptian and the pro-Babylonian factions:

Zedekiah son of Josiah, whom King Nebuchadrezzar of Babylon made king in the land of Judah, succeeded Coniah [Jehoiachin] son of Jehoiakim. But neither he nor his servants nor the people of the land listened to the words of the LORD that he spoke through the prophet Jeremiah. (Jer 37:1–2)

Zedekiah had affection for Jeremiah, and the prophet in turn never condemned the king. One of the most poignant scenes in the book of Jeremiah is the meeting between the king and the prophet:

Then King Zedekiah sent for him [Jeremiah], and received him. The king questioned him secretly in his house, and said, "Is there any word from the LORD?" Jeremiah said, "There is!" Then he [Jeremiah] said, "You shall be handed over to the king of Babylon [Nebuchadrezzar]." (Jer 37:17)

In 594 B.C.E., Zedekiah, who had been enthroned by Babylonia, made the tactical error of convoking in Jerusalem an anti-Babylonian conference of neighboring states, including Edom, Moab, Ammon, Tyre, and Sidon (Jer 27:3). Egypt may have been responsible for stirring up anti-Babylonian sentiments in Zedekiah.

Early in his reign Pharaoh Apries (Hophra) prodded King Zedekiah of Judah to revolt against the Babylonians. He supported Judah for the moment but then withdrew. Zedekiah's revolt was fatal, leading to the fall of Jerusalem and the conquest of Judah. Jeremiah alluded to Apries' brief intervention:

> Meanwhile, the army of Pharaoh [Apries] had come out of Egypt; and when the Chaldeans [Babylonians] who were besieging Jerusalem heard news of them, they withdrew from Jerusalem. (Jer 37:5)

On January 15, 588 B.C.E., Nebuchadrezzar laid siege to Jerusalem, but the city was able to hold out for a year and a half. Siege walls were built around the city to force the inhabitants into starvation:

> On the ninth day of the fourth month the famine became so severe in the city [Jerusalem] that there was no food for the people of the land. (Jer 52:6)

After Jerusalem's walls had been breached, the capital city and its Temple were destroyed by fire. The Temple was ravaged about August 5, 586 B.C.E. Between August 14 and 17, 586 B.C.E., Jerusalem was totally destroyed. Discrepancy of dates is attributed to different chronological calculations.

Zedekiah fled Jerusalem in the direction of the Jordan River, but he was intercepted by the Babylonian army and then compelled to witness the execution of his two sons. With his eyes gouged out, Zedekiah was taken in chains to Babylon, where he succumbed (2 Kings 25:4–7):

> The king of Babylon [Nebuchadrezzar] killed the sons of Zedekiah before his eyes, and also killed all the officers of Judah at Riblah. He put out the eyes of Zedekiah, and bound him in fetters, and the king of Babylon took him to Babylon, and put him in prison until the day of his death. (Jer 52:10–11)

Riblah (modern Ribleh), a city in the Lebanese Beqaa valley, is about twenty miles south of Homs (Syria). It was strategically located in ancient times on the cross-section of military highways. Neco had imprisoned King Jehoahaz at Riblah.

Exile

The second deportation from Judah to Babylon followed the destruction of 586 B.C.E. Among the people of Judah only the leading citizens went into exile. Excavations of the Judahite towns and fortresses, located in the She-phelah (low hill separating the coastal plain from the central mountain ridge), the Negev (the southern part of Judah), and the Judean Desert (bordering on the Dead Sea), reveal signs of their destruction during the Babylonian invasion. Not everything was destroyed, however, as archaeology attests. At Ketef Hinnom, a site facing Jerusalem's walls, the Iron Age II culture continued through the late sixth century B.C.E., quite long after the devastation wrought by the Babylonians in 586 B.C.E.

The book of Jeremiah also attests that life went on in Judah and Jerusalem after the Babylonian invasion. The peasants who remained behind in Judah were able to continue their life, and some pilgrims worshiped amidst the ruins of the Jerusalem Temple:

> On the day after the murder of Gedaliah [Babylonian-appointed governor of Judah], before anyone knew of it, eighty men arrived from Shechem and Shiloh and Samaria [in the northern province], with their beards shaved and their clothes torn, and their bodies gashed, bringing grain offerings and incense to present at the temple of the LORD. (Jer 41:4–5)

This graphic description of the pilgrims suggests they were participating in mourning rites.

In the aftermath of the fall of Jerusalem and the destruction of the Temple, Judah became a Babylonian province, with Gedaliah, a non-Babylonian, appointed as governor. He was headquartered at Mizpah (Tell en-Nasbeh), eight miles north of Jerusalem in the territory of Benjamin, on the border between Judah and Israel. This indicates that the Babylonians had not destroyed Benjamin. Mizpah became the capital of the new Babylonian province, replacing Jerusalem. William Badè conducted important excavations at Tell en-Nasbeh between 1926 and 1935.

Nebuzaradan, a Babylonian high official, gave Jeremiah the choice of going to Babylon or to Mizpah to join Gedaliah:

> Then Jeremiah went to Gedaliah son of Ahikam at Mizpah, and stayed with him among the people who were left in the land. (Jer 40:6)

With the collusion of Baalis, king of the Ammonites (in Transjordan), Ishmael, a member of the royal family and a nationalist fanatic, murdered Gedaliah in 582 B.C.E.:

> In the seventh month, Ishmael son of Nethaniah son of Elishama, of the royal family, one of the chief officers of the king, came with ten men to Gedaliah son of Ahikam, at Mizpah. As they ate bread together there at Mizpah, Ishmael son of Nethaniah and the ten men with him got up and struck down Gedaliah son of Ahikam son of Shaphan with the sword and killed him, because the king of Babylon had appointed him governor in the land. (Jer 41:1–2)

After the assassination of Gedaliah, Jeremiah was taken against his will to Egypt, where he prophesied that Nebuchadrezzar would invade that land:

> He [Nebuchadrezzar] shall come and ravage the land of Egypt, giving those who are destined for pestilence, to pestilence, and those who

are destined for captivity, to captivity, and those who are destined for the sword, to the sword. . . . He shall break the obelisks [pillars] of Heliopolis, which is in the land of Egypt; and the temples of the gods of Egypt he shall burn with fire. (Jer 43:11, 13)

Heliopolis is the Greek name of the ancient city of On ("city of the pillar"), seven miles northeast of Cairo.

During the reign of Pharaoh Amasis II (570–526 B.C.E.), Nebuchadrezzar attacked Egypt in 568 B.C.E., as Jeremiah had prophesied:

The word that the LORD spoke to the prophet Jeremiah about the coming of King Nebuchadrezzar of Babylon to attack the land of Egypt. (Jer 46:13)

Amel-Marduk (Evil-merodach), son of Nebuchadrezzar, succeeded his father in 562 B.C.E. The book of Jeremiah ends with a note about the captivity of Jehoiachin, indicating he was pardoned after thirty-seven years:

In the thirty-seventh year of the exile of King Jehoiachin of Judah, in the twelfth month, on the twenty-fifth day of the month, King Evilmerodach of Babylon, in the year he began to reign [562 B.C.E.], showed favor to King Jehoiachin of Judah and brought him out of prison; he spoke kindly to him, and gave him a seat above the seats of the other kings who were with him in Babylon. So Jehoiachin put aside his prison clothes, and every day of his life he dined regularly at the king's table. For his allowance, a regular daily allowance was given him by the king of Babylon, as long as he lived, up to the day of his death. (Jer 52:31–34)

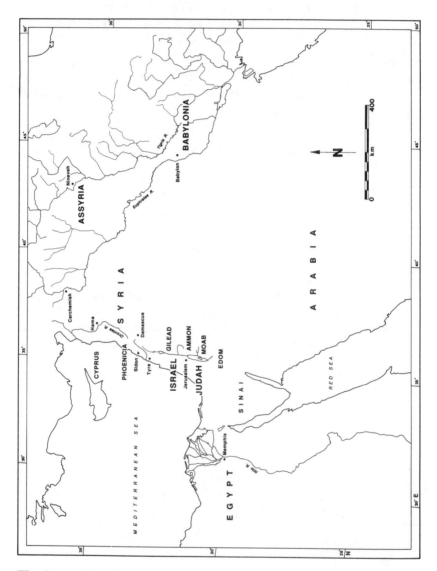

The Ancient Near East

3

Geographical Setting

Biblical narratives are often rich in geographical details. The contents of the Bible are so closely related to their geographical setting that the study of the place-names from the Bible is a valuable scholarly discipline, known as toponomy. Determining the historical identification of archaeological sites requires the application of combined evidence garnered from relevant disciplines, including historical philology, linguistics, archaeology, and physical geography.

One of the purposes of a topographic survey is to establish the location of ancient sites. In the process the surveyors photograph and plan the remains of sites, collect surface potsherds and other artifacts, and sketch maps. Far more detailed study follows upon these preliminary steps. Today, regional surveys are complementing, when not replacing in some cases, the excavation of isolated mounds (tells). The surface survey provides a far more comprehensive understanding of the region as a whole.

Only in the second half of the nineteenth century did the geography of Palestine become a scholarly quest. Edward Robinson, an American biblical scholar, was responsible in large measure for demonstrating the importance of biblical geography. On the basis of only two visits to Palestine, in 1838 and again in 1852, Robinson made a lasting contribution to the historical geography of the Bible. He described the physical and historical geography of Palestine as well as identifying many biblical sites. His traveling companion Eli Smith, an American missionary in Syria who was fluent in Arabic, was able to recognize ancient biblical place-names preserved in Arabic forms.

As a consequence of Robinson's pioneer work, the Palestine Exploration Fund, based in London, conducted between 1871 and 1878 a survey of most of western Palestine. Later, Nelson Glueck's survey of Transjordan, begun in the 1930s, produced valuable insights into the historical geography of that region. Today, a large number of regional surveys are under way in both

Israel and Jordan and to a lesser degree in Syria and adjacent countries of the Middle East. These recent surveys are correcting some conclusions of earlier ones on the basis of new evidence. With respect to Transjordan (Ammon, Moab, and Edom), the archaeology of the Bronze and Iron ages is just at the beginning, despite what archaeologists have already accomplished.

Oracles Against the Nations (Jeremiah 46–51)

The book of Jeremiah contains a long list of place-names, concentrated in the final section known as "oracles against the nations" (Jer 46:1–51:64). This segment begins with the formula: "The word of the LORD that came to the prophet Jeremiah concerning the nations" (Jer 46:1). Elsewhere in the prophetic books (Isaiah, Ezekiel, Amos, Nahum, Obadiah, Zephaniah), as well as in nonbiblical literature, "oracles against the nations" appear. Jeremiah's "oracles against the nations," beginning with Egypt and ending with Babylon, form a geographical pattern that moves from west to east.

Not every "oracle against the nations" is necessarily from the lips of Jeremiah, at least not *ipsissima verba* (the exact words). As already stated, the collection is composite, with a complicated literary history.

Judgment on Egypt (Jer 46:2–28)

In the case of Egypt, Jeremiah's knowledge is based on firsthand experience in that land. He resided in Egypt for some time after the fall of Jerusalem in 586 B.C.E. According to Eliezer Oren, who conducted, over several years, a systematic archaeological survey coupled with excavations between the Suez Canal and the Gaza Strip:

> Jeremiah's intimate acquaintance with the Egyptian Delta is reflected in a number of references concerning the location of Jewish garrisons and their direct involvement in the political and military affairs of the Saite kings of Egypt. (Jeremiah 43–46)[1]

The following are the principal place-names that occur in Jeremiah's oracle against Egypt (Jer 46:2–28):

Carchemish, the first-mentioned site, was the scene of Nebuchadrezzar II's decisive victory over Neco II of Egypt in 605 B.C.E., making Babylonia the principal power in the ancient Near East. Previously, in 717 B.C.E., Sargon II had annexed Carchemish to Assyria. Carchemish, occupying over 230 acres, commanded the main ford across the Euphrates. Being in a militarily sensitive location on the border between Turkey and Syria today, the site is not easily accessible to visitors. Carchemish's magnificent art work, including reliefs celebrating a victorious battle against the Assyrians, is on display in the Museum of Anatolian Civilizations in Ankara (Turkey).

Cush and Ethiopia are confusing terms. The Hebrew term Cush (Kush) was the ancient Egyptian name for Nubia, and the equivalent of Ethiopia, which was the ancient Greek name (not to be confused with modern Ethiopia). Nubia in northeastern Africa extended from the Nile Valley (in Upper Egypt) eastward to the Red Sea, southward to Khartoum, and westward to the Libyan desert. Located in the region south of Egypt, Cush corresponds roughly to present-day Sudan, also known as Ethiopia. However, that is not always the case. Cush in some texts is parallel with Midian, thus locating it in northern Arabia/southern Jordan.

Put has a disputed identification. As a geographical designation, Put probably refers to part of Libya, west of Egypt.

Lud is also an uncertain designation. It may be a reference to distant Lydia in Asia Minor, although some would understand "Libyans."

Gilead as a geographical designation is used loosely in the Bible; it may refer to all of Transjordan. In the more restricted sense, Gilead, located between Bashan and Moab, is the region in Transjordan extending from the Arnon to the Yarmuk rivers. The Jabbok (Zerqa) River divided Gilead in two. This highland region was good pastureland and was also famous for balm, as Jeremiah mentions (Jer 8:22; 46:11; 51:8).

Migdol, meaning "tower" or "fortress," may be either a proper or a common noun in both Hebrew and Egyptian. A Jewish settlement in the time of Jeremiah, Migdol was thought to have been situated at Tell el-Heir, thirteen miles northwest of Kantara in Lower (northern) Egypt. However, Oren's North Sinai Expedition has discovered a more plausible location for Migdol. It is a twenty-five-acre site with a large, fortified, mudbrick structure located about a mile north of Tell el-Heir, west of the Eastern Frontier Canal. Local Egyptian pottery of the Saite period uncovered there attests that the site was occupied in the time of Jeremiah. This site also bears close affinities with Tahpanhes with respect to military architecture, pottery, and metallurgy.

Memphis is situated on the west bank of the Nile River, about fifteen miles south of Cairo. It was the ancient capital of Lower Egypt. The Hebrew form of the name Memphis is Noph, which appears frequently in the Bible. Foreigners were settled at this site during the lifetime of Jeremiah. Memphis ceased to be the principal city after Alexander the Great built Alexandria in the fourth century B.C.E.

Tahpanhes is a city on the eastern frontier of the Lower Delta, located on the caravan route leading to Palestine and Mesopotamia. Known as Daphne in Greek, Tahpanhes is located at Tell Defneh. Flinders Petrie excavated the site at the end of the last century. In Jeremiah's time, Jews had settled at Tahpanhes, and the prophet sought refuge there after the destruction of Jerusalem in 586 B.C.E. The fact that Jeremiah mentioned Tahpanhes several times (Jer 2:16; 43:7; 44:1; 46:14) indicates its importance as an Egyptian settlement. Psammetichus I built this prominent commercial center.

Jeremiah also mentioned Thebes, the magnificent capital of Egypt, located about four hundred miles south of Cairo in Upper Egypt. The three areas known today as Luxor, Karnak, and the West Bank constitute the ancient city of Thebes. "No," the Hebrew name, is a transcription of the Egyptian word for "the City," the common designation of Thebes. In Jeremiah's day Thebes was in decline. In 663 B.C.E., Ashurbanipal sacked Thebes and carried off its riches to Assyria.

Describing the menacing march of Nebuchadrezzar against Egypt, Jeremiah compared the Babylonian king to the rugged heights of Mount Tabor and Mount Carmel:

> As I live, says the King, whose name is the LORD of hosts, one is coming like Tabor among the mountains, and like Carmel by the sea. (Jer 46:18)

The point of the comparisons is somewhat obscure. Both Tabor and Carmel rise above their surroundings. Tabor in the northeast corner of the Valley of Jezreel is about 1,750 feet above sea level. Because of its imposing appearance it is often compared with Mount Hermon, which in fact is much higher. Carmel, a limestone mountain range jutting into the East Mediterranean sea, is about 1,650 feet above sea level. The Plain of Acco lies to its north, and the Plains of Sharon and Philistia to the south.

Judgment on the Philistines (Jer 47:1–7)

The Philistines are numbered among the Sea Peoples who migrated from the Aegean region to the southern coastal plain of Canaan sometime after 1175 B.C.E. and survived for about six hundred years. Jeremiah specified Caphtor, that is, the Aegean island of Crete, as the Philistines' place of origin. The Philistines and the Israelites, both inhabiting Canaan, were in continuing conflict over the land. Archaeological evidence, especially from current excavations at Ashkelon and Ekron, is shedding light on the Philistines, but to date no major written material originating with the Philistines has been recovered. A few undeciphered texts generally called Philistine with similarities to Linear A (a simplified form of pictographic script) have been found, for example, at Tell Deir 'Alla as well as in Philistia proper. At Ekron the archaeologists have discovered sixteen inscriptions with scripts similar to Hebrew and Phoenician.

The name Palestine is, ironically, derived from the name of Israel's enemies, the Philistines, who settled in the southwest coast of Canaan adjacent to the East Mediterranean, where the five principal Philistine city-states are situated: Ashdod, Ashkelon, Gaza, Gath, and Ekron. Today, archaeologists use "Palestine" as a convenient geographical term for the ancient territories that now comprise the modern states of Israel and Jordan. Archaeologists have determined the location of the Philistine cities, with the exception of

Destruction of Ashkelon in 604 B.C.E. In the 1992 excavations at Ashkelon, the Philistine seaport on the Eastern Mediterranean, Lawrence Stager uncovered graphic evidence of destruction by the Babylonian army under King Nebuchadrezzar. Among the gruesome remains was this complete male skeleton, lying on its back with arms and legs extended. The skeleton's crushed skull amid scattered and smashed pottery corresponds to Jeremiah's description in his Judgment on the Philistines (Jer 47:1–7), where he speaks of the demolition of Ashkelon by an enemy from the north. *Photograph by Carl Andrews. Courtesy of the Leon Levy Expedition to Ashkelon.*

Gath, which may be identified with Tel es-Safi (Tel Zafit), halfway between Gezer and Lachish.

Gaza, the southernmost city of the Philistine pentapolis, is identified with the modern Tell Kharubeh. The location of modern Gaza atop the ancient city makes excavation impossible during these politically tense times. The site, strategically situated on the trade route from Egypt to western Asia, was occupied from the Late Bronze Age to the Byzantine period (1500 B.C.E.– 635 C.E.). Egypt controlled Gaza in Jeremiah's day.

Ashkelon, one of the largest archaeological sites in modern Israel, encompasses 150 acres. Occupied for about 3,500 years between 2000 B.C.E. and 1500 C.E., the site contains remnants of many cultures, including Canaanite, Philistine, Phoenician, Roman, Byzantine, Islamic, and Crusader. The only Philistine city with a harbor, Ashkelon is located twelve miles north of Gaza and ten miles south of Ashdod. During most of the Iron Age (1200–586 B.C.E.), Ashkelon was under the control of the Philistines. Nebuchadrezzar destroyed both Ashkelon and Gaza in 604 B.C.E. Jeremiah had prophesied the devastation of Ashkelon (Jer 25:17–20; 47:1–7).

In the context of Jeremiah's judgment on the Philistines, the Phoenician cities of Tyre and Sidon are mentioned. Linking these two important Phoenician seaports with Philistia seems strange at first, but commentators speculate that Philistia and Phoenicia may have been connected by an alliance as well as by trade.

Tyre, fifty-two miles south of Beirut in modern Lebanon, was the principal seaport on the Phoenician coast. It was a center of commerce and culture. The city was built partly on the mainland and partly on an island. Jeremiah prophesied Tyre's conquest by Nebuchadrezzar (Jer 25:22; 27:1–11). After a siege of thirteen years (585–573 B.C.E.) Nebuchadrezzar was still unable to conquer the island portion of Tyre, but Tyre submitted to him.

Sidon, situated twenty-five miles north of Tyre on the Mediterranean coast, was at times the ancient Phoenician capital. Hegemony seems to have fluctuated between Tyre and Sidon. Close ties existed between the two cities, although they were also rivals. Nebuchadrezzar captured Sidon on his way to besiege Judah in 586 B.C.E., as Jeremiah prophesied (Jer 25:22; 27:3; 47:4).

Judgment on Moab (Jer 48:1–47)

Moab apparently was not occupied to any degree after 701 B.C.E. Nor is it well known archaeologically despite the number of explorations that have been conducted, especially during the past decade. Among the intrepid early nineteenth-century explorers were Ulrich Seetzen, who located the ruins of ancient Gerasa (Jerash) and Philadelphia (Amman), and Ludwig Burckhardt, who rediscovered the lost city of Petra. In the 1930s Glueck, as mentioned, explored in a more systematic way the formerly unknown land of Transjordan, including Moab. Beginning in 1978, J. Maxwell Miller directed a thorough archaeological exploration of Moab, concentrating on the southern Moabite plateau. During this survey he studied over 400 sites, and the results are now published.[2]

Moab designates the rolling plateau east of the Dead Sea, rising 3,000 feet above sea level. It lay between the rivers Arnon (Wadi el-Mojib) and Zered (Wadi el-Hesa), although in certain periods Moab extended even north of the Arnon. This northern Moab region is more familiar from the Bible. The southern Moabite plateau is located in an isolated region between the Wadi el-Mojib and the Wadi el-Hesa. The land of Moab was favorable for growing wheat and barley as well as for sheep farming. Moab and Israel were in continuous conflict. In his oracle of judgment on Moab, Jeremiah preserved the names of many Moabite towns.

At Dibon (modern Dhiban), three miles north of the Arnon River and thirteen miles east of the Dead Sea, the Moabite Stone (now in the Louvre), known also as the Mesha Stele, came to light in 1868. Mesha, the king of Moab, erected this monument to honor Chemosh, the god of the Moabites. The king also commemorated on this black basalt stele his liberation from Israelite domination in the middle of the ninth century B.C.E. In his study of the Mesha inscription, J. Andrew Dearman points out that of the seventeen place-names appearing on the Moabite Stone, twelve are found in the Bible.[3] Excavations conducted at Dibon in the 1950s revealed occupation at the site extending from 3000 B.C.E. to 1400 C.E., although not continuously.

The site of the ancient town of Nebo, the mount from which Moses viewed the Promised Land, is usually identified with Khirbet al-Mukhaiyat, northwest of Madaba and two miles southeast of Mount Nebo. Here the Franciscans uncovered a church and monasteries as well as Iron Age tombs.

The identity of Kiriathaim ("two cities") is uncertain, but it may be Khirbet el-Qureiya, an Iron Age site six miles west of Madaba, on the bank of the Wadi 'Uyun ed-Dhib, according to Dearman. In Jeremiah's lifetime this town was under the rule of the Moabites.

Heshbon (modern Hesban) in northern Moab was excavated during several seasons beginning in 1968 as part of the Madaba Plains Project. Occupation of the site extended from the Iron Age until the Muslim period (1200 B.C.E.–1456 C.E.), although not continuously. In Jeremiah's time, Heshbon was a prosperous town. The prophet referred to Heshbon as belonging to Ammon as well as to Moab (Jer 49:3).

The identity of the place-name Madmen is unknown.

Horonaim's identity is also uncertain, but it may be located at modern el-Iraq, nine miles east of the southeast corner of the Dead Sea. The text of Jeremiah suggests that Horonaim was at the foot of a descent (Jer 48:5). Since Horonaim is mentioned together with Zoar and the waters of Nimrin, it would appear to have been a settlement south of the Wadi el-Mojib, situated in southern Moab. Dearman suggests that Horonaim was perhaps an

Tell Hesban (biblical Heshbon) in Iron Age II. The header-stretcher reservoir wall of Heshbon's famous pool (*to right*) associated with the Song of Songs 7:4. In Iron Age II the reservoir was thirty-three feet deep. *Courtesy of Lawrence Geraty, the Andrews University Excavations.*

Iron Age fortress at Tell Meidan, west of Kathrabba, or it is to be identified with 'Ai, east of Kathrabba.

The identity of Luhith is uncertain, but Dearman suggests Kathrabba as a possibility.

'Aroer, one of several Aroers in Palestine, designates a fortress guarding the King's Highway on the north bank of the Arnon. It is identified with modern Khirbet 'Ara'ir, about a mile southeast of Dhiban on the north edge of the Wadi el-Mojib. The site, excavated in the 1960s, was occupied as early as 2250 B.C.E.

Holon is tentatively identified with Aliyan, seven miles northeast of Dibon.

Jahzah (Jahaz), the site where Sihon, king of the Amorites, was killed in battle with the Israelites (Num 21:23–26), is identified tentatively with Khirbet Medeiniyeh, located on a bend of the Wadi eth-Themed, southeast of Heshbon and Madaba. According to Dearman, "The size of the site [Khirbet Medeiniyeh], with its implied importance for the entire area, and its Iron-Age occupational history suit its identification with a well known name such as Jahaz."[4]

Mephaath is thought to be modern Khirbet Jawa, six miles south of Amman (capital of present-day Jordan).

Beth-diblathaim is believed to be identical with Almon-diblathaim, one of the stopping places of the Israelites en route to the land of Canaan (Num 33:46–47). It cannot be identified with certainty, but Dearman suggests Um al-Walid, southeast of Madaba.

Beth-gamul may be modern Khirbet el-Jemeil, north of the Arnon River.

Beth-meon is believed to be an alternate designation for Beth-baal-meon and Beon. It is identified with the tell located in the modern village of Ma'in, five miles southwest of Madaba.

Kerioth, often identified with present-day el-Qureiyat, northwest of Dibon, is mentioned on the Moabite Stone as the chief sanctuary of the Moabite god Chemosh. As the site's identification Dearman suggests Khirbet 'Aleiyan, five miles east-northeast of Dhiban.

Bozrah is not to be confused with the Edomite fortress city of Bozrah (Jer 49:13). It may be the same as Bezer, situated perhaps at present-day Umm el-'Amad, eight miles northeast of Madaba.

Kir-heres (Kir haraseth), an ancient capital of Moab, is equated with present-day el-Kerak, where the famous Crusader castle is located. Situated on the summit of a mountain, it is surrounded by walls. Modern Kerak is 3,110 feet above sea level. Albright and Glueck found Iron Age potsherds on the slopes of this site.

Geographers have offered several suggestions about the location of the Moabite town of Jazer. It is tentatively identified with Khirbet es-Sar, eight miles west of Amman.

Sibmah (Shebam), famous for wine and vines, may be located at Quran el-Kibsh, a few miles west of Heshbon.

Elealeh, identified with present-day el-'Al, is two miles northeast of Heshbon. Excavated briefly, it is traditionally mentioned together with Heshbon.

Zoar is one of the five cities of the plain, together with Sodom (Jer 49:17), Gomorrah (Jer 49:17), Admah, and Zeboiim. Thought to be somewhere south of the Dead Sea, Zoar may be identified with es-Safi, five miles south of the Dead Sea. No traces of the other four cities have been uncovered, but the situation may change as excavations continue south of the Dead Sea. According to the Bible, these five cities, Zoar excepted, were destroyed by God for their wickedness (Gen 19:24–29).

Eglath-shelishiyah ("the third Eglath") is unknown.

The "waters of Nimrin" designate a desert stream in the land of Moab. The specific reference may be to the Wadi en-Numeira, about ten miles south of the Dead Sea. The context of Jeremiah suggests a location in southern Moab (Jer 48:34). Dearman, too, suggests that the "waters of Nimrin" correspond to modern Wadi en-Numeira flowing to the Dead Sea.

Judgment on the Ammonites (Jer 49:1–6)

Even before the Archaeological Survey of Greater Amman began in 1988, much was already known about this region. Projects at such sites as Sahab, Siran, Deir 'Alla, Tell Mazar, Tell es-Sa'idiyeh, and the Beq'ah (Valley) have added greatly to archaeological knowledge about Iron Age II, the period of Jeremiah.

The territorial boundaries of Ammon, located in central Transjordan, are not clearly delineated. Ammon extended along the north bank of the Jabbok River. The Ammonites settled in this land at the beginning of the thirteenth century B.C.E. For most of their history, Ammon and Israel were in conflict. During the seventh century B.C.E. the Transjordan states, as vassals of Assyria, paid tribute. Nonetheless it was a time of prosperity for the Ammonites. Also, archaeological evidence indicates that they did not suffer repercussions from the Neo-Babylonian campaign in Judah; rather, they prospered under both Neo-Babylonian domination and subsequent Persian rule. As a consequence of the collapse of the Northern Kingdom of Israel in 721 B.C.E. and of the Southern Kingdom of Judah in 586 B.C.E., Ammon appeared to flourish. The kingdom of the Ammonites was strongly fortified by circular towers during Iron Age II.

Inscriptions illuminating the history and culture of Ammon have surfaced recently. A notable example is Tell Siran on the outskirts of modern Amman where a bottle-shaped object incised with eight lines of Ammonite came to light. Dating about 600 B.C.E., the inscription refers to a construction project by a king named Amminadab. Also, Deir 'Alla in the Jordan Valley yielded fragments of wall plaster inscribed in a Northwest Semitic dialect, perhaps Ammonite, although some would say Aramaic. This mural inscription dates from the mid-eighth century B.C.E.

Rabbah of the Ammonites (modern Amman), also known as Rabbath Ammon, was the capital of the Ammonites. When rebuilt in the third century B.C.E. by Ptolemy II Philadelphus, Rabbah was renamed Philadelphia and flourished as a Hellenistic city. In 635 C.E., at the time of the Arab conquest, the name was changed back to Ammon.

Located twenty-five miles east of the Jordan River, Rabbah was strategically situated at the crossroads of the trade routes running both north-south and east-west. Its agriculture was enriched by water from the Jabbok (modern Zerqa River), one of the chief eastern tributaries of the Jordan, rising in a spring near Amman. The reference to the "daughters of Rabbah" (Jer 49:3) describes the villages surrounding Rabbah. While most of the archaeological remains at the capital city date from the Roman period, evidence of the Iron Age II occupation to which Jeremiah alluded (Jer 49:2–3) is increasing. Abundant artifacts, including pottery, sculpture, and tombs, have surfaced in the area of Amman.

Jeremiah mentioned 'Ai ("the ruin," 49:3) together with Heshbon. 'Ai is to be distinguished from the Canaanite town of the same name located near Bethel, across the Jordan. Jeremiah may have had in mind the city of 'Ai, east of Kathrabba in Transjordan.

Judgment on Damascus (Jer 49:23–27)

This, the briefest of the "oracles against the nations" found in the book of Jeremiah, dating probably from the eighth century B.C.E., describes the Assyrian conquests of that century. In this oracle Damascus stands for the whole nation. Damascus, the capital of modern Syria, is one of the oldest, continuously occupied cities in the world. A fertile oasis situated on a plateau 2,300 feet above sea level, Damascus was strategically located on the principal trade routes, which accounted for its economic prosperity. The city reached its zenith in the ninth century B.C.E. A century later, in 732 B.C.E., Tiglath-pileser III conquered Damascus, making it an Assyrian province.

The ancient city of Hamath, present-day Hama, is situated on the east bank of the Orontes River, between Aleppo (to the north) and Damascus (to the south). In the course of history Hamath had been the center of an independent kingdom. Jeroboam II of Israel conquered Hamath in 780 B.C.E. Later, it fell victim to the imperialism of the Neo-Assyrian empire. In 740 B.C.E., Tiglath-pileser III conquered Hamath; then in 720 B.C.E., Sargon II destroyed the city. When Assyria conquered the city, the people from Hamath were transferred to Israel. Pharaoh Neco occupied Hamath before the battle of Carchemish. The Babylonian Chronicle reports that Nebuchadrezzar intercepted the Egyptians at Hamath as they fled from Carchemish in 605 B.C.E.

Arpad (present-day Tell Rif'at) is an Aramean city in northwestern Syria, located twenty miles northwest of Aleppo. The Bible always mentions Arpad and Hamath together as examples of cities destroyed by the Assyrians. In 720 B.C.E., Arpad revolted unsuccessfully against Sargon II.

Judgment on Kedar and Hazor (Jer 49:28–33)

Kedar designates a nomadic tribe, and Jeremiah refers to an alliance of nomadic Arab tribes living in the northwest Arabian desert. The Bible mentions Kedar and the Kedarites frequently. If one pieces these references together, a composite of Kedar emerges. Kedar was the son of Ishmael, born of Abraham and Hagar. The Kedarites were desert dwellers who lived in tents made of black goat hair (the Hebrew name "Kedar" suggests blackness). They herded sheep, goats, and camels, and also had a reputation as skilled archers.

In Jeremiah they are cited contemptuously as "those who have shaven temples" (Jer 49:32). This pagan practice was forbidden to the Israelites, and some Orthodox Jews to this day continue to observe the ban (Lev 19:27).

Jeremiah referred to Kedar in conjunction with Cyprus in an accusation against Judah:

> Cross to the coasts of Cyprus and look, send to Kedar and examine with care; see if there has ever been such a thing. (Jer 2:10)

Cyprus and Kedar represent the geographic extremes of west and east. Jeremiah's references to Kedar in this passage and in the "oracles against the nations," in addition to frequent allusions to Kedar in the Assyrian and Neo-Babylonian sources, underscore the importance of Kedar. From the eighth to the fourth century B.C.E., the Kedarites were an influential force. Nebuchadrezzar defeated the Kedarites in 599 B.C.E., confirming Jeremiah's announcement of judgment (Jer 49:28). A century later, Kedarite territory extended as far as the border of Egypt.

Hazor (*hasor*) is not the renowned city nine miles north of the Sea of Galilee. In the present context this Hazor would designate an unknown site in the Arabian desert, east of the Jordan. Some commentators suggest that *hasor* should be read *haserim* and then translated "unwalled villages" instead of the proper place-name, on the analogy of Isa 42:11, reading "the villages (*haserim*) that Kedar inhabits."

Judgment on Elam (Jer 49:34–39)

Elam is located in the fertile hill country east of the Tigris River, with Susa as its capital and administrative center. The Elamites and the ancient Medes inhabited the land that is now western Iran. The Elamites had a reputation as skilled archers. With the resurgence of Assyria in the eighth century B.C.E., the Elamites were in constant conflict with the Assyrians. After the defeat of Susa at the hands of Ashurbanipal in 645 B.C.E., the Elamites joined the Assyrian campaigns against Judah (Isa 22:6). Jeremiah, as well as Ezekiel (32:24–25), foretold the fall of Elam.

Judgment on Babylon (Jer 50:1–51:64)

The great city of Babylon (*Babel* in Hebrew), the political and religious capital of Babylonia, is located about fifty-four miles south of modern Baghdad (Iraq), and twelve miles east of the present course of the Euphrates River. The ancient city was situated on both sides of the Euphrates River, connected by a stone bridge. The region was also called Chaldea, especially during the last Babylonian dynasty (626–539 B.C.E.). Tell Babil preserves the ancient name of Babylon, which designates either the city or the empire.

Babylon reached its peak under Nebuchadrezzar, when it became the most prominent city in Mesopotamia. Jewish captives from Judah were brought to Babylon in 597 B.C.E. and again in 586 B.C.E. Babylon fell to the Persians in 539 B.C.E. Alexander the Great conquered Babylon in 331 B.C.E.

The physical remains of Babylon extend over three and a half square miles. The ancient gate, named Ishtar in honor of one of the principal deities of Babylon, was erected by Nebuchadrezzar. A reconstruction of the Ishtar gate stands at the entrance to ancient Babylon today. Both Isaiah and Jeremiah predicted that Babylon would be reduced to a heap of ruins.

Speaking of the restoration of Israel, Jeremiah named four non-Babylonian sites notable for lush pastureland: Carmel, Bashan, Ephraim, and Gilead (Jer 50:19).

Carmel, the limestone hills on the northern coast of Palestine jutting into the Mediterranean Sea near modern Haifa, has dense vegetation. The Hebrew word *karmel*, meaning "garden land," is used in the Bible, including Jeremiah, as a common noun with this connotation:

> I [the LORD] brought you into a plentiful (*hakkarmel*) land to eat its fruits and its good things. But when you entered you defiled my land, and made my heritage an abomination. (Jer 2:7)

> I [the LORD] looked, and lo, the fruitful land (*hakkarmel*) was a desert, and all its cities were laid in ruins before the LORD, before his fierce anger. (Jer 4:26)

Bashan is the region northeast of the Jordan River lying to the north of Gilead and extending to Mount Hermon. Its fertile plateau is excellent for growing wheat and raising cattle. Bashan is also famous for oak trees.

Ephraim (meaning "to bear fruit") denotes the territory of the tribe of Ephraim and later the Northern Kingdom of Israel and surrounding territory.

This is the central hill country of Palestine whose principal city was Shechem. "The hills of Ephraim" (Jer 50:19) coincide with the territory of the tribe of Ephraim. It was a fertile area ideal for the cultivation of grapes and fruit trees, vegetable gardening, and wheat farming.

As already stated, the Yarmuk River forms the boundary between Bashan and Gilead. Boundaries fluctuated from time to time, but Gilead ordinarily designates the mountainous area extending from the Arnon to the Yarmuk, between Bashan and Moab. The balm that made Gilead famous (Jer 8:22; 46:11; 51:8) refers to the resin of the balsam tree. It was used to scent oils and perfumes and also as a medicament. Since balsam is not indigenous to the region, Gilead must have been an export center.

Merathaim denotes the region in southern Babylonia, near the mouth of the Tigris and the Euphrates. Merathaim may be a play on words meaning "double rebellion."

Pekod denotes a small Aramean tribe dwelling on the east bank of the Lower Tigris River.

Leb-qamai (literally, "the heart of those who rise against me") is an artificial word or cryptogram for Kasdim, that is, Chaldea. This is a late Masoretic device:

> Thus says the LORD: I am going to stir up a destructive wind against Babylon and against the inhabitants of Leb-qamai. (Jer 51:1)

The Medes came from the highlands east of Babylonia, in present-day northwestern Iran. Ecbatana was the capital. In the time of Cyrus the Great (mid-sixth century B.C.E.), Media became part of the Persian empire. Today's Kurds consider themselves the direct descendants of the ancient Medes, who migrated two millennia ago to the mountainous regions of modern Turkey, Iraq, and Iran.

Jeremiah referred to the kingdoms of Ararat (Urartu), Minni, and Ashkenaz as nations that would form an alliance against Babylonia. At the time this poem was composed, these nations were under the control of the Medes. Ararat denoted the area surrounding Lake Van in east Anatolia (Turkey). Minni, perhaps to be associated with the Manneans, is located in northwestern Iran. This is the only reference to Minni in the Bible.

Ashkenaz may refer to a people later known as Scythians, ancient nomads, who were notorious for their savagery. As well as fierce warriors, the Scythians were horse breeders. From the sixth to the third century B.C.E., this enigmatic people, who spoke an Indo-European language, flourished from eastern Siberia to the Danube River. Anthropologists are currently conducting an archaeological search for the ancient Scythians in the region known until recently as the Soviet Union.

Sheshach is mentioned twice in Jeremiah: in a "judgment on the nations" (Jer 25:26) and again in the "judgment on Babylon":

How Sheshach is taken, the pride of the whole earth seized! How Babylon has become an object of horror among the nations! (Jer 51:41)

This is another cryptogram; here it stands for "Babylon." The technical term for this device is athbash, that is, the substitution of Hebrew letters in reverse alphabetical order. These cryptograms in the book of Jeremiah are a late scribal device.

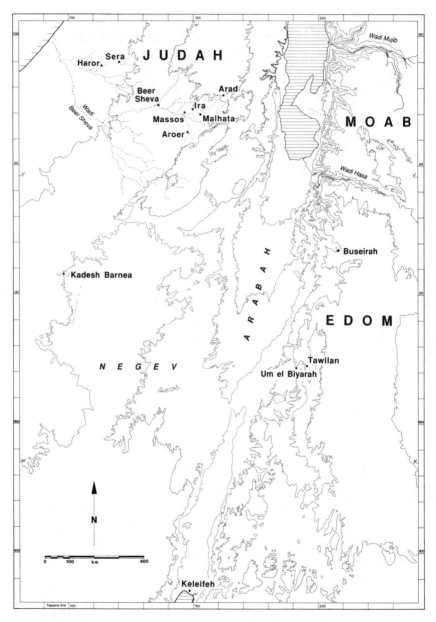

Edom and Judah

4

Edom and Judah

Edom and Judah were in close contact throughout their history. The book of Jeremiah alone has over forty references to Edom. The two kingdoms, according to the biblical authors, hated each other as only close neighbors can. The abiding hostility between Edom and Judah is all too evident in the Bible, especially in the prophetic books (Isaiah, Jeremiah, Ezekiel, Amos, Joel, Obadiah, and Malachi), which, of course, are not completely objective sources. Typical of the animosity is Jeremiah's judgment on Edom:

> Edom shall become an object of horror; everyone who passes by it will be horrified and will hiss because of all its disasters. As when Sodom and Gomorrah and their neighbors were overthrown, says the LORD, no one shall live there, nor shall anyone settle in it. (Jer 49:17–18)

These verses are only part of Jeremiah's longer judgment on Edom, included among his "oracles against the nations" (Jer 49:7–22). The wickedness of Sodom and Gomorrah has become proverbial. Counted among the five cities of the Jordan Plain, Sodom and Gomorrah have not been identified, despite surveys and excavations conducted in the vicinity of the Dead Sea. Some scholars have supposed these sites were submerged in the waters at the southern end of the Dead Sea. On the other hand, they may be purely legendary.

The enmity between Edom and Israel can be traced as far back as the time of Moses and the exodus, when Edom denied the Israelites passage through their territory (Num 20:14–21).

Ammon, Moab, and Edom constitute the three "nation-states" of Transjordan. Judah's political relations seem to have been worse with Edom than with Ammon and Moab. The biblical kingdom of Edom, also known as Seir, is situated on a high plateau 3,500 feet above sea level; it is a rugged, mountainous region. Boundaries cannot be identified precisely, but Edom extended over a hundred miles from the Brook Zered (Wadi el-Hesa) in the north to the Gulf of Aqaba in the south, stretching across both sides of the Arabah (Rift Valley). After the Babylonian exile, Idumea, the word the Septuagint (Greek Old Testament) uses for Edom, designated the area in Judea, west of the Arabah, from Beth-zur to south of Beer-sheba, where the Edomites settled. The Edomites apparently moved west when the Nabateans settled in Edomite territory. In the Hellenistic and Roman periods the Edomites were known as the Idumeans.

Excavations have not yet uncovered Edomite sites with evidence that predates the eighth century B.C.E., although surveys have revealed the remains of Edomite villages as early as the twelfth century B.C.E. The third phase of the Neo-Assyrian period (745–627 B.C.E.) was the most prosperous era in Edom's history. From the seventh through the early sixth century B.C.E., Edomite presence increased significantly in the Negev of Judah and attained the height of its development both politically and economically. In the seventh century B.C.E. the Judahites also settled intensively in the mountains of Judah as well as in the Negev. Along with the Edomites, the Ammonites and the Moabites also thrived during this period.

The economy of Edom was based on trade and agriculture, although its agriculture was inferior to that of Ammon and Moab. Also, copper was mined in Edom. The fact that the trade routes reaching from India and South Arabia to Egypt passed through Edom was a distinct economic advantage.

Archaeological excavations and surveys attest that the Judahites and Edomites intermingled in the seventh to sixth centuries B.C.E., when the Edomites were actually present in the territory of Judah. Edomite presence among their traditional enemies may be explained in terms of commercial relations existing between the two, or the Edomite settlement in Judahite land, or the Edomite conquest of Judahite territory. The difficulty of reconciling the association of Edomites and Judahites with long-standing mutual antipathy may be explained partially by the fact that the biblical accounts reflect a long and complex tradition. Then, too, international relations and interpersonal relations are quite different matters, as history attests. Ironically, the people of Judah fled to Edom for safety at the time of the Babylonian destruction of Jerusalem.

David (1000–961 B.C.E.), Jehoshaphat (873–849 B.C.E.), Amaziah (800–783 B.C.E.), and Uzziah (Azariah, 783–742 B.C.E.), all kings of Judah, gained control over Edom during their reigns. When Jehoram (849–843 B.C.E.) was king of Judah, Edom rebelled. Consequently, for about sixty years (849–790 B.C.E.) the Edomites enjoyed independence. Later, when the Edomites defeated Judah in Ahaz's reign (735–715 B.C.E.), they were again autonomous until the Babylonians conquered Edom, apparently in the early sixth century B.C.E.

After 735 B.C.E., Edom became a vassal state of Assyria. It appears that the Edomites joined Judah in a conspiracy against Babylon in 594/593 B.C.E., during the reign of King Zedekiah, who convened an anti-Babylonian meet-ing in Jerusalem. Such an alliance of small states did not represent a serious threat to Babylonia. In connection with this alliance Jeremiah received the following instruction from the Lord:

> Send word to the king of Edom, the king of Moab, the king of the Ammonites, the king of Tyre, and the king of Sidon by the hand of the envoys who have come to Jerusalem to King Zedekiah of Judah. . . . Now I [the LORD] have given all these lands into the hand of King Neb-uchadnezzar of Babylon. . . . All the nations shall serve him and his son and his grandson. (Jer 27:3, 6, 7)

The people of Judah felt a deep resentment toward Edom for their fail-ure to come to their assistance during the second siege of Jerusalem by the Babylonians in 586 B.C.E. Instead, Edom profited from Jerusalem's demise by occupying towns in southern Judah. Whether Edom participated in the actual razing of Jerusalem is debatable, although the psalmist appears to have little doubt:

> Remember, O LORD, against the Edomites the day of Jerusalem's fall, how they said, "Tear it down! Tear it down! Down to its foundations!" (Ps 137:7)

John Bartlett in a recent and valuable synthesis, incorporating all available archaeological and documentary evidence on Edom and the Edomites, dis-associates them from the destruction of Jerusalem and Judah in 586 B.C.E.:

> In fact, Edom played no direct part in the events of 587 BCE. The only firm evidence suggests that some Judean refugees found sanctuary in Edom. For the destruction of Jerusalem and Judah in 587 [or 586] BCE Edom cannot be held responsible.[1]

Jeremiah confirmed that refugees from Judah had fled to Edom in 586 B.C.E.:

> Likewise, when all the Judeans who were in Moab and among the Ammonites and in Edom and in other lands heard that the king of Babylon had left a remnant in Judah and had appointed Gedaliah son of Ahikam son of Shaphan as governor over them, then all the Judeans returned from all the places to which they had been scattered and came to the land of Judah, to Gedaliah at Mizpah; and they gathered wine and summer fruits in great abundance. (Jer 40:11–12)

Much remains to be learned about Edom's history. Although Edomite inscriptions (seals, ostraca, tablets, weights) have surfaced, no monumental inscriptions comparable to the Moabite Stone have come to light. The avail-able written evidence emanates, for the most part, from Edom's enemies— the Assyrians, Babylonians, and Judahites—who were somewhat tendentious in their reporting.

Excavations in Jordan

Archaeological excavations and surface explorations of Edom are still at an early stage; consequently, much remains to be learned. Completed excavations have been published only in a preliminary way. The excavations of Crystal-M. Bennett at Umm el-Biyara, Tawilan, and Buseirah, sites that flourished in the Iron Age from about 721 to 539 B.C.E., as well as in the Persian period, are being prepared for publication posthumously. These sites which had become fully Edomite give indication of eventual destruction by fire. However, they remained occupied long after 586 B.C.E., perhaps even as late as 332 B.C.E.

Although these sites did not contain artifacts earlier than 800 B.C.E., finding Iron Age I remains in the future at sites like Buseirah is quite possible. Recent surveys have unearthed Iron Age I pottery at sites in northern Edom. Glueck speculated erroneously that much of Transjordan was not occupied in the Neo-Babylonian and Persian periods.

Umm el-Biyara, Tawilan, Buseirah

Umm el-Biyara was a domestic settlement situated on a mountain, a thousand feet above the valley floor, overlooking Petra from the west. This one-period site, dating from the second quarter of the seventh century B.C.E., was excavated by Bennett between 1963 and 1965. It yielded a seal impression, decorated with a winged sphinx, from the first half of the seventh century B.C.E.; it reads "Belonging to Qaus Gabar, king of Edom." Qaus (Qos) was the principal deity of Edom. The theophoric (bearing the name of a god) component "Qaus" occurs in many of the Edomite inscriptions that have been recovered.

Tawilan, settled in the seventh to sixth centuries B.C.E., may be identified with Teman, but this is not at all certain. Tawilan is located on the eastern outskirts of Petra. According to Bennett, Tawilan was a prosperous agricultural settlement in Iron Age II. Jeremiah placed Teman in parallel with Edom:

> Therefore hear the plan that the LORD has made against Edom and the purposes that he has formed against the inhabitants of Teman: Surely the little ones of the flock shall be dragged away; surely their fold shall be appalled at their fate. (Jer 49:20)

Some scholars suggest that Teman was not a specific town; rather, it was a regional term referring to southern Judah.

Buseirah, identified with biblical Bozrah, was a large (nineteen acres), fortified town, about twenty-one miles southeast of the Dead Sea. A royal capital, it was the principal town in northern Edom. Bozrah flourished in the seventh to sixth centuries B.C.E. Excavations from 1971 to 1976 revealed some of Bozrah's history. The destruction of buildings by fire, probably at the hands of Nebuchadrezzar, can be detected on the site's acropolis. Jeremiah used Bozrah to symbolize the whole of Edom:

> For by myself I have sworn, says the LORD, that Bozrah shall become an object of horror and ridicule, a waste, and an object of cursing; and all her towns shall be perpetual wastes. (Jer 49:13)

Jeremiah also named Bozrah in parallel with the land of Edom itself:

> Look, he [the invading army] shall mount up and swoop down like an eagle, and spread his wings against Bozrah, and the heart of the warriors of Edom in that day shall be like the heart of a woman in labor. (Jer 49:22)

Dedan

Included in Jeremiah's judgment on Edom (49:7–22) are the inhabitants of Dedan, an Arabian people (49:8–11):

> Flee, turn back, get down low, inhabitants of Dedan! For I [the LORD] will bring the calamity of Esau upon him, the time when I punish him. . . . But as for me, I have stripped Esau bare, I have uncovered his hiding places, and he is not able to conceal himself. His offspring are destroyed, his kinsfolk and his neighbors; and he is no more. (Jer 49:8, 10)

Esau was the ancestor of Edom. Dedan, located in northwest Saudi Arabia, is identified with present-day al-'Ula, about fifty miles southwest of Tema (modern Teima). Dedan was well known for caravan trade throughout the Arabian Peninsula. Inasmuch as Edomite territory did not extend so far as northwest Arabia, a clan of Dedanites may have settled in Edom.

The inhabitants of Tema and Dedan, oases situated on the Arabian trade routes, were the objects of Jeremiah's ominous predictions against the nations under the symbol of a cup of wine representing divine judgment:

> For thus the LORD, the God of Israel, said to me [Jeremiah]: Take from my hand this cup of the wine of wrath, and make all the nations to whom I send you drink it. . . . So I took the cup from the LORD's hand, and made all the nations to whom the LORD sent me drink it: . . . Dedan, Tema, Buz, and all who have shaven temples. (Jer 25:15, 17, 23)

Surveys in Jordan

Between 1933 and 1935 Glueck surveyed Edom. Unlike earlier explorers, because of his knowledge of pottery chronology he was able to date the occupation of the Edomite sites. Inevitably, more recent surveys have led to significant reinterpretations of Glueck's conclusions, especially that

Transjordan was abandoned during the Middle Bronze and Late Bronze ages. Despite the fact that during the last decade archaeologists have been conducting extensive surveys as well as some excavations in Transjordan including the Edomite region, relatively few sites in Jordan have yet been excavated.

In addition to Miller's survey of central and southern Moab, extending from the Wadi el-Mojib (Arnon River) to the Wadi el-Hesa (Zered River), other areas surveyed include the northern Jordan region between the Yarmuk and Zerqa (Jabbok) rivers by Siegfried Mittmann, and the East Jordan Valley from the Yarmuk River to the Dead Sea by Moawiyah Ibrahim, James Sauer, and Khair Yassine.

Burton MacDonald conducted the Wadi el-Hesa Archaeological Survey, including northern Edom, between the Wadi el-Hesa and Tafila, together with the northern Arabah. MacDonald's survey is complemented by his ongoing project of identifying biblical sites in southern Jordan (Edom). Stephen Hart surveyed the central region of Edom from Tafila to Naqb esh-Shtar. W. J. Jobling surveyed the Wadi Hisma region between Ras en-Naqb and Aqaba. Walter Rast and Thomas Schaub surveyed the Wadi Arabah and the Ghor (the main part of the Jordan Valley), around the southeast coast of the Dead Sea.

Tell el-Kheleifeh

In addition to his survey, Glueck excavated two sites in Transjordan between 1938 and 1940. One of these sites is Tell el-Kheleifeh, a low mound situated at the head of the Red Sea, near the center of the north shore of the Gulf of Elath (also spelled Eilat). It is equidistant from the port of modern Eilat in Israel and the port of modern Aqaba in Jordan. Owing to questions about the stratigraphy of the site, the identity of Tell el-Kheleifeh is still debated. Glueck, following the lead of Fritz Frank who discovered Kheleifeh in 1932, equated it with Solomonic Ezion-geber; at the same time, Glueck considered Elath to be the later name for Ezion-geber. Ezion-geber was a way station of the Israelites during their wanderings in the wilderness. Also, it was at Ezion-geber that Solomon built a fleet of ships.

The identification of Tell el-Kheleifeh continues to be a problem. Bartlett is inclined to identify Tell el-Kheleifeh with the Elath founded in the eighth century B.C.E. by King Uzziah (783–742 B.C.E.) and then seized by Edom about 735 B.C.E. Beno Rothenberg, following the conjecture of earlier scholars, identifies Jezirat Fara'un, seven miles south of modern Eilat, as the harbor of Solomon's Ezion-geber.

Gary Pratico, who is conducting a reappraisal of Glueck's conclusions, questions the identification of Tell el-Kheleifeh with Ezion-geber. Whereas some archaeologists equate Tell el-Kheleifeh with biblical Elath, others suggest that Elath is located at Aqaba and Ezion-geber at Tell el-Kheleifeh.

Aerial view of Tell el-Kheleifeh. At the end of Nelson Glueck's last season of
excavation in 1940. The ruins preserve the basic outlines of the offsets/insets
fortified settlement that dates between the eighth and sixth centuries B.C.E.
Note the four-chambered gate complex in the western end of the southern
wall. The western, southern, and eastern lines of the earlier casemate fortress
are also visible in the northwestern corner (*upper left*) of the excavated area.
The monumental "four-room" building, originally identified by Glueck as a
smelter, is discernible in the center of the casemate fortress. *From the
Collections of the Harvard Semitic Museum. Courtesy of Gary Pratico.*

At Tell el-Kheleifeh, Glueck identified six periods of occupation,
extending from Iron Age I through the Persian period (eleventh to the
fifth century B.C.E.). According to Pratico's revision, the pottery of Tell
el-Kheleifeh does not date earlier than the eighth century B.C.E. It continues to the early sixth century B.C.E., with some pottery dating as late
as the fourth century B.C.E.

Pratico divided the occupational history of the site into two principal architectural phases, the earlier level being the "casemate fortress" and the later
level the "fortified settlement." The casemate wall consisted of a double line

of walls divided into internal rooms by cross walls. The solid wall of the "fortified settlement," dating from the eighth to the early sixth century B.C.E., was an offset-inset wall, so called because it was constructed of salients and recesses, which are sawtooth projections breaking the straight line of the wall. The latter phase bears similarities with the fortress at Arad (below). A later occupation continued to the fourth century B.C.E.

During his excavation of the site, Glueck discovered a square building at the northwest corner of the mound. Noticing two horizontal rows of apertures in the walls of the building, Glueck interpreted them as flue holes and concluded the building must have functioned as a smelter or copper refinery. Rothenberg disproved Glueck's metallurgical interpretation, and then he demonstrated convincingly that the structure was a storehouse and/or granary.[2]

In addition to Edomite pottery in Stratum IV, Edomite presence at Tell el-Kheleifeh is evident in the appearance of twenty-two jar handles stamped with the same Edomite seal bearing the name Qaws'anal, an Edomite official. This inscription is divided into two registers, separated by a double horizontal line, and reads in full "Belonging to Qaws'anal, servant of the king (*lqws'nl 'bd hmlk*)." Qaus, of course, was the well-known Edomite deity. The seal's West Semitic script is dated to the late seventh or early sixth century B.C.E.

Detail of the Tell el-Kheleifeh excavations. Looking southwest. A view of the western perimeter of the casemate fortress. Five casemate rooms are visible. The figure is standing outside the fortress complex. The northern shoreline of the Gulf of Aqaba is just visible in the upper left. *From the Collections of the Harvard Semitic Museum. Courtesy of Gary Pratico.*

Tell el-Kheleifeh was probably a Judahite stronghold or fortified caravansary, built in the eighth century B.C.E., and was then taken over by the Edomites during the seventh century B.C.E., before being destroyed in the early sixth century B.C.E. Its purpose, according to Amihai Mazar, was to control the approach to the Red Sea.

Excavations in Israel

Excavations and surveys by Israeli archaeologists on the western side (modern Israel) of the Arabah are also casting light on Edomite history, especially the latter half of the seventh century B.C.E. when settlements in that region increased. Among the excavated sites with Edomite finds are Tel 'Ira, Tel Malḥata, Tel Masos, Tel Arad, Tel 'Aroer, Ḥorvat 'Uza, and Ḥorvat Qitmit, all located in the eastern Negev, as well as Kadesh-barnea in the southwest Negev Highlands. Most of these forts flourished in the seventh century B.C.E., and some show signs of town planning. The majority of Judahite towns and fortresses in the Judean Desert were destroyed by the Babylonians in 586 B.C.E. For the most part, these sites have been only partially published to date.

Edomite pottery dating from the seventh to the early sixth century B.C.E. has been found in the Israelite strata of these sites. Itzhaq Beit-Arieh theorizes that the Edomites seized and occupied land belonging to Judah about 600 B.C.E.

The largest of these sites is Tel 'Ira, which Anson Rainey has identified as Ramat-negeb. Covering eighteen acres, it is described by Moshe Kochavi as the largest walled settlement of the biblical Negev. He calls it "a fortified eagle's nest dominating the Beer-sheba valley."[3] Tel 'Ira was inhabited and fortified in the late eighth and seventh centuries B.C.E.

Tel Malḥata and Tel Masos are located on lowland along the Beer-sheba Brook. After the early Israelite city at Malḥata was destroyed, rebuilt walls continued in use until this fortified town was conquered by the Babylonians.

At Tel Masos, identified tentatively with biblical Hormah, a small fortress, built during the seventh century B.C.E., was destroyed at the beginning of the sixth century B.C.E.

Arad

Tel Arad, situated eighteen miles northeast of Beer-sheba and seventeen miles south of Hebron, controlled the main road to Edom. The site consists of two settlements: a large, fortified lower city that reached its peak from 2900 to 2700 B.C.E. during the Early Bronze Age II; and an Iron Age frontier fortress on the southeast ridge that served as both an administrative and a military outpost. Two Hebrew ostraca containing the name

"Arad" confirm the identity of this Israelite site. Beginning in 1962, Ruth Amiran excavated the twenty-two-acre lower city, while Yohanan Aharoni directed the excavations of the royal Israelite fortress on the upper tell.

According to the excavators, six successive Israelite fortresses were constructed on the hill between the tenth and the sixth century B.C.E. The latest was thought to have been built in 594/593 B.C.E., the fourth year of King Zedekiah's reign. Israelite occupation of Arad came to an end in 586 B.C.E. when the Babylonians or Edomites destroyed the fortress.

Within the fortress was a small Israelite temple (or shrine) in the northwest quadrant. According to Aharoni, it was founded in Stratum XI and dates from King Solomon (961–922 B.C.E.). This temple was the first ever uncovered on an archaeological excavation. The Arad temple comprised a large courtyard with a sacrificial altar therein, a broad room (*hekal*), and the Holy of Holies or cella (*debir*). Opposite the eastern entrance was a niche formed by a recess in the center of the western, long wall of the nave; this was the Holy of Holies. Two limestone incense altars flanked the entrance of the *debir* which was approached by three steps in front. Within the *debir* were a *bamah*, or platform, and two standing stones, called *maṣṣebot*, situated against the rear wall.

The Solomonic Temple in Jerusalem was a long-axis type, with the entrance located on one of the short sides. In contrast, the Arad temple was a broad-room plan, with the entrance in the middle of a long side.

According to Aharoni, the altar at Arad was destroyed in the late eighth century B.C.E., and the shrine was abolished a century later during the religious reform of King Josiah (640–609 B.C.E.).

Questions and uncertainties surround the dating and interpretation of the Arad fortress and temple. The most recent dissenting voice is that of David Ussishkin, who disagrees with Aharoni's dating of the Arad shrine. Denying that it was built in the Solomonic era, he claims it could not have been founded before the end of the eighth century B.C.E. and more probably not before the beginning of the seventh century B.C.E. In other words, the shrine may have existed only from the seventh century to the early sixth century B.C.E.

Ussishkin's dating of the shrine suggests that neither its construction nor destruction relates to the religious reform of Hezekiah or Josiah. He observes that "a shrine had been allowed to be built and used in the peripheral fort of Arad during the later part of the Judean kingdom till its final destruction."[4] This raises the question of how inclusive the reform of Josiah was with respect to the centralization of worship in the Jerusalem Temple. Ussishkin asserts, in addition, that the final destruction of the shrine by fire occurred simultaneously with the destruction of the fort, at the beginning of the sixth century B.C.E.

Fortress at Arad. This is an aerial view of the Arad fortress during excavation. *Photograph by S. J. Schweig. Courtesy of the Institute of Archaeology, Tel Aviv University.*

Among the historic discoveries at Arad were approximately two hundred ostraca (inscribed potsherds) found in various levels. Over half of the ostraca were inscribed in Aramaic and date from the Persian period (400 B.C.E.). The remainder, written in Hebrew, include letters and documents from the royal archives of the citadel. The Hebrew inscriptions are said to have spanned a period of more than 350 years. These ostraca are an excellent source of information about language, epigraphy, and paleography.

Iron Age fortress at Arad. The fortress in this photograph is restored to its ninth century B.C.E. appearance. A series of fortresses were built and rebuilt on the northeast hill of Arad between the tenth and sixth centuries B.C.E., according to the excavators of the site. The Arad sanctuary was located in the northwest corner of the fortress. *Courtesy of Ze'ev Herzog.*

The Holy of Holies at Arad. Steps flanked by two limestone incense altars lead to a niche in the sanctuary's back wall, which constituted the Holy of Holies (*debir*). Note the two standing stones (*maṣṣebot*) against the rear wall. *Courtesy of the Institute of Archaeology, Tel Aviv University.*

A group of seventeen ostraca were found in one room of the fortress. Belonging to the archive of Eliashib son of Eshyahu, the Israelite commander of the Arad fort, they reveal what life was like in the Judahite fortress during the reign of King Zedekiah. Some of these ostraca were notes addressed to Eliashib, directing him to issue rations (oil, wine, bread, etc.) from the storehouses of the fortress.

Typical of this genre is the ostracon (Number 1) ordering Eliashib to provide supplies of bread and wine to a group called the Kittim (*ktym*, the Hebrew name for Cypriots), who are mentioned on ten Arad ostraca from the archive of Eliashib. The inscription reads:

> To Eliashib: And now, give the Kittiyim 3 baths of wine, and write the name of the day. And from the rest of the first flour, send one homer of flour in order to make bread for them. Give them the wine from the aganoth [large banquet bowls] vessels.[5]

Kittiyim (Kittim) is preserved in the name of Kition (present-day Larnaca), a Phoenician city on the southeast coast of Cyprus. Jeremiah referred to the Kittim as an illustration of the geographical extremes extending from west to east: "Cross to the coasts of Cyprus (*kittiyim*) and look, send to Kedar and examine with care" (Jer 2:10).

Provisions were supplied to the Kittiyim for a journey to a distant location. Aharoni supposed that the Kittiyim were Greek or Cypriot mercenaries serving in the army of Judah. Na'aman suggests that these mercenaries were serving in the Egyptian army and were being furnished supplies by the king of Judah, as vassal to Egypt.

The most important inscription (Number 24) in the archive was a letter ordering the fortress commander to dispatch reinforcements from Arad and neighboring Kinah to a certain Elisha, so as to help defend Ramat-negeb against an Edomite attack. This letter reads in part:

> From Arad 50 and from Kinah. . . . And you shall send them to Ramat-Negeb by the hand of Malkiyahu the son of Qerab'ur and he shall hand them over to Elisha' the son of Yirmiyahu in Ramat-Negeb, lest anything should happen to the city. And the word of the king is incumbent upon you for your very life! Behold, I have sent to warn you [Eliashib] today: [Get] the men to Elisha': lest Edom should come there![6]

Ramat-negeb, meaning "the height of the Negeb," may, according to some scholars, be identified with Horvat 'Uza, five miles southeast of Arad, which was situated on the frontier. As noted, Rainey suggests that Ramat-negeb is located at Tel 'Ira. Ussishkin would date the archive of Eliashib to the final destruction level of the fortress.

The frequent appearance of the name Edom in the Arad inscriptions, as well as at other Judahite sites, underscores the prominence of the Edomites in the eastern Negev during the seventh to sixth centuries B.C.E. It is apparent that Edom was a real menace to Judah at that time.

Also, ostraca found in the Arad sanctuary contain two names from priestly families, Pashhur and Meremoth. Pashhur, a name probably of Egyptian origin, would have been fairly common in Jeremiah's time. The prophet refers to more than one Pashhur:

> Now the priest Pashhur son of Immer, who was chief officer in the house of the LORD, heard Jeremiah prophesying these things. Then Pashhur struck the prophet Jeremiah, and put him in the stocks that were in the upper Benjamin Gate of the house of the LORD. The next morning when Pashhur released Jeremiah from the stocks, Jeremiah said to him, The LORD has named you not Pashhur but "Terror-all-around" (*magor missabib*). . . . And you, Pashhur, and all who live in your house, shall go into captivity, and to Babylon you shall go. (Jer 20:1–3, 6)

In this passage Jeremiah is engaging in wordplay on the name of the priest Pashhur. This Pashhur was chief officer in the Temple of Jerusalem, second in rank to the high priest.

King Zedekiah sent another Pashhur son of Malchiah to Jeremiah to inquire of the LORD on Judah's behalf (Jer 21:1–2). Pashhur son of Malchiah, and Gedaliah son of another Pashhur, were among those who imprisoned Jeremiah in the cistern (Jer 38:1–6).

Ḥorvat 'Uza

Beit-Arieh, assisted by Bruce Cresson, conducted in 1982 the first season of excavation at Ḥorvat 'Uza (city of Kinah mentioned in an Arad document?), a Judahite fortress situated on the southeastern border of the Kingdom of Judah, about six miles southeast of Tel Arad. The fortress, constructed during the seventh century B.C.E., had three principal phases of occupation: the end of the Iron Age (seventh to sixth century B.C.E.), the Hellenistic period (second century B.C.E.), and the Roman period (second to third century C.E.). None of the pottery dates before the seventh century B.C.E. An adjacent Iron Age settlement was uncovered, together with five Hebrew ostraca, three in the fort and two in the settlement. One of these, consisting of thirteen lines, appears to be complete, but it is still undeciphered.

In the course of six seasons of excavations (1982–1986), the most important finds at Ḥorvat 'Uza were the ostraca. In all, there were twenty-eight in Hebrew, one in Edomite, and one in Aramaic.

In the 1983 season the excavators concentrated on the gate area of the Iron Age fortress. The pottery of this area dated from the seventh century B.C.E. During this excavation season five ostraca inscribed in Hebrew and one in Edomite, all dating from the Iron Age, were discovered. The Edomite ostracon dates from the end of the seventh and the beginning of the sixth century B.C.E.

This relatively complete inscription consists of six lines of text. The writer invokes the blessing of Qaus. It appears that an Edomite official addressed this letter to "Blbl," the fortress commander, who was also an Edomite. The recipient is directed to deliver some food (possibly unleavened dough) to the messenger who brought the letter. The text, despite some illegibility, reads as follows:

> Thus said Lumalak: Say to Blbl! Are you well? I bless you by Qaus. And now give the food that Ahi'ma . . . And may Uziel lift it upon the altar . . . lest the food become leavened.[7]

The excavators are convinced that the presence of this Edomite ostracon at Ḥorvat 'Uza is evidence that this Judahite fortress had been captured by the Edomites about the time of the Babylonian conquest of Judah (588/586 B.C.E.). "The ostracon furnishes the first clear and direct historical evidence for Edomite penetration into the Negev."[8]

The so-called ostracon of Aḥiqam was also discovered at Ḥorvat 'Uza. It was found in the front guardroom of the fortress gate. The text, consisting of four lines, is similar to Arad ostracon Number 24 in that both deal with

The ostracon of Aḥiqam from Ḥorvat 'Uza. This ostracon, found in the front guardroom of the fortress gate, was addressed to Aḥiqam who may have been commander of the fort. The excavators interpret this Hebrew-language ostracon as an administrative document dealing with military organization. *Courtesy of Itzhaq Beit-Arieh and Bruce Cresson.*

the deployment of troops. The ostracon of Ahiqam is "an administrative document providing information on the scope of the military organization in Judah towards the end of the First Temple period."[9]

Horvat Qitmit

The first Edomite shrine ever excavated was at Horvat Qitmit, located in ancient Judah, not in Edom. Between 1984 and 1986, Beit-Arieh excavated at this eastern Negev site which is situated on a flat-topped hill overlooking the Malḥata Valley, slightly southwest of Horvat 'Uza. The site, comprising two building complexes and two enclosures, consists of only one stratum with two phases; it dates from the last days of the Kingdom of Judah.

The presence of a large quantity of Edomite pottery, as well as fragmentary inscriptions containing the name of the Edomite god Qaus, convinced the excavators that the site was Edomite, even though it lay in Judahite territory. Apparently Edom conquered large portions of Judahite land around 586 B.C.E. when the Southern Kingdom was extremely vulnerable, according to Beit-Arieh.

"Qitmit" is related to the Arabic word "Qatamat," meaning dusty, ashy sand, which is an apt description of the region. As a shrine it sheds valuable light on Edomite religious practices. The fact that it was in Judahite territory demonstrates that the Edomites were conquering Judahite land about the same time the Babylonians were vanquishing Judah (586 B.C.E.).

In addition to Edomite pottery, the remains at the site included about five hundred clay figurines as well as fragments of figurines and reliefs. Among the cultic objects were clay cult stands, an ostrich figurine, a lifesized hand attached to a flexed arm, a dagger, and heads from human figurines.

The most spectacular discovery was the head of a goddess with a three-horned miter painted red with black features. This head was found in the rectangular enclosure. The function of the third horn on the divine miter is still not understood. Pirhiya Beck described the goddess's face in these words:

> The asymmetry of the face is particularly noticeable in the unequal eyes; they were incised on bits of clay that were then applied to the face. Again, there is no symmetry in the eyebrows and locks of hair. This lack of symmetry is also evident in the modeling of the mouth, which gives the face a lively expression enhanced by a captivating smile.[10]

Only one (Complex A) of the two areas that constitute the cultic center at Qitmit has been excavated thus far. The sacred precinct, designated Complex A, consists of the following: a three-room rectangular structure; a circular enclosure including a basin (probably used for water storage), a pit, and an altar (for animal sacrifices); and a *bamah* (a low platform of fieldstones) surrounded by walls on three sides. The cultic objects were discovered in the *bamah* enclosure. The excavator thinks that the shrine's Complex A functioned as a place for animal sacrifice, ritual meals, and the offering of prayers. It would have served the Edomites located in Judahite territory toward the end of the First Temple period.

Head of a goddess from Ḥorvat Qitmit. This head is wheel-made from clay. Found in the cult precinct of Ḥorvat Qitmit, the first Edomite shrine ever excavated, the horned miter identifies the head as a deity. With respect to the three horns, one is located on each side of the head and a third in the middle of the forehead. *Courtesy of Itzhaq Beit-Arieh and Bruce Cresson.*

'Aroer

'Aroer is a five-acre site located in the Negev of Israel, fifteen miles southeast of Beer-sheba. This fortified outpost, situated on a Negev trade route, is identified with modern 'Ar'arah. It occupies the top of a hill, 1,300 feet above sea level. Inasmuch as it is surrounded on three sides by wadis (dry riverbeds), it was well protected.

Three towns mentioned in the Bible are known by the name 'Aroer, two of them in Transjordan. 'Aroer of the Negev is mentioned specifically in connection with David when he sent some of the spoils to the elders of 'Aroer, after his victory over the Amalekite raiders (1 Sam 30:26–28). However, the remains at 'Aroer do not date so early as David. Apparently, Davidic 'Aroer is located at Tel Esdar, about a mile and a half north of 'Aroer.

Between 1975 and 1981, Avraham Biran and Rudolph Cohen conducted an emergency excavation at 'Aroer. On the basis of their investigations, the site was

Jasper seal and impression. Found at 'Aroer, this seal bears the name *lqosa'* ("belonging to Qosa"), the Edomite deity. The name of the seal's owner apparently included the deity's name. The seal may have come from Edomite territory. On the left is a wax impression of the seal. *Courtesy of the Hebrew Union College–Jewish Institute of Religion, Jerusalem.*

Astarte, goddess of fertility. This figurine was found at 'Aroer. Made in a mold, it dates from the late seventh to the early sixth century B.C.E. Astarte is portrayed wearing a pointed hat. *Courtesy of the Hebrew Union College–Jewish Institute of Religion, Jerusalem.*

first settled in the seventh century B.C.E., after Sennacherib's destruction of Judah in 701 B.C.E. Biran thinks the fortress at 'Aroer may have been built by Josiah. Because of its location on the trade route, 'Aroer may have served as an administrative center in southern Judah. Biran believes that 'Aroer was linked culturally and commercially with the Mediterranean coast as well as with Edom.

'Aroer was settled again in the Herodian period (from the first century B.C.E. to the first century C.E.). The pottery found at Stratum II of 'Aroer pertains to the same period as En-gedi (Stratum V), Lachish (Stratum II), Tell Beit Mirsim (Stratum A3), and Jerusalem (Stratum X), all dating from the late seventh to the early sixth century B.C.E., when those cities enjoyed a certain prosperity.

Among the important finds at 'Aroer was a cone-shaped jasper seal belonging to an Edomite. It was inscribed *lqosa'*, that is, "belonging to Qosa," the Edomite deity. Again, this seal indicates some connection between Edom and Judah before the Babylonian conquest of Judah in 586 B.C.E. Five intact Astarte figurines, representing the goddess of fertility, were also uncovered at 'Aroer. Their date ranges from the late seventh to the early sixth century B.C.E.

Remains of a house at 'Aroer. Dating from the late seventh century B.C.E., these remains were found immediately below the surface. *Courtesy of the Hebrew Union College–Jewish Institute of Religion, Jerusalem.*

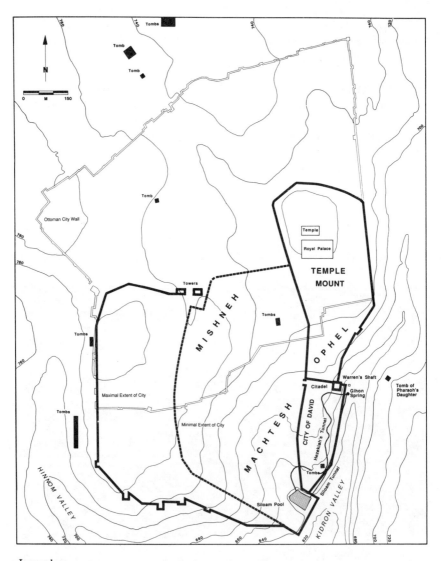

Jerusalem

5

Cities of Judah

Then the prophet Jeremiah spoke all these words to Zedekiah king of Judah, in Jerusalem, when the army of the king of Babylon was fighting against *Jerusalem* and against all the cities of Judah that were left, *Lachish* and *Azekah*; for these were the only fortified cities of Judah that remained. (Jer 34:6-7)

The capital city of Jerusalem was the greatest city of the Kingdom of Judah. The large fortified city of Lachish was second in importance to Jerusalem in the Southern Kingdom. Azekah, neighbor of Lachish, was one of the last two fortress-cities to withstand the assaults of the Babylonians in 586 B.C.E.

Jerusalem

The book of Jeremiah contains a great deal of information about Jerusalem; in fact, it has more than one hundred references to the city. The seventh century B.C.E., the era of Jeremiah, was a time of prosperity for Jerusalem, when the city attained the height of its development. There was increased building activity in both Judah and Jerusalem in the last half of the seventh century B.C.E. The special status accorded Jerusalem is illustrated by the frequent occurrence of the expression "Judah and Jerusalem," already used by Isaiah. In the following verse Jerusalem is the only city mentioned by name alongside the specific districts:

And the people shall come from the towns of Judah and the places around Jerusalem, from the land of Benjamin, from the Shephelah, from the hill country, and from the Negeb, bringing burnt offerings and sacrifices, grain offerings and frankincense, and bringing thank offerings to the house of the LORD. (Jer 17:26)

Jeremiah also witnessed the destruction of Jerusalem at the hands of the Babylonians:

> And many nations will pass by this city [Jerusalem], and all of them will say one to another, "Why has the LORD dealt in this way with that great city (*ha'ir haggedolah hazzo't*)? (Jer 22:8)

Donald Wiseman notes that "in the Old Testament the adjective 'great' (*gdl*) before 'city' is used to point to the status of an 'important' royal capital . . . and not necessarily to emphasise [*sic*] its colossal size."[1]

Location and Extent

The topography of Jerusalem is crucial for the proper understanding of the book of Jeremiah. Jerusalem, built on a hilltop, is situated on a limestone plateau 2,400 feet above sea level in the central hill country of Palestine. After David conquered Jerusalem at the beginning of the tenth century B.C.E., making it his royal capital, Jerusalem became known as the City of David. Like the earlier settlements of Jerusalem that date back at least five thousand years, the City of David, constricted to an area of about fifteen acres, was located on the narrow hill southeast of the Temple Mount. Today, the City of David is outside the walls of the Old City.

The presence of the perennial Gihon (in Hebrew, literally "gusher") spring outside the walls at the foot of the southeast ridge of Jerusalem accounts for the location of the original settlement of Jerusalem in that narrow area of the city. In the Iron II period (1000–586 B.C.E.), the Gihon, the only source of fresh water in the area, fed three interconnected subterranean waterworks, and they still function today. Warren's Shaft, the earliest of these systems, connected the northern part of the City of David with the water source. It was presumed to date from the end of Solomon's reign (961–922 B.C.E.). On the basis of recent geological investigations, however, Warren's Shaft could date as early as the Canaanite period. Consisting of a shaft and connecting tunnels, Warren's Shaft is named after Charles Warren, who rediscovered it in 1867. In times of siege this shaft enabled Jerusalemites, while remaining within the wall, to draw water from the Gihon spring, which was outside the wall. If Warren's Shaft was actually in existence before David's time, then Joab, commander of David's army, may have gained entrance to Jerusalem through Warren's Shaft (*ṣinnor*), thereby capturing the Jebusite city for David (2 Sam 5:8).

Jerusalem's second hydraulic system was the Siloam Channel, which provided water for irrigation. It served as an aqueduct carrying water along the Kidron Valley to reservoirs at the southern end of the city.

The third system was Hezekiah's rock-hewn tunnel, a 1,750-foot-long passage, dating from 701 B.C.E. This meandering aqueduct diverted water from the Gihon spring to the Siloam pool, a reservoir within the city walls, located

Aerial view of the City of David. Looking north. "City of David" designates the fifteen-acre, southeastern spur, below the Temple Mount (with the Dome of the Rock at its center), outside the present walls of the Old City. The road on the right cuts through the Kidron Valley which divides the City of David from the village of Silwan. The road on the left marks the Tyropoeon or Central Valley which serves as the western boundary of the City of David. *Photograph by Zev Radovan.*

at the southwest corner of the City of David. Until recently, the construction of Hezekiah's tunnel was considered a remarkable engineering feat for its time. However, the study of Dan Gill of the Geological Survey of Israel concludes that the tunnel was only a modification of natural caves already formed in Jerusalem's limestone bedrock.[2]

Hezekiah constructed this enclosed aqueduct to protect Jerusalem's water supply during the anticipated attack by the Assyrian king Sennacherib in 701 B.C.E. A few details about the tunnel's construction are contained on a monumental inscription, discovered in 1880, near the southern entrance to the tunnel.

Jerusalem is surrounded by precipitous valleys, five hundred feet deep, on three sides. However, the northern side of the city, lacking natural defenses, has always been vulnerable. In their initial attack on the city in 588/586 B.C.E., the Babylonians breached the northern wall of Jerusalem.

The city is bounded on the east and part of the north by the Kidron Valley, which separates Jerusalem from the Mount of Olives. King Josiah, having eradicated from the Temple all illicit cult objects, ordered them to be destroyed in the Kidron Valley.

Lying to the south and southwest of Jerusalem is the Hinnom Valley. It acquired a sinister reputation by association with the shameful Tophet shrine where children were apparently sacrificed as burnt offerings.

The Tyropoeon is the small north-south valley in the center of Jerusalem; shallower than the Kidron and the Hinnom, today it is only a slight depression. Running southward through the heart of the Old City, the Tyropoeon divided the eastern hill (Lower City) from the western hill (Upper City).

The western hill, lying between the Hinnom and Tyropoeon valleys, was broader than the eastern hill. The Jewish historian Josephus described Jerusalem as a city divided into two parts: the Lower City and the Upper City. The Lower City encompassed the City of David and the Temple Mount. The Upper City or western hill incorporated the present Jewish and Armenian Quarters, the Citadel, and Mount Zion. In time, the Lower City was intensely populated and became the residential quarter of the poor, while the more prosperous lived in the Upper City.

The population of the original City of David numbered about 2,000. In Solomon's reign (961–922 B.C.E.), Jerusalem, including the Temple Mount, was about thirty-two acres in extent, with a population of about 5,000. When Hezekiah was king (715–687 B.C.E.), Jerusalem expanded considerably, extending to the western hill (Upper City). The city may have been as large as one hundred and forty acres, with a population numbering about 15,000. Jerusalem's demographic growth in that period is accounted for by the influx of immigrants from the Northern Kingdom after the fall of Samaria in 721 B.C.E. as well as by those emigrating from the west after Sennacherib's siege in 701 B.C.E., when the provinces of Judah were ceded to Philistia.

Biblical texts together with excavations help to determine the extent of Jerusalem in the time of Jeremiah and later. One of the prophetic texts envisions in detail the rebuilt and enlarged city of Jerusalem. However, it may date to Nehemiah, governor of Jerusalem, in the Persian period (539–332 B.C.E.):

> The days are surely coming, says the LORD, when the city shall be rebuilt for the LORD from the tower of Hananel to the Corner Gate. And the measuring line shall go out farther, straight to the hill Gareb, and shall then turn to Goah. The whole valley [the Hinnom] of the dead bodies and the ashes, and all the fields as far as the Wadi Kidron, to the corner of the Horse Gate toward the east, shall be sacred to the LORD. It [Jerusalem] shall never again be uprooted or overthrown. (Jer 31:38–40)

This description of the new boundaries of Jerusalem moves in a counterclockwise direction, beginning at the northwest corner of the Temple enclosure and terminating at the southeast corner of the palace area, south of the Temple. Hananel designates a tower at the northwest corner of the Temple Mount. The Corner Gate would have been on the west side of the city, and the Horse Gate on the southeast corner of the Temple enclosure. The Gareb hill and Goah are otherwise unknown. According to Gabriel Barkay, the Gareb and Goah may describe the northern suburbs of Jerusalem that were outside the city wall before the destruction of the city in 586 B.C.E.

Archaeology

Jerusalem, occupied for almost six thousand years, is one of the most intensively excavated cities in the world. The results of 125 years of excavation help shed light on this complex city. As the pace of excavation quickened with the reunification of Jerusalem after the Arab-Israeli War of 1967, more has been learned about Jerusalem during the past twenty-five years than in the preceding hundred years.

Before the nineteenth century, Jerusalem was not well known. The American biblical scholar Edward Robinson, who visited Jerusalem for the first time in 1838, played a key role in the rediscovery of Jerusalem. As a result, his name is associated with three important monuments in Jerusalem. He was the first explorer in modern times to investigate Hezekiah's tunnel by actually crawling through it; he discovered the remains of Jerusalem's Third Wall in the northern part of the city; he noted the spring of an arch ("Robinson's Arch"), near the southwest corner of the Temple platform, associated with a broad stairway ascending from the Tyropoeon valley to the Temple Mount. Robinson may have accomplished even more in Jerusalem had he not dismissed in principle "all ecclesiastical tradition" concerning religious sites such as the Holy Sepulchre.

Inspired by Robinson's achievements, England established in 1865 the

Palestine Exploration Fund to investigate Palestine systematically and scientifically. British engineers illuminated the historical topography of Jerusalem, identifying some of the principal monuments and boundaries of the city as well as the water systems. Charles Wilson and Charles Warren, clarifying the ancient topography of Jerusalem, investigated the northeast corner of the City of David, in the vicinity of the Temple Mount. Around the four sides of the Temple enclosure, Warren, between 1867 and 1870, made soundings by means of an intricate series of vertical shafts and lateral tunnels, so as not to disturb existing structures or arouse the suspicions of the Turkish authorities.

Several other archaeologists, including Charles Clermont-Ganneau, Frederick Bliss, Archibald Dickie, R. A. S. Macalister, John Crowfoot, Gerald Fitzgerald, and Raymond Weill, continued the work of the pioneers, but their conventional methodology remained deficient.

A new era began in the 1960s with the systematic excavations of Kathleen Kenyon. Utilizing modern scientific techniques, she cut a major trench the length of the eastern slope of the City of David, and in the process she conducted ceramic, stratigraphic, and architectural analyses. Kenyon succeeded in solving some of the historical problems relating to the City of David's history; at the same time, she laid the foundations for future archaeological investigation. Because of the limitations of her method, she inevitably came to some erroneous conclusions.

With the reunification of East and West Jerusalem in 1967, Israeli archaeologists undertook the intensive investigation of the Old City in East Jerusalem during three long-term excavations as well as several smaller projects. Besides the three principal digs described below, the other short-term undertakings centered on the Armenian Quarter, Mount Zion, the Jaffa Gate Citadel, and the Damascus Gate.

Benjamin Mazar, concentrating on the southwestern corner of the Temple Mount, extended his probes along the western and southern retaining walls of the Temple enclosure. The important discoveries from this major project pertain principally to the Herodian period (36 B.C.E.–70 C.E.), but valuable light has also been cast on the Iron Age through the Arab period.

Nahman Avigad's dig in the center of the Jewish Quarter of the Old City marked the first time that area had ever been excavated. Important information for the period of Jeremiah came to light in this extensive project. The excavator established that as early as the eighth century B.C.E. Jerusalem's western hill had been settled and subsequently enclosed within a wall. In the eighth to the seventh century B.C.E., Jerusalem expanded to four times its former size.

Evidence for this development hinges on Avigad's uncovering in the Jewish Quarter (in the northern part of the western hill) a massive fortification wall, known from Nehemiah's postexilic restoration of Jerusalem's city wall as the "Broad Wall" (Neh 3:8). This stone wall (213 feet long, 25 feet wide, and 10 feet high), the first city wall ever constructed on the western hill, is attributed to Hezekiah (2 Chr 32:5). In the late eighth century B.C.E. this wall protected the western side of Jerusalem from Assyrian attack.

Avigad believed this wall surrounded the entire plateau of the western hill, including perhaps the Second Quarter (Mishneh) and the Mortar (Maktesh) mentioned by the prophet Zephaniah, a contemporary of Jeremiah (Zeph 1:10–11). Huldah, a Jerusalemite prophetess during the reign of Josiah (640–609 B.C.E.), resided in the Second Quarter or elusive Mishneh (2 Kings 22:14). Mishneh and Maktesh may have constituted the center of

The "Broad Wall." This massive stone wall was exposed by Nahman Avigad in 1970 during his excavations of the Jewish Quarter (Upper City) of Jerusalem. Constructed by King Hezekiah in the late eighth century B.C.E., it protected the western suburbs of Jerusalem against Assyrian attack. *Courtesy of Nahman Avigad, Institute of Archaeology, Hebrew University, Jerusalem.*

political and commercial activity during Josiah's reign. Apparently they were located on the northern side of Jerusalem, the direction from which the Babylonian attackers approached the city. The Mishneh, then, would have been the first quarter captured by the Babylonians after breaching the northern wall of Jerusalem.

In confirmation of reports in 2 Kings 25:9–10 and Josephus' *Antiquities of the Jews,* Avigad uncovered dramatic evidence of the two-year Babylonian siege of Jerusalem. Amidst ashes at the base of a defense tower erected to protect the northern side of the city four arrowheads were buried. One was iron and three were bronze, all shot by Babylonian archers. One of the bronze arrowheads was a so-called "Scythian type." The Scythians, whom Jeremiah (51:27) referred to under the name "Ashkenaz," were a nomadic tribe of

A "Scythian type" arrowhead. Found in Jerusalem, this cast, bronze arrowhead is distinguished by its three triangular fins and hollow socket. This is tangible evidence of the ferocity of the Babylonian siege in 586 B.C.E. *Courtesy of* Biblical Archaeology Review.

Indo-European origin who moved from Central Asia to southern Russia where they established an empire that lasted from the eighth and seventh centuries to the second century B.C.E. The Scythians, known for their savagery, used a double-curved bow, and their arrows had trefoil-shaped heads. The one found by Avigad had three triangular fins and a hollow socket into which a shaft was inserted.[3]

Beginning in 1978, Yigal Shiloh continued the earlier archaeological investigations of Kenyon. He concentrated on the southeastern hill above the Gihon spring, the oldest occupied area of the city. Shiloh also reinvestigated Jerusalem's three water systems, all connected with the Gihon spring. Further, Shiloh uncovered a monumental stepped-stone structure rising over fifty feet. It may have served as a podium to support the administrative buildings constructed by David on the royal acropolis. Shiloh was inclined to date this mammoth structure no later than the tenth century B.C.E., but additional evidence supports an earlier date in the fourteenth to the thirteenth century B.C.E. (Late Bronze Age). This was Macalister's Jebusite construction and Kenyon's "Maccabean" one.

Shiloh uncovered in Stratum X (seventh to the sixth century B.C.E.) unquestionable evidence of the destruction of the First Temple and of the city of Jerusalem by Nebuchadrezzar in 588/586 B.C.E. Several other archaeological digs in the Southern Kingdom of Judah provide historical-archaeological parallels for this same destruction, notably Stratum II at Lachish. The other sites that show traces of destruction in that same time frame include Ramat Raḥel (Stratum V), En-gedi (Stratum V), Arad (Stratum VI), 'Aroer (Stratum II), and Tel 'Ira (Stratum VI).

Jerusalem's Stratum X revealed layers of ash covering the building structures. On the floors of these buildings were the burnt remains of wooden furnishings and ceiling beams. Israelite houses, built into the lower part of

The stepped-stone structure. This terraced structure, founded in the fourteenth-thirteenth century B.C.E., is situated on the northeast extremity of the City of David. Preserved to a height of over fifty feet, it may have served as the supporting foundation for Jerusalem's acropolis. Israelite residences of the seventh and sixth centuries B.C.E., including Aḥiel's House (marked by the two upright pillars), the Burnt Room, and the Bullae House, were built along the edges of the stepped-stone structure. *Photograph by Zev Radovan.*

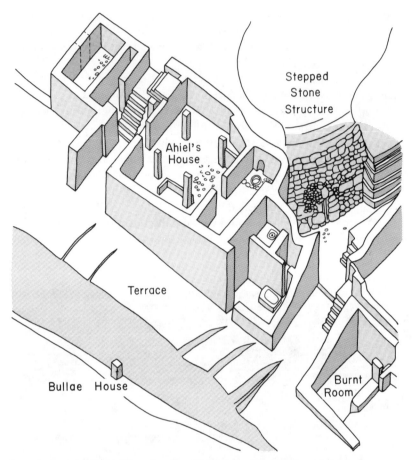

Isometric reconstruction of strip of buildings, City of David. Iron Age houses at base of stepped-stone structure: Aḥiel's House (with four pillars supporting the upper story) and Burnt Room on upper terrace; Bullae House on lower terrace. *Courtesy of City of David Archaeological Project.*

the stepped-stone structure, were destroyed by fire in 588/586 B.C.E. The excavators gave appropriate names to three of these houses. "Aḥiel's House," a large four-room house, was so called because a Hebrew ostracon bearing the name "Aḥiel" was found within. The "Burnt Room" was so denoted because of the carbonized wood and ash accumulated on its floors. The excavators traced the remains of the charred wood to local trees, identified as *Pistacia atlantica*, as well as to imported boxwood. The "Bullae House" received its name from the fifty-one bullae (seals originally appended to papyrus documents) lying in its northern corner. Bronze and iron arrowheads (exactly like those found by Avigad in the Jewish Quarter

Aḥiel's House in the City of David. The large four-room house in the left half of the photograph, so designated because an ostracon bearing his name was discovered inside. The house measures twenty-six by forty feet. *Photograph by Zev Radovan. Courtesy of the City of David Archaeological Project.*

Burnt Room in the City of David. Located at the base of the stepped-stone structure, this room is so designated because of the layer of dark ash found on the floor. This carbonized wood and ash were the residue from the room's wood furnishings and ceiling beams. *Photograph by Y. Harari. Courtesy of the City of David Archaeological Project.*

dig), attesting to the ferocity of the Babylonian siege, were also uncovered in the Burnt Room and the Bullae House.

Arrowheads in the City of David. Arrowheads were also found in the burnt layer of the Burnt Room and the House of the Bullae. Most are of iron, while the "Scythian" arrowhead on the extreme right is of bronze. *Photograph by Zev Radovan. Courtesy of the City of David Archaeological Project.*

Manasseh and Josiah

From the mid-eighth century B.C.E. to its demise in 586 B.C.E., the Kingdom of Judah enjoyed a renaissance, although always under the threat of attack from its imperial neighbors— Assyria, Egypt, and Babylonia. Accordingly, the kings of the late Judahite monarchy built up the defenses of Jerusalem.

Manasseh, son and successor of Hezekiah, had the longest reign of any Judahite king (687–642 B.C.E.). This was a period of increased building activity in Jerusalem. His regime served as the link between the prophets of the eighth and seventh centuries B.C.E. The Bible gives a strongly negative assessment of Manasseh's theology but says almost nothing about the economic and political conditions of the times. This Assyrian vassal-king refortified Jerusalem, building a new defensive wall:

> Afterward he [Manasseh] built an outer wall for the city of David west of Gihon, in the valley, reaching the entrance at the Fish Gate; he carried it around Ophel, and raised it to a very great height. (2 Chr 33:14)

Ophel designates the topographic saddle connecting the City of David with the royal precinct on the Temple Mount. Manasseh's outer wall, situated on the eastern slope of the southeastern hill, continued north around the Temple area. Kenyon uncovered this wall on the eastern slope of the hill of the City of David. Designating it "Wall NA," she attributed it to King Hezekiah. Dan Bahat is convinced this wall was built by Manasseh.[4]

Jerusalem reached its zenith under King Josiah (640–609 B.C.E.). His religious reform conferred special status on Jerusalem and its Temple, making it the exclusive place of sacrifice in Judah. Several places in Jerusalem figure in the account of Josiah's reform, but they cannot be identified today.

Fortifications

In his description of the devastation of Jerusalem by the Babylonians, Jeremiah mentioned the siege ramp (*sollah*) three times:

> For thus says the LORD of hosts: Cut down her trees; cast up (*šipku*) a siege ramp (*sollah*) against Jerusalem. This is the city that must be punished; there is nothing but oppression within her. (Jer 6:6)

The root *špk*, literally "to pour out," refers to the building of a siege ramp in the sense of "to heap up." Behind the directive in this text are Deuteronomy's rules for the conduct of warfare forbidding the destruction of trees. Only trees no longer producing fruit could be cut down "for use in building siegeworks" (Deut 20:19–20). Wood from the local trees would also have been used in the construction of war machines.

> See, the siege-ramps (*hassollot*) have been cast up against the city [Jerusalem] to take it. (Jer 32:24)

> For thus says the LORD, the God of Israel, concerning the houses of this city [Jerusalem] and the houses of the kings of Judah that were torn down to make a defense against the siege-ramps (*hassollot*) and before the sword. (Jer 33:4)

This last text is describing the construction of a counterramp built against the inner wall of the defending city.

Ancient cities were fortified by surrounding mudbrick walls on all sides. During the Iron Age II period (1000–586 B.C.E.), Judah used the casemate wall, consisting of two parallel walls, joined at intervals by short cross walls to form chambers. The casemates or small chambers functioned as living quarters or were used for storage. Houses were often built into the city walls—for example, the house of Rahab the harlot (Josh 2:1–21).

The Assyrians perfected the art of warfare, and the neighboring peoples, including Israel, learned from them. In the conduct of siege warfare (*maṣor*), there were siege works, siege towers, and siege mounds. *Sollah*, translated "siege ramp," derives from the root *sll*, "to heap up."

In antiquity there were several ways to attack and defend a city, including the siege ramp. The attackers would gain access by surrounding the besieged city with an earthen ramp or mound formed by a pile of stones (*sollah*). *Dayeq*, another word for a mound, is synonymous with *sollah*. The ramp would be reinforced with wooden planks (Jer 6:6), so it could support the siege machines, such as the battering rams (*karim*), that were used for breaching the defenders' walls or sapping under the walls to gain entrance. The wooden beam of the battering ram, equipped with a metal point, was suspended from the war machine by thick ropes. The body of the battering ram, mobilized by four to six wheels, was enclosed to protect its operators from the defenders' missiles.

Siege and Fall

When Zedekiah (597–586 B.C.E.), the last king of Judah, rebelled against Babylon despite Jeremiah's advice, Nebuchadrezzar began a siege in 588 B.C.E. of the Southern Kingdom that lasted eighteen months, resulting in the almost complete destruction of Jerusalem:

> In the fifth month, on the tenth day of the month—which was the nineteenth year of King Nebuchadrezzar, king of Babylon—Nebuzaradan the captain of the bodyguard who served the king of Babylon, entered Jerusalem. He burned the house [the Temple] of the LORD, the king's house, and all the houses of Jerusalem; every great house he burned down. All the army of the Chaldeans [Babylonians], who were with the captain of the guard, broke down all the walls around Jerusalem. (Jer 52:12–14)

In a parallel passage describing the destruction by fire of the Upper City, Jeremiah stated:

> The Chaldeans [Babylonians] burned the king's house (*bet hammelek*) [the royal palace] and the houses of the people (*bet ha'am*), and broke down the walls of Jerusalem. (Jer 39:8)

This verse, as B. Mazar explains, refers to two extensive complexes—*bet hammelek* and *bet ha'am*. The phrase "the houses of the people," a translation based on an emendation of the text, should be rendered in the singular, "the house of the people" (*bet ha'am*), referring to the meeting place of the "people of the land" (*'am ha'areṣ*). Mazar describes *'am ha'areṣ* as "an assembly, comprised of the landed gentry of Judah, which held an important position in the political life of the Judean kingdom." He continues, "It had functioned alongside the Davidic kings, most noticeably since the reign of Josiah." According to Mazar, *'am ha'areṣ* constituted an anti-Egyptian faction supporting Josiah and his son and successor Jehoahaz, both of whom were anti-Egyptian.[5]

Concerning the demise of Zedekiah when the Babylonians took Jerusalem, Jeremiah relates:

> When King Zedekiah of Judah and all the soldiers saw them [the Babylonians], they fled, going out of the city at night by way of the king's garden through the gate between the two walls; and they [Zedekiah and his soldiers] went toward the Arabah [the area of the Dead Sea]. (Jer 39:4)

"The gate between the two walls" was located in the southeast wall of the City of David. The double wall may refer to the wall built by Hezekiah to protect the Siloam pool.

After the destruction in 586 B.C.E., Judah and its capital, Jerusalem, continued to be inhabited. Gedaliah was appointed governor of Judah but unfortunately was murdered (2 Kings 25:22–26). According to Jeremiah, pilgrims continued to arrive in Jerusalem from the north in the garb of mourners and to offer sacrifice at the site of the Temple:

> On the day after the murder of Gedaliah, before anyone knew of it, eighty men arrived from Shechem and Shiloh and Samaria, with their beards shaved and their clothes torn, and their bodies gashed, bringing grain offerings and incense to present at the temple of the LORD. (Jer 41:4–5)

Lachish

Both biblical and nonbiblical texts mention the strategic Canaanite and Israelite city of Lachish. Its location was uncertain until W. F. Albright, in 1929, proposed Tell ed-Duweir as the site of Lachish, an identification that has stood the test of time. This imposing mound in the foothills of Judah is situated about thirty miles southwest of Jerusalem and fifteen miles west of Hebron. The tell is rectangular in shape and quite large, measuring thirty acres at the base and eighteen acres at the summit. Occupation of Lachish extended from the Chalcolithic period (fourth millennium) until its final abandonment about 150 B.C.E. Deep valleys protect the mound on all sides, except the southwest corner near where the city gate was located. This vulnerable area was the natural target of hostile assaults, as happened with the Assyrian attack in 701 B.C.E. and again with the Babylonian incursion in 588/586. B.C.E.

James Starkey conducted systematic excavations at Lachish from 1932 to 1938, concentrating on the city-gate complex and the Judahite palace-fort. With respect to the gate, he was able to distinguish and date the superimposed city-gate Levels II and III, the Level II complex having been constructed above (and thereby subsequent to) Level III. Level II was a sparsely populated Judahite city, whereas the Level III city was much larger. Starkey correctly ascribed the destruction of Level II to the Babylonian siege in 588/586 B.C.E. when the city was totally destroyed by fire. Subsequent excavations demonstrated that Starkey had erred in dating Level III to the Babylonian campaign against King Jehoiachin in 597 B.C.E.

In 1973, David Ussishkin undertook long-term excavations at Lachish, giving special attention to the city-gate complex. He speculates that the new city represented by Level II, including the city wall and city gate, may have been partly built by King Josiah (640–609 B.C.E.). At the same time, he concurs with Starkey that the destruction of Level II was wrought by

The Lachish roadway. The roadway leading up to the Judahite city gate at Lachish (Levels III and II) under reconstruction. A broad road, flanked by massive walls, extended from the bottom of the mound to the gate complex. Levels III and II were approached by the same roadway. *Courtesy of David Ussishkin.*

the Babylonian siege in 588/586 B.C.E. In addition, Ussishkin has established, to the satisfaction of most archaeologists, that the controversial Level III dated from 701 B.C.E. when the Assyrians under Sennacherib besieged Lachish, completely destroying the fortified city by fire.

Restoration of Lachish's city gate is in progress under the direction of Ussishkin. The work includes the inner and the outer gateway, the road leading to the gate, and a portion of the Iron Age city wall.

Ostraca (Letters)

Among the most significant written finds in the burnt rubble of Level II at Lachish, which was rebuilt sometime during the seventh century B.C.E., were twenty-one ostraca or storage jar fragments inscribed in black ink. These well-known Lachish Letters (most were letters, and the remainder were lists of names) date from about 590 B.C.E., during the reign of Zedekiah, the last king of Judah, and immediately before the Babylonian siege of Lachish. Eighteen of the inscribed potsherds, blackened by fire, were found in 1935 lying on the floor and covered with ashes in a guardroom in the piazza between the outer and the inner city gate, destroyed by the Babylonians in

586 B.C.E. The remaining three inscribed fragments were discovered in 1938 in the vicinity of the palace-fort.

Hoshaiah, stationed in a garrison somewhere between Lachish and Jerusalem, dispatched these letters to Yaosh, military commander of Lachish, during the final days of Judah. The garrison of Hoshaiah may have been located at Kiriath-jearim (usually identified with the village of Abu Ghosh). Written in Hebrew prose like that of the Bible, these invaluable ostraca illuminate Hebrew philology and epigraphy and at the same time shed light on the era of Jeremiah.

As almost always happens with epigraphic finds, especially when problems of decipherment are involved, scholars are divided in their interpretation. So,

Level II city gate at Lachish. Pictured is the forecourt in front of the inner gate of Level II, the gate where the Lachish Letters were found. *Courtesy of David Ussishkin.*

Restoration of the Lachish city gate. The Judahite city gate of Lachish
(Levels III and II) under reconstruction. The largest and most impressive city
gate in ancient Israel is at Lachish. Several gates were built, one on top of the
other, at the southwest corner of the city. The restoration incorporates the
remains of two of the superimposed gates, namely, Level III (destroyed by
Sennacherib in 701 B.C.E.) and Level II (destroyed by Nebuchadrezzar II in
586 B.C.E.). Note the massive tower of the outer gate. The fortifications at
Lachish consisted of a double fortification wall and a double gateway
complex. *Courtesy of David Ussishkin.*

too, with the Lachish Letters (not to mention the Dead Sea Scrolls). Yigael
Yadin suggested that these ostraca were only drafts of a letter dispatched
not *to* but *from* Lachish to Jerusalem. In this scenario, Hoshaiah would have
been commander of Lachish, and Yaosh a prominent official in Jerusalem.
Among other reasons, Yadin argued that papyrus, not potsherds, was used
for official documents. In his view, the written material on the potsherds
was transcribed onto papyrus before being dispatched to Jerusalem.[6]

The specific document under discussion here is Lachish Letter IV, which
reads:

> May Yahweh bring my lord this very day good tidings! And now, in
> accordance with all that my lord hath written, so hath thy servant
> done. I have written on the door (*delet*) in accordance with all that
> [my lord] hath directed me. And with regard to what my lord hath
> written about Beth-haraphid, there is nobody there. And as for

> Semakyahu, Shemayahu hath taken him and brought him up to the capital [Jerusalem], and thy servant . . . send thither. . . . And [my lord] will know that we are watching *for* the [fire] signals (*mas'et*) of Lachish, according to all the signs which my lord hath given, for we cannot see Azekah.[7]

The corresponding biblical citation is the following:

> . . . when the army of the king of Babylon was fighting against Jerusalem and against all the cities of Judah that were left, *Lachish* and *Azekah*; for these were the only fortified cities of Judah that remained. (Jer 34:7)

The historical assumption is that the Babylonians had already captured Azekah, situated eleven miles northeast of Lachish, and Lachish was about to be taken.

With respect to "the [fire] signals (*mas'et*)," the word *mas'et* (literally, "lifting") occurs in Jeremiah where the prophet warns of an imminent invasion from the north. There it is translated "[fire] signal" on the basis of Lachish Letter IV:

> Flee for safety, O children of Benjamin, from the midst of Jerusalem! Blow the trumpet in Tekoa, and raise a signal (*mas'et*) on Beth-haccherem; for evil looms out of the north, and great destruction. (Jer 6:1)

Crucial to Yadin's argument is the phrase "we are watching for the [fire] signals of Lachish" (*'el mas'et lakiš naḥnu šomerim*). He maintained, on the basis of biblical parallels, that the preposition *'el* should be translated "over" and not "for," in the sense that the writer (Hoshaiah) "is tending" the fire signals of Lachish. According to Yadin's reading, Hoshaiah (mentioned by name only in Lachish Letter III) was commander of Lachish, and Yaosh an official in Jerusalem.

Frank Cross disagrees with Yadin's interpretation on the basis of Hebrew orthography. At the same time, he considers Lachish Letter III as "a letter from a junior officer, Hoshaiah, to his commander at Lachish, Ya'osh."[8]

Lachish Letter III contains the first occurrence outside the Bible of *nabi'*, the common Hebrew word for "prophet."

> . . . And as for the letter of Tobyahu, servant of the king, which came to Shallum, son of Yaddua, through the instrumentality of the prophet (*nabi'*), saying, "Take care!" thy servant [Hoshaiah] hath sent it to my lord [Yaosh].[9]

Some interpreters have suggested that the prophetic reference here is to Jeremiah, but this conjecture cannot be sustained. There were other prophets, some known and others anonymous, who were contemporaries of Jeremiah.

Azekah

Lachish and Azekah, cities of the Shephelah (Lowlands), mentioned both in Jeremiah and in the Lachish Letters, lie between the Philistine plain and the mountains of Judah. The fortress-city of Azekah, identified with Tell Zakariyah, is situated on a high hill, 1,214 feet above sea level, northeast of Lachish. According to Jeremiah, Azekah and Lachish were the last two Judahite fortresses to succumb to the siege operations of the Babylonians just before their assault on Jerusalem. Bliss, assisted by Macalister, excavated at Tell Zakariyah during three seasons in 1898–1899. The nine-acre site was settled from about 1500 B.C.E. through the Byzantine period (324–635 C.E.). One can locate from the topography alone, even without excavation, the siege ramp at Azekah.

One of the important discoveries at Tell Zakariyah was an Israelite fortress with eight towers. The chronology of the site is somewhat uncertain, but a study of comparable Israelite fortresses found at Kadesh-barnea and elsewhere suggests that the fortress at Tell Zakariyah dates from the eighth century B.C.E.

6

Inscriptions and Literacy

Writing

In the ancient Near East, writing was invented as early as the third millennium, appearing first in Mesopotamia and a little later in Egypt. The alphabet dates from the first part of the second millennium. Writing emerges in ancient Israel from the twelfth century B.C.E., but it does not imply that literacy was widespread in Palestine; such a phenomenon is difficult to measure. Compared with the wealth of written materials found in Egypt and Mesopotamia, Israel was relatively poor in inscriptions during the period of the monarchy (1020–586 B.C.E.), but this may be due in part to the use of perishable writing materials such as papyrus and leather.

From the eighth century B.C.E. onward, the knowledge of writing among the people of Israel and Judah was on the increase. The majority of extant texts come from the late eighth to the sixth century B.C.E., especially during the period of Jeremiah. Among the eighth-century epigraphic materials are the Samaria ostraca, which are inscribed potsherds that list quantities of fine oil and wine, as well as the Siloam inscription, carved on the east wall of Hezekiah's tunnel in Jerusalem.

Seals (objects with writing cut into their surface) are devices used for establishing personal ownership. Again, a large number of seals date from the late eighth century B.C.E., and especially from the seventh century B.C.E. and later. Important for their cultural significance, these seals convey valuable information about government, administration, and religious practice.

The book of Jeremiah, especially chapter 36 (dating from Jehoiakim's reign) and chapter 32 (dating from Zedekiah's reign), discloses specific information about ancient writing. Jeremiah 36, one of the most informative chapters of the book, describes, among other events, the prophet's dictation of a scroll. It furnishes insight into the process involved in writing a biblical

85

book. Jeremiah 32 provides detailed information about the legal transaction of buying property, including the signing of the deed and other requirements.

Dictating his first scroll, Jeremiah committed to writing the word of the Lord, with Baruch, the son of Neriah, acting as secretary:

> In the fourth year [605 B.C.E.] of King Jehoiakim son of Josiah of Judah, this word came to Jeremiah from the LORD: Take a scroll (*megillat seper*) and write on it all the words that I have spoken to you against Israel and Judah and all the nations. . . . Then Jeremiah called Baruch son of Neriah, and Baruch wrote on a scroll (*megillat seper*) at Jeremiah's dictation all the words of the LORD that he had spoken to him. (Jer 36:1–2, 4)

Sometime after the completion of the scroll, it was read successively to three audiences. Baruch read it within the hearing of the populace from the chamber (*liškah*) of Gemariah son of Shaphan, situated in the upper court of the Temple, near the New Gate. Then Baruch read it to the administrative officials, who were so disturbed by Jeremiah's ominous predictions that they alerted King Jehoiakim.

Jehudi, one of the king's servants, did the third reading of the scroll in the presence of King Jehoiakim. Before that, the royal officials interrogated Baruch:

> "Tell us now, how did you write all these words? Was it at his [Jeremiah's] dictation?" Baruch answered them, "He dictated all these words to me, and I wrote them with ink (*deyo*) on the scroll." (Jer 36:17–18)

As the scroll was being read to King Jehoiakim, he reacted disdainfully:

> Now the king was sitting in his winter apartment (it was the ninth month), and there was a fire burning in the brazier before him. As Jehudi read three or four columns (*delatot*), the king would cut them off with a [scribe's] penknife (*ta'ar hassoper*) and throw them into the fire in the brazier, until the entire scroll (*megillah*) was consumed in the fire that was in the brazier. Yet neither the king, nor any of his servants who heard all these words, was alarmed, nor did they tear their garments. Even when Elnathan and Delaiah and Gemariah urged the king not to burn the scroll, he would not listen to them. And the king commanded Jerahmeel the king's son and Seraiah son of Azriel and Shelemiah son of Abdeel to arrest the secretary (*hassoper*) Baruch and the prophet Jeremiah. But the LORD hid them. (Jer 36:22–26)

Jeremiah defied the king's contemptuous act of burning the scroll by starting his dictation anew:

> Then Jeremiah took another scroll and gave it to the secretary Baruch son of Neriah, who wrote on it at Jeremiah's dictation all the words of

the scroll that King Jehoiakim of Judah had burned in the fire; and many similar words were added to them. (Jer 36:32)

Writing Materials

Several writing surfaces were utilized in ancient Israel; among them were papyrus, animal skins in the form of leather and parchment (a refined type of leather), wooden tablets, potsherds (pieces of broken pottery), ostraca (inscribed potsherds), clay tablets, stone, and metal. Archaeology has recovered samples of all of them. The more important documents would have been written on papyrus or on leather.

Since the scroll of Jeremiah is not preserved, it is uncertain whether it was written on papyrus or on leather, although arguments are offered in favor of each. Hebrew documents written on both leather and papyrus have been discovered. The oldest is a Hebrew papyrus at Wadi Murabba'at in the vicinity of the Dead Sea, dating from the late eighth or early seventh century B.C.E. Most of the Dead Sea Scrolls, discovered since 1947 in caves west of the Dead Sea in the vicinity of Qumran, were written on parchment; some were on papyri.

Scholars who maintain that Baruch wrote Jeremiah's scroll on papyrus argue that this writing material would have been more easily cut and burned, in accord with the description of King Jehoiakim's scornful action. It is argued further that leather would have produced an intolerable stench when burned. Scholars who suggest that the canonical scriptures were written on leather argue that leather scrolls would have been more durable than papyrus, withstanding better the wear and tear of climate and constant handling. They maintain that cutting leather was not a problem when done at the sutures used for joining the sheets of parchment. R. Lansing Hicks[1] argues in favor of leather over papyrus on the basis of economics: it was more expensive to import papyrus from Egypt, especially since leather was already available in Palestine. None of these arguments, however, is of itself compelling.

The word "paper" is derived from "papyrus." Papyrus, which is associated with swamp or marsh land, is cultivated in the Nile Delta of Egypt. In fact, the hieroglyphic sign for Lower Egypt (the Delta) is the papyrus plant. This aquatic plant is also known in the marshes of Lake Huleh situated in Upper Galilee (Israel). The white pith or spongy tissue in the stem of the plant was used for writing material. It was cut into strips, glued together, pressed, and dried. A second layer was imposed on the first at right angles, creating a lattice pattern of horizontal and vertical layers. Single sheets pasted end to end formed a papyrus roll (*megillat seper*, in Hebrew). Papyrus was an expensive writing material. The dry climate of Egypt was conducive to the preservation of documents written on papyrus, unlike the damper climate of Palestine that caused the papyrus to deteriorate.

The Hebrew word *delatot* is translated as "columns" (of writing) in Jer 36:23: "As Jehudi read three or four columns (*delatot*), the king would cut them off with a penknife and throw them into the fire in the brazier." Since the Hebrew word is used with this meaning only in the present biblical verse, the argument is not decisive. It does occur with this same meaning, however, in Lachish Letter IV. The singular form of *delatot* is *delet*, most often translated "door." Hicks argues that *delet* is an appropriate technical term for a writing board because "a column of writing resembled in shape a single writing tablet and a written scroll looked like a hinged, multi-leaved writing board when extended." Hicks's proposal is based on an earlier article by Philip Hyatt.[2]

Ink (*deyo*), applied with a brush, was utilized in writing on both leather and papyrus. The preferred color of ink was black made from carbon. In the preparation, soot was mixed with a thin solution of gum, and water was added to reduce the thickness of the mixture. In the Lachish Letters the ink consisted of a mixture of carbon ink and iron ink.

Analysis of the ink inscription on a plastered wall of a large building at Tell Deir 'Alla sheds light on the kind of ink and writing instruments used in antiquity. Deir 'Alla, situated in the middle of the Jordan Valley, midway between the Sea of Galilee and the Dead Sea, may have been a center of religious instruction. The religious text, dating from the mid-eighth century B.C.E., and mentioning Balaam, son of Beor (Numbers 22–24), was written in a West Semitic dialect, perhaps Aramaic.[3]

The Deir 'Alla text was inscribed in red and (mostly) black ink. J. A. Mosk, reporting in the *editio princeps* on the analysis of the ink, noted that the red pigment was identified as red iron oxide and that black iron oxide may have been among the black compounds.

The scribe of the Deir 'Alla text may have used a small stick, a reed, or a rush (a tufted marsh plant), most likely the latter, as a writing instrument. The nib is described as having a chisel-shaped (broad) edge, measuring one tenth of an inch in width and consisting of numerous small fibers that are both soft and stiff.

Pens discovered in Egypt were fashioned from the stem of the rush, which botanists identify as a member of the genus *Juncus*, designating any of several flowering plants distinguished by cylindrical stalks or hollow, stemlike leaves. *Juncus maritimus*, which grows in wet soil, is present in Palestine and Syria. The Jordan Valley, the Dead Sea, and Lake Huleh produce these plants.

With respect to the scribe's pen (*'et*), Jeremiah referred to two kinds of tools used for engraving inscriptions on stone:

> The sin of Judah is written with an iron pen (*'et barzel*); with a diamond point (*sipporen šamir*) it is engraved on the tablet of their hearts, and on the horns of their altars. (Jer 17:1)

Expressing a desire to have his testimony recorded for the future, Job wanted it incised with an "iron pen": "O that with an iron pen ('*eṭ barzel*) and with lead they were engraved on a rock forever!" (Job 19:24).

The translation "diamond point" (above) is not to be understood literally; it refers to a very hard substance such as flint.

The scribe's penknife (*ta'ar hassoper*) was used for cutting the papyrus sheets and rolls and also for fashioning and sharpening the reed pens. The Hebrew word for penknife (*ta'ar*) is derived from the verb '*arah* (in Pi'el), meaning "to uncover," "to make bare." The noun may also be translated as "razor."

Recording Property Transfer

Jeremiah 32 is important historically for its detailed description of the legal procedure involved in the transfer of property. Jeremiah's cousin Hanamel was forced to sell his field in the ancestral hometown of Anathoth:

> Jeremiah said, The word of the LORD came to me: Hanamel son of your uncle Shallum is going to come to you and say, "Buy my field that is at Anathoth, for the right of redemption by purchase (*mišpaṭ hagge'ullah liqnot*) is yours." (Jer 32:6–7)

As next of kin (*go'el*), Jeremiah had the obligation of buying back the land, as prescribed in Lev 25:25–32, lest the estate be alienated from the family:

> If anyone of your kin falls into difficulty and sells a piece of property, then the next of kin shall come and redeem what the relative has sold. (Lev 25:25)

The institution of the *go'el* was at the center of family solidarity in biblical times; the tradition of the *go'el* lies behind this property transaction involving Jeremiah. Basic to *go'el* in this context is that real property is a religious concept. The word *go'el* derives from a Hebrew root meaning "to buy back," "to redeem," or more basically "to protect." By purchasing the estate of his cousin Hanamel, Jeremiah was acting in his capacity as the *go'el*. The *go'el* was also obliged to redeem his kin from slavery as well as to enforce blood vengeance.

The preparation of Jeremiah's deed of sale is then described in detail:

> And I [Jeremiah] bought the field at Anathoth from my cousin Hanamel, and weighed out the money to him, seventeen shekels of silver. I signed the deed, sealed it, got witnesses, and weighed the money on scales. Then I took the sealed deed of purchase ('*et-seper hammiqnah 'et-heḥatum*), containing the terms and conditions, and the open copy (*haggaluy*); and I gave the deed of purchase to Baruch son of Neriah son of Mahseiah, in the presence of my cousin Hanamel, in the presence of the witnesses who signed the deed of purchase, and in the

presence of all the Judeans who were sitting in the court of the guard. In their presence I charged Baruch, saying, Thus says the LORD of hosts, the God of Israel: Take these deeds, both this sealed deed of purchase and this open deed, and put them in an earthenware jar (*keli ḥares*), in order that they may last for a long time. For thus says the LORD of hosts, the God of Israel: Houses and fields and vineyards shall again be bought in this land. (Jer 32:9–15)

Basically, four steps were followed in this transaction: writing the document, signing witnesses to it, sealing it, and storing it. The contract was written in two copies. The first was the signed deed, designated as "the sealed deed of purchase"; it was rolled and then sealed on the outside. The duplicate copy, called the "open deed," was available for reference in case of a dispute.

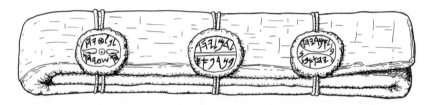

Conjectural reconstruction of a sealed deed. This papyrus from the period of the Judahite monarchy is sealed with three bullae attached to string that secures the rolled papyrus. *Original drawing by Nahman Avigad. Courtesy of the Israel Exploration Society.*

While coinage began to appear in Asia Minor in the mid-seventh century B.C.E., stamped or minted coins had not yet reached the Levant (countries along the eastern Mediterranean shores). Monetary value was determined by weighing (*šql*) ingots or scraps of precious metals. Silver was the principal form of payment in Israel. A hoard of silver ingots was found at En-gedi in a cooking pot secreted below the floor of a house dating from the time of Jeremiah (late seventh century B.C.E.). In the 1992 excavation season at Tel Miqne-Ekron the archaeologists uncovered a hoard of silver ingots dating from the seventh century B.C.E.

Baruch was to safeguard the sealed deeds by depositing them in an earthenware jar; a practice reminiscent of the manner of preservation of the Dead Sea Scrolls (Qumran Scrolls). In keeping with an ancient custom, numerous Qumran Scrolls had been stored in clay jars, measuring more than two feet high and ten inches wide. In addition, these leather scrolls were wrapped in linen cloth for safekeeping.

Ingots found at Tel Miqne-Ekron. Just before the Babylonian siege of the
Philistine city of Ekron (in the south central part of modern Israel) in 603
B.C.E., seventy-seven silver ingots were hidden in a jug nestled within another
vessel. This extraordinary silver treasure was discovered during the 1992
excavation season beneath the floor of a seventh-century B.C.E. building.
Photograph by Ilan Sztulman. Courtesy of the Tel Miqne-Ekron Excavations.

Ingots found at En-gedi. A hoard of silver ingots, dating late in the seventh century B.C.E., was found in a pottery cooking pot hidden below the floor of a house at En-gedi, an oasis on the western shore of the Dead Sea. *Photograph by David Harris. Courtesy of the Israel Museum, Jerusalem.*

Inscribed Seals and Seal Impressions

Almost four hundred seal inscriptions, most dating from the eighth to the sixth century B.C.E., have been published. Basically, seals are the equivalent of personal signatures. First employed in Mesopotamia, they had several uses in the ancient world: to establish personal possession of objects; to witness documents, as with Jeremiah's sealed deed of purchase; and to secure documents. Hebrew seals were commonly oval in shape, in imitation of the scaraboid (dung beetle) seals of Egypt, where the dung beetle was venerated as a sacred symbol of resurrection. Seals were cut from precious or semiprecious stones, local limestone, metal, ivory, and glass. Most of the seals found in Palestine are undecorated and bear only two-line inscriptions, including the name of the owner of the seal, the name of the father (patronymic), and the title of the seal's owner.

Seals are of two kinds: cylinder seals and stamp seals. Cylinder seals are so called because they are in the form of a cylinder. The owner of the seal wore it on a cord around the neck and affixed it to a document by rolling it in damp clay. Stamp seals ordinarily were set in rings, whence the term "signet ring." Jeremiah used "signet ring" (*hotam*) metaphorically to describe something precious:

> As I live, says the LORD, even if King Coniah [Jehoiachin] son of Jehoiakim of Judah were the signet ring (*hotam*) on my right hand, even from there I would tear you off. (Jer 22:24)

Seal inscriptions have assumed great importance, since they sometimes contain names of persons already familiar from the biblical text. As Avigad noted, "The seal inscriptions are the only Hebrew epigraphic source that mentions contemporary persons known from the Bible."[4] He cautioned that the identification of persons mentioned in Hebrew epigraphic sources with biblical figures would always be conjectural, unless confirmed by other evidence, such as a title or a genealogical sequence of three generations. Also, the seal must date from the same period when the biblical person lived.

Seal impressions on clay, known as bullae, continue to be discovered in large numbers. Bullae were used to seal documents written on parchment or papyrus. After the document had been rolled and secured with string, a glob of soft clay was applied to the knot and then sealed. Many of the recently discovered seal impressions bear the marks of the papyrus fibers and the strings to which they had been attached on the reverse side. In many cases, when a city was burned, the fire destroyed the scrolls; at the same time, the intense heat of the fire hardened the clay sealings, thereby preserving them. On the other hand, bullae (unbaked clay) can and do survive without a fire.

In most of the Mediterranean zone—Jerusalem to the coast—parchment or papyrus would not survive in the nondesert environment, even if there were not a fire. Damp soil is also destructive of bullae, whereas drier conditions are conducive to their preservation. Archaeologists have retrieved several from Ashkelon and elsewhere, for example. However, the real reason few bullae have been found is that bullae are small, and sieving is not yet widely practiced. Also, to the uninitiated, an unbaked clay bulla looks like an ordinary lump of clay if it is not carefully examined.

House of the Bullae

The House of the Bullae was perhaps the most extraordinary discovery in Jerusalem's City of David excavations. In 1982, Shiloh unearthed a hoard of fifty-one bullae, which, until then, lay stacked away for more than twenty-five hundred years in this House which the archaeologists appropriately dubbed the House of the Bullae. Forty-one of those bullae, each the size of a fingernail, are well preserved and quite legible. This is the only collection found in a stratified archaeological context (Stratum X) in Israel, in contrast to finds made during illicit excavations.

The House of the Bullae, situated on Jerusalem's narrow but steep southeastern slope above the Gihon spring, is located at the base of the monumental stepped-stone structure. This is designated Area G on the surveyors' grid. When Nebuchadrezzar and his Babylonian army destroyed Jerusalem in 586 B.C.E., the House of the Bullae was burned in the resultant conflagration. The intense fire destroyed the papyrus scrolls stored in the House of the Bullae but baked and thereby preserved the precious bullae. The ashes recall the biblical description of the disaster:

In the fifth month, on the seventh day of the month—which was the nineteenth year of King Nebuchadnezzar, king of Babylon—Nebuzaradan, the captain of the bodyguard, a servant of the king of Babylon, came to Jerusalem. He burned the house of the LORD, the king's house, and all the houses of Jerusalem; every great house he burned down. All the army of the Chaldeans who were with the captain of the guard broke down the walls around Jerusalem. (2 Kings 25:8–10)

The date of the bullae, the mid-seventh to the early sixth century B.C.E., has been established by three criteria: their stratified context in a controlled excavation (Stratum X), the script in which they were written, and the personal names on the bullae.

Bulla of Gemaryahu son of Shaphan. Among the fifty-one bullae found on the plastered floor of the City of David's House of the Bullae was this small clay disk inscribed "Gemaryahu son of Shaphan." This name, occurring frequently in Jeremiah, designates the scribe in the court of King Jehoiakim. *Photograph by Zev Radovan. Courtesy of the City of David Archaeological Project.*

Jeremiah 36 is especially helpful in determining the precise date of these bullae from the City of David; one need only turn to the book of Jeremiah:

Then, in the hearing of all the people, Baruch read the words of Jeremiah from the scroll, in the house of the LORD, in the chamber of Gemariah son of Shaphan the secretary (*hassoper*), which was in the upper court, at the entry of the New Gate of the LORD's house. When Micaiah son of Gemariah son of Shaphan heard all the words of the LORD from the scroll, he went down to the king's house, into the secretary's chamber; and all the officials were sitting there: Elishama the secretary, Delaiah son of Shemaiah, Elnathan son of Achbor, Gemariah son of Shaphan, Zedekiah son of Hananiah, and all the officials. . . . And the king commanded Jerahmeel the king's son and Seraiah son of Azriel and Shelemiah son of Abdeel to arrest the secretary Baruch and the prophet Jeremiah. (Jer 36:10–12, 26)

Of the fifty-one bullae found in the City of David, one bears the name Gemariah son of Shaphan ([Belonging] to Gemaryahu son of Shaphan). This same name appears four times in Jeremiah 36. Baruch read Jeremiah's initial scroll to the populace from Gemariah's chamber situated in the Temple precinct. Whether Gemariah himself was a scribe (*soper*) is uncertain; his seal does not bear a title. Avigad, noting the unlikelihood of a royal scribe omitting his title from his own seal, speculated that the father Shaphan was the scribe, and not Gemariah the son.[5] Shiloh, the excavator of the City of David, assumed Gemariah was a scribe of King Jehoiakim.

Gemariah was a strong supporter of Jeremiah at the court of King Jehoiakim:

> Even when Elnathan and Delaiah and Gemariah urged the king [Jehoiakim] not to burn the scroll, he would not listen to them. (Jer 36:25)

Other Bullae

Unlike Gemariah son of Shaphan's seal which was found in a controlled excavation, over two hundred and fifty other clay bullae, inscribed in Hebrew and dating from the same period, have appeared on the antiquities market. Although their provenience is not disclosed, they almost certainly come from clandestine digging in the City of David. As with Gemariah, the names of two other individuals can be identified with certainty, according to Avigad. They are Baruch son of Neriah the scribe (Jer 36:4) and Jerahme'el the son of the king (Jer 36:26), whose names appear on seal impressions.

The first of these two seal impressions, consisting of three lines, reads "Belonging to Berekyahu (Baruch) son of Neriyahu (Neriah) the scribe." He was none other than the friend and confidant of Jeremiah. The seal, made of dark-brown clay, is oval in shape. His name is written in the formal-cursive Hebrew of the seventh century B.C.E. Since Baruch is mentioned only in association with Jeremiah, scholars have assumed that he was not a royal scribe but merely the personal secretary of Jeremiah. However, since his bulla was found among others of royal officials, Baruch may have been an official scribe as well.

With respect to the second bulla, "Belonging to Jerahme'el son of the king," it consists of two lines of script separated by a double line. Jehoiakim sent Jerahmeel to arrest Jeremiah and Baruch:

> And the king commanded Jerahmeel the king's son and Seraiah son of Azriel and Shelemiah son of Abdeel to arrest the secretary Baruch and the prophet Jeremiah. But the LORD hid them. (Jer 36:26)

"Son of the king" was an official title but not necessarily to be understood in the literal sense. According to Avigad, persons bearing this title were assigned to the royal family, without being the natural sons of the king.

Two other seals of unknown provenience bear names that appear in the book of Jeremiah. The first seal reads "Belonging to Neriyahu (Neriah) son of the king," inscribed on a scaraboid (ovaled shape) of dark-brown stone. The two-line inscription is written in ancient Hebrew characters. The name Neriah occurs several times in Jeremiah as the designation of Baruch's father:

> And I [Jeremiah] gave the deed of purchase to Baruch son of Neriah son of Mahseiah, in the presence of my cousin Hanamel. (Jer 32:12; 36:4; etc.)

The name Neriah occurs once in the book of Jeremiah as the designation of Seraiah's father:

> The word that the prophet Jeremiah commanded Seraiah son of Neriah son of Mahseiah, when he went with King Zedekiah of Judah to Babylon, in the fourth year of his reign. Seraiah was the quartermaster. Jeremiah wrote in a scroll all the disasters that would come to Babylon, all these words that are written concerning Babylon. And

Bulla of Berekyahu son of Neriyahu the scribe. The bulla is of dark-brown clay. Its inscription, which is complete, is divided by two double lines into three registers. *Photograph by David Harris. Courtesy of the Israel Museum, Jerusalem.*

לברכיהו
בן נריהו
הספר

Line drawing of the Berekyahu seal. The original seal was oval-shaped. The inscription makes clear that "Baruch" is a shortened form ("pet name") of the scribe's full name "Berekyahu." *Original drawing by Nahman Avigad. Courtesy of the Israel Exploration Society.*

Jeremiah said to Seraiah: "When you come to Babylon, see that you read all these words, and say, 'O LORD, you yourself threatened to destroy this place so that neither human beings nor animals shall live in it, and it shall be desolate forever.' When you finish reading this scroll, tie a stone to it, and throw it into the middle of the Euphrates, and say, 'Thus shall Babylon sink, to rise no more, because of the disasters that I am bringing on her.' " (Jer 51:59–64)

A two-line seal bearing the Hebrew inscription "Belonging to Seraiah (son of) Neriah" (*sryhw/nryhw*) has also come to light, although its provenience is unknown. The owner of the seal may be the same Seraiah who accompanied King Zedekiah to Babylon, carrying with him Jeremiah's oracle against Babylon. Sinking the written oracle in the Euphrates symbolized the inevitable doom of Babylon. Seraiah son of Neriah was the brother of Baruch son of Neriah, and both were the grandsons of Mahseiah. Jeremiah was on good terms with both brothers.

Bulla of Jeraḥme'el son of the king. The seal consists of two lines of script separated by a double line. *Courtesy of the Israel Exploration Society.*

לירחמאל
בן המלך

Line drawing of the Jeraḥme'el seal. *Original drawing by Nahman Avigad. Courtesy of the Israel Exploration Society.*

Three other seal impressions relating to the failed anti-Babylonian revolt at Mizpah, immediately following the Babylonian destruction of Judah in 586 B.C.E., have turned up in different places. The three names appearing on these seals—Gedaliah, Ishmael, and Baalis—are also found in Jeremiah:

> Now Johanan son of Kareah and all the leaders of the forces in the open country came to Gedaliah at Mizpah and said to him, "Are you at all aware that Baalis king of the Ammonites has sent Ishmael son of Nethaniah to take your life?" But Gedaliah son of Ahikam would not believe them. . . . In the seventh month, Ishmael son of Nethaniah son of Elishama, of the royal family, one of the chief officers of the king, came with ten men to Gedaliah son of Ahikam, at Mizpah. As they ate bread together there at Mizpah, Ishmael son of Nethaniah and the ten men with him got up and struck down Gedaliah son of Ahikam son of Shaphan with the sword and killed him, because the king of Babylon had appointed him governor in the land. (Jer 40:13–14; 41:1–2)

King Nebuchadrezzar appointed Gedaliah as provincial governor of Judah after the fall of Jerusalem in 586 B.C.E. Mizpah is identified with Tell en-Nasbeh eight miles north of Jerusalem. Situated on the border between Judah and Israel, it became the Babylonian provincial capital. Ishmael, described as a descendant of the royal family, together with his nationalistic cohorts assassinated Gedaliah because they suspected that he was a Babylonian collaborator. Baalis, king of the Ammonites, was part of the conspiracy to murder Gedaliah, apparently as a way of gaining more influence over the devastated land of Judah. Earlier the Ammonites had joined in forming an anti-Babylonian coalition with King Zedekiah and the kings of the neighboring countries of Edom, Moab, Tyre and Sidon (Jer 27:3).

In the destruction debris of Lachish, the excavator James Starkey discovered in 1935 a stamp seal bearing the two-line inscription "Belonging to Gedalyahu, the one over the house (*Gedalyahu 'ašer 'al habbayit*)." The fiber marks of the papyrus document it sealed are still evident on the underside of this clay bulla. Like Jerusalem (Stratum X) and most of the other cities of Judah, Lachish (Stratum II) was destroyed by the Babylonian army.

Although the name Gedaliah is quite common, this may be the actual seal of Gedaliah, the governor of Judah, who functioned as "the royal steward" during the reign of Zedekiah before the tragic events of 586 B.C.E. The Hebrew title "(the one) over the house," denoting a royal administrative official, has been the subject of a recent study by Scott Layton, who concludes: "In the course of time, the office of royal steward seemed to have increased in importance; eventually the royal steward became a senior administrator, one of the highest officials in the state."[6]

A clay bulla reading "Belonging to Ishmael the son of the king" is part of a private collection in Jerusalem, and its provenience is unknown. The Hebrew script dates from the end of the seventh or early sixth century B.C.E.

The name Ishmael occurred frequently on seals and seal impressions of that period. Barkay,[7] who studied this bulla in detail, is convinced that its owner was Ishmael son of Nethaniah, a member of the royal family:

> In the seventh month, Ishmael son of Nethaniah son of Elishama, of the royal family, one of the chief officers of the king, came with ten men to Gedaliah son of Ahikam, at Mizpah. (Jer 41:1)

A third bulla, inscribed with the words "Belonging to Milkomur servant of Baalis," was discovered in 1984 at Tell el-Umeiri, an Ammonite city in the Madaba Plains of central Transjordan. This Ammonite seal impression dates about 600 B.C.E. The name Milkomur may possibly mean "light of Milkom," the national god of Ammon.

Instead of the generic title "servant of the king," here the king is actually named. He is Baalis, an Ammonite king, mentioned in Jeremiah and appearing here for the first time in an extrabiblical inscription.

"Servant" (*'ebed*), title of the owner of the seal, does not mean "slave" in this context but someone in a dependent (or inferior) position to the king. Vertical or patron/client, master/servant relationships were common in the biblical world. According to Avigad, *'ebed* was the title of a high-ranking officer in the royal court.

The book of Jeremiah mentions Baalis:

> Now Johanan son of Kareah and all the leaders of the forces in the open country came to Gedaliah at Mizpah and said to him, "Are you at all aware that Baalis king of the Ammonites has sent Ishmael son of Nethaniah to take your life?" But Gedaliah son of Ahikam would not believe them. (Jer 40:13–14)

A fitting conclusion to a study of Hebrew bullae has been well expressed by the late Nahman Avigad, who spent much of his life deciphering inscriptions, especially seals and bullae from the time of Jeremiah:

> In conclusion I cannot refrain from expressing my own feelings when handling and deciphering these two bullae [Baruch the scribe, and Jerahmeel the king's son] for the first time. One has the feeling of personal contact with persons who figure prominently in the dramatic events in which the giant figure of Jeremiah and his faithful follower Baruch were involved at a most critical time preceding the downfall of Judah.[8]

Ostraca

In addition to papyrus and leather, potsherds (pieces of broken pottery) were used as writing surfaces in the ancient Near East. Inscribed potsherds, known as ostraca, are the most common forms of documents that archaeologists unearth. During the past two decades, inscribed potsherds have been discovered with even greater frequency. This is a consequence of Aharoni's technique of dipping pottery. As director of excavations at Beersheba and elsewhere in Israel, he introduced the practice of soaking and dipping sherds in water and then inspecting them carefully for possible inscriptions before proceeding with the more vigorous washing process. The traditional procedure of scrubbing the pottery with a brush without dipping in advance may have obliterated countless inscriptions from ostraca.

The fact that potsherds were both inexpensive and readily available may account for their frequent use as writing surfaces. Written with a reed in black ink, the inscriptions on potsherds are a rich source of historical information. That the ostraca are practically indestructible over a long period of time enhances their historical value. Potsherds appear to have been used for brief notes, whereas leather or papyrus was reserved for transmitting longer documents.

The two principal collections of ostraca, written in biblical Hebrew prose and contemporary with Jeremiah, are the Arad Ostraca (see chapter 4) and the Lachish Letters (see chapter 5). Both of these collections are valuable for Hebrew epigraphy (the study of ancient inscriptions) as well as for understanding the historical situation in the days of Jeremiah.

Two Amulets from Jerusalem

In 1979, during excavation of burial caves at Ketef Hinnom (see chapter 8) facing Jerusalem's walls, Barkay and his team discovered two small, rolled, silver amulets or ornaments. These silver talismans, found with other items in burial cave Number 25, are in the form of small cylindrical silver plaques, rolled into scrolls. The Hebrew inscriptions were incised lightly on them with a sharp instrument, reminding one of Jeremiah's comment on the sin and punishment of Judah:

> The sin of Judah is written with an iron pen (*'et barzel*); with a diamond point it is engraved on the tablet of their hearts, and on the horns of their altars. (Jer 17:1; also Job 19:24)

Dating from either the mid-seventh or the early sixth century B.C.E., the amulets are incised with the personal name of the God of Israel. This is the first occurrence of Yahweh on an object excavated in Jerusalem. It appears within the Priestly Benediction, which is also inscribed on the amulets. The wording is almost the same as the Priestly Benediction in Numbers:

> The LORD bless you and keep you; the LORD make his face to shine upon you, and be gracious to you; the LORD lift up his countenance upon you, and give you peace. (Num 6:24–26)

Divine Name found in Jerusalem. Excavators at Ketef Hinnom recovered from a tomb repository (Cave 25) two amulets (rolled-up strips of silver) inscribed with the Divine Name (YHWH). Pictured here is the smaller of the two silver plaques (unrolled). *Courtesy of Gabriel Barkay.*

According to Ada Yardeni, who deciphered the text after Barkay had identified fifty-one letters on the large plaque and forty-eight on the small plaque, "The text on the plaques is the earliest text found so far with an almost identical parallel in the biblical text."[9]

Just as today some individuals wear biblical verses in lockets around the neck for blessings and divine protection, so too in Jeremiah's time these amulets were placed in small cases and worn as a necklace to preserve the owner from evil and to invoke the divine blessing.

7

Worship and Architecture

Roland de Vaux defined worship, and its synonym "cult," as "all those acts by which communities or individuals give outward expression to their religious life, by which they seek to achieve contact with God."[1] More simply stated, worship is the human response to the transcendent being. The purpose of worship is to maintain the relation between the human being and the Holy One. The main focus of Israelite worship was on Yahweh (the Lord), who could not be represented by any image.

Reverence paid to the divine being was accompanied by both creed and ritual. Israelite ritual assumed multiple forms, some of them adapted from practices of neighboring peoples. However, Israelite worship was essentially different: it was not merely external, but imposed moral demands. The prophets, including Jeremiah, constantly inveighed against the people of Judah for neglecting the ethical requirements of religion, while at the same time being scrupulous in external observances.

The vocabulary of worship is extensive, but two Hebrew words are basic: *'abodah*, signifying "service"; and *hištaḥawayah*, meaning "bowing" or "prostration," that is, assuming a posture of reverence. As the vocabulary suggests, service to the deity is founded on the analogy of service to an earthly ruler or master.

Queen of Heaven

While Jeremiah, like the other prophets, impugned several of the rituals adopted by the people of Judah, one apostasy that was especially repugnant was the ancient cult to the Queen of Heaven. The prophet denounced the worship of this mother goddess of pagan religion on two specific occasions, once during the reign of Jehoiakim (609–598 B.C.E.), following the death of Josiah, and again after the fall of Jerusalem (586 B.C.E.) when the people sought refuge in Egypt.

The first account follows Jeremiah's famous temple sermon. A direct quotation from the Lord, it forbade the prophet to intercede on behalf of the people of Judah because of their adherence to the cult of the Queen of Heaven:

> As for you [Jeremiah], do not pray for this people [Judahites], do not raise a cry or prayer on their behalf, and do not intercede with me [the LORD], for I will not hear you. Do you not see what they are doing in the towns of Judah and in the streets of Jerusalem? The children gather wood, the fathers kindle fire, and the women knead dough, to make cakes (*kawwanim*) for the queen of heaven; and they pour out drink offerings to other gods, to provoke me to anger. (Jer 7:16–18)

The religious reform of Josiah came to an end with his tragic death in 609 B.C.E. The reign of Jehoiakim was marked by a return to idolatry. The word *kawwanim*, which occurs only here and in Jer 44:19, is a loanword from the Akkadian *kamanu*. Akkadian, an East Semitic language, was spoken in Mesopotamia from about 2000 to 500 B.C.E. *Kawwanim* denote sweetened cakes used in the cult of the mother goddess Ishtar as practiced in Mesopotamia. Offering cakes to deities was a common practice.

Walter Rast,[2] commenting on Jeremiah's description of baking the *kawwanim*, observes that the cakes were baked directly on the embers of the fire, since the text does not mention an oven (*tannur*). The oven would have been the ordinary way of baking bread in Palestine during the Iron Age.

The worship of the Queen of Heaven appears to have been a family cult: the children gathered the firewood; the fathers ignited the fires; the women made the dough. At the same time, it was a feminine cult, with the women playing the leading role. Susan Ackerman[3] suggests that the prominence of women in the cult of the Queen of Heaven, as described in Jeremiah, reflects the special place of women in the worship of the Mesopotamian Tammuz. Tammuz, the Sumerian deity of spring vegetation, was the lover of Ishtar.

The prophet Ezekiel alluded to an annual lament ritual, practiced especially by women, commemorating the loss of the god Tammuz who was detained in the underworld. The women in Ezekiel were mourning Tammuz in the north gate of the Jerusalem Temple. Ezekiel considered this an abomination:

> Then he [God] brought me [Ezekiel] to the entrance of the north gate of the house of the LORD; women were sitting there weeping for Tammuz. Then he said to me, "Have you seen this, O mortal? You will see still greater abominations than these." (Ezek 8:14–15)

Jeremiah's second censure of the cult of the Queen of Heaven was addressed to the Jewish refugees scattered throughout Egypt, but they refused to heed the prophet's words:

Then all the men who were aware that their wives had been making offerings to other gods, and all the women who stood by, a great assembly, all the people who lived in Pathros in the land of Egypt, answered Jeremiah: "As for the word that you have spoken to us in the name of the LORD, we are not going to listen to you. Instead, we will do everything that we have vowed, make offerings to the queen of heaven and pour out libations to her, just as we and our ancestors, our kings and our officials, used to do in the towns of Judah and in the streets of Jerusalem. We used to have plenty of food, and prospered, and saw no misfortune. But from the time we stopped making offerings to the queen of heaven and pouring out libations to her, we have lacked everything and have perished by the sword and by famine." And the women said, "Indeed we will go on making offerings to the queen of heaven and pouring out libations to her; do you think that we made cakes (*kawwanim*) for her, marked with her image (*leha'aṣibah*), and poured out libations to her without our husbands' being involved?". . . "Thus says the LORD of hosts, the God of Israel: You and your wives have accomplished in deeds what you declared in words, saying, 'We are determined to perform the vows that we have made, to make offerings to the queen of heaven and to pour out libations to her.' By all means, keep your vows and make your libations!" (Jer 44:15–19, 25)

Pathros is the Hebrew transcription of the Egyptian phrase meaning "land of the south." It is a designation for Upper Egypt. The Nile Valley, lying north-south between Cairo and Aswan, constitutes Upper Egypt. Mizraim is the name for Lower Egypt, which forms the Delta region of the Nile Valley.

"We used to have plenty of food, and prospered" (Jer 44:17) is interpreted as a reference to the fertility aspects of the Queen of Heaven cult.

Jeremiah refers to "the pouring out of libations" in this passage and elsewhere. In the context of providing the daily sustenance of the Lord, the book of Numbers mentioned the drink offering or libation poured out over the sacrifice itself to enhance the pleasant fragrance:

Moreover, you shall offer one-fourth of a hin [about a gallon and a half] of wine as a drink offering with the burnt offering or the sacrifice, for each lamb. . . . And as a drink offering you shall offer one-third of a hin of wine, a pleasing odor to the LORD. (Num 15:5, 7)

In Jer 44:19 the cakes are described as bearing the image (*leha'aṣibah*) of the goddess. Although the exact meaning of this reference is debatable, this feature can be traced to the cult of Ishtar in Mesopotamia. There are several possibilities. The cakes may have been shaped like a star, since Ishtar, Astarte's Mesopotamian counterpart, was an astral deity. The dough for the cakes may have been formed by hand into the likeness of the deity. Or the cakes may have been made in a clay mold in the shape of the goddess.

Archaeologists have discovered in the palace kitchen at Mari (Tell el-Hariri), an ancient city located in the Middle Euphrates region, just north of the modern Syro-Iraqi border, as many as forty-seven clay molds. Mold 1044 may rep-

The Mari mold. This mold for cakes, representing a goddess, was discovered in a royal kitchen at the Mari palace. *From André Parrot,* Mission archéologique de Mari, II: Le Palais– documents et monuments *(1959), Pl XIX, 1044. Courtesy of the Louvre.*

resent the nude goddess Ishtar, with her hands supporting her breasts. Cakes were baked in the image of Ishtar and offered to the goddess in the sacrificial cult. In keeping with another ancient practice, these cakes may have been shaped like the pubic triangle, suggesting the female genitalia.[4]

Rast describes the nude goddess on the Mari mold as follows:

> The depiction of the female is realistic, with eyes and facial features appearing as in a normal human being. A heavy gathering of hair, suggestive of a turban, is found on the head. That it is hair is indicated by what appear to be cross-braided locks. The neck is covered with a broad necklace five rings wide. There appear to be bracelets on the wrists. The figure is in a seated position facing frontally. Buttocks are heavy with knees and feet held closely together.[5]

In addition to biblical texts, archaeology attests to the Israelite use of cult figurines. A large number of nude goddesses, dating from the eighth and seventh centuries B.C.E., have been discovered at Israelite sites, even in Jerusalem in the vicinity of the Temple Mount.

Jeremiah and the Jewish refugees in Egypt were on a theological collision course over the interpretation of history. Jeremiah considered the cultic practice of the Queen of Heaven as responsible for the disaster of 586 B.C.E. in Judah and Jerusalem. In the eyes of the people of Judah, all their troubles began with the reform of Josiah, which outlawed the cult to the Queen of Heaven, a religious devotion that had been the reason for their earlier prosperity. Jeremiah insisted that exclusive loyalty to the Lord, the God of Israel, had been the only reason for success in the past. Despite Jeremiah's denunciation of the Queen of Heaven, the Jewish refugees persisted in worshiping the mother goddess as the way to guarantee security and prosperity in Egypt.

The exact identity of the mother goddess, the Queen of Heaven, denounced by Jeremiah on two occasions, has been the subject of scholarly discussion. Several candidates have been suggested, including the West Semitic Astarte, Ishtar, Anat, and Asherah. Astarte is the Greek and Latin form of the Hebrew name Ashtoret, written with the vowels of the word *bošet*, "shame," to be read instead of the proper name of the pagan deity. Astarte was worshiped under a variety of names in the ancient Near East. She was the consort of the storm god Baal. Astarte, goddess of sexual love and fertility, also a war goddess, was, according to Mark Smith,[6] the only West Semitic goddess bearing the title Queen of Heaven in the Iron Age. Astarte was identified in the Greek world with Aphrodite.

Ishtar, the East Semitic goddess, who was the Babylonian-Assyrian equivalent of Astarte, is commonly identified with the West Semitic Astarte. Ishtar, a fertility goddess, was also associated with war. Ackerman suggests that the Queen of Heaven may represent a syncretistic (fusion of different forms of belief) deity combining traits of both Ishtar and Astarte.

Frank Cross favors the identification of the Queen of Heaven with Hurrian Astarte. In 1963 the Archaeological Museum of Seville (Spain) acquired a bronze statuette portraying a naked female figure, identified as Astarte. This seated figurine, interpreted as a product of Phoenician centers of northern Syria, sheds light on the Phoenician colonization of Spain. An eighth-century B.C.E. Phoenician inscription is carved on the statuette's base. Commenting on the text's reference to Aštart-Hor, Cross states: "The goddess cannot be separated, however, from the Hurrian Ištar." He adds that she is probably to be identified with Ištar of Nineveh.[7]

In his comparative study of the evidence on the Queen of Heaven from the first millennium, Saul Olyan observes:

> The identification of the Queen of Heaven . . . is no simple task, and in fact must remain uncertain. Nonetheless, the best case can be made

for West Semitic Ashtart. The case which can be made in favor of Ishtar is suggestive, but flawed in some serious respects. The cases for Asherah or Anat are far less impressive.[8]

The name of the West Semitic goddess Anat occurs in personal names in Israel; for example, "Shamgar son of Anat," one of the predynastic judges in Israel (Judg 3:31; 5:6); also "Anatyahu" at Elephantine Island on the Nile; and, of course, "Anathoth" (the name derived from the Canaanite goddess Anat), the birthplace of Jeremiah (Jer 1:1).

Although Asherah may have been Yahweh's consort, evidence is slight that she was identified with the Queen of Heaven. Asherah was an ancient Canaanite fertility goddess, mentioned frequently in the Hebrew Bible where she is linked with Baal. Her manifestations take various forms: as a figurine representing the goddess, or as a wooden likeness of the goddess in the form of a green tree (Deut 16:21), or as tree trunks (Hebrew *'ašerim*, in the plural form). Jeremiah in an indictment of Judah alluded to *'ašerim*: "while their children remember their altars and their sacred poles (*'ašerim*)" (Jer 17:2). King Manasseh erected an image of Asherah in the temple (2 Kings 21:7). King Josiah, as part of his reform, removed the image of Asherah and had it burned in the Kidron Valley (2 Kings 23:6).

During excavations in 1975–1976 at Kuntillet 'Ajrud (Ḥorvat Teman), a religious center located thirty miles south of Kadesh-barnea in the Sinai desert, Ze'ev Meshel investigated a large building, dating from about 800 B.C.E. Inscriptions and drawings were found on wall plaster, on two large jars (pithoi), and on a stone vat. Among the writings was the following: *lyhwh šmrn wl'šrth*, meaning "[I have blessed you] by Yahweh of Samaria and his Asherah."

Ruth Hestrin, in her study of the iconography (pictorial documents) of the Asherah at Kuntillet 'Ajrud and elsewhere, concluded that the Asherah at Kuntillet 'Ajrud does not designate a divine name but refers to an object or cult symbol.[9]

In addition to Jeremiah, the cult of the Queen of Heaven is known from a contemporary inscription,[10] originating in Kition, situated on the southern coast of Cyprus, buried under modern Larnaca. Brian Peckham,[11] who identifies the Queen of Heaven as Astarte, draws attention to the parallels between the book of Jeremiah and this inscription; they have several elements in common. The inscription describes a festival, consisting of a procession through the city streets, accompanied by singing and lighting a fire to the Queen of Heaven. Also, bread is baked for Astarte as well as cakes for the participants.

Baking Bread

Since bread (*leḥem*) was one of the staples of the ancient diet, bread making became a craft in Palestine, and the public bakeries were located on a specially designated street:

So King Zedekiah gave orders, and they [royal officials] committed Jeremiah to the court of the guard; and a loaf of bread was given him daily from the bakers' street, until all the bread of the city was gone. (Jer 37:21)

Lest bread become stale, it was baked daily, a task usually performed at home by women of the household. Bread was made from various cereal grains like barley, wheat, or millet. Wheat, by far the most common grain for bread, was also the best, while barley meal served the needs of the poor. Dough for the bread was prepared by kneading flour (or meal) and water with leaven, which was derived from old fermented dough. Leaven was not used in the bread intended for liturgical rituals—for example, in the case of the Showbread (Bread of the Presence), which consisted of twelve loaves of unleavened bread, arranged in two rows of six in the Temple, and replaced every Sabbath. Salt was added for seasoning. The bread was normally shaped into flat, round loaves (pita), about eighteen inches in diameter. The Bible often refers to these flat loaves as cakes, for want of a better word.

In the Bible, bread often signifies food in general. In addition to being a dietary staple, bread also functioned as a utensil for eating. As today in the Middle East, bread was never cut; it was always broken, as Jeremiah attests in describing the funeral feast (*marzeaḥ*): "No one shall break (*yipresu*) bread for the mourner" (Jer 16:7).

Ovens

Various methods were used for baking bread. Most bread was not made in molds but laid on the sides of bread ovens. Bread was normally baked in an oven (*tannur*, in both Hebrew and Arabic). Sometimes a griddle of metal or earthenware, supported by a few stones and placed over the fire, was utilized for baking; or baking was done on heated stones of the hearth. Hearth cakes were made by placing the dough under the hot ashes. The oven was usually located in the courtyard or in front of the house.

The oven (*tannur*) was a conical cylinder in which the dough was either baked on heated stones or stuck to the inside wall of the oven. This kind of oven, shaped like a large inverted earthenware jar and called *tabun* in Palestinian Arabic, is still used in villages. Besides the more or less cylindrical form of the aboveground *tannur*, there is, according to Gustaf Dalman,[12] an egg-shaped design, in which the opening where the bread goes in is located not on top but in front near the top. Stubble, dry grass, twigs, or animal dung bound with straw was used to heat the oven. The baking process required only a few minutes. Archaeologists have uncovered ovens, dating from Iron Age I and II (1200–586 B.C.E.), at nearly every site in Palestine.

On a related subject, the more affluent homes were furnished with braziers, not for the purpose of cooking but for heating, as in the case of King Jehoiakim:

Now the king was sitting in his winter apartment (it was the ninth month [Kislev, i.e., December]), and there was a fire burning in the brazier (*ha'aḥ*) before him. (Jer 36:22)

Into this fire the king contemptuously threw the pieces of Jeremiah's scroll. The brazier was probably a portable firepan made of metal or clay for warming a room.

Describing King Solomon's palaces, Ussishkin comments:

Another feature typical of contemporary throne rooms is an open hearth near and in front of the throne. . . . Other throne rooms contained "movable hearths," a small metal "cart" with wheels which could be moved nearer to or further from the throne on a specially built platform or "stone-rails." . . . It seems reasonable to assume that such a hearth—whether fixed or movable—was in use in Jerusalem as well. This conclusion is strengthened by the story of King Jehoiakim.[13]

"Other Gods"

Worship of the Queen of Heaven was but one manifestation of Israelite foreign cult. Obviously the Israelites did not restrict their worship to the Lord (Yahweh) alone but had "other gods" as well, as recently excavated fertility figurines attest. The following is the divine indictment of the people of Judah for breaking the covenant by practicing non-Israelite worship in various ways despite Josiah's reforms:

And the LORD said to me [Jeremiah]: Conspiracy exists among the people of Judah and the inhabitants of Jerusalem. They have turned back to the iniquities of their ancestors of old, who refused to heed my words; they have gone after other gods (*'elohim 'aḥerim*) to serve them; the house of Israel and the house of Judah have broken the covenant that I made with their ancestors. (Jer 11:9–10)

Pillar Figurines

Nude pillar figurines were counted among the forms of worship of "other gods." Symbolizing the mother goddess, they were common in Judah during the eighth and seventh centuries B.C.E. Several examples of pillar figurines with large breasts supported by the hands, perhaps to emphasize the maternal aspects, have surfaced in Jerusalem. The pendulous breasts suggest they depict fertility goddesses. Pillar figurines are so called because of their pillar-shaped body which may represent the trunk of a tree, suggestive of the goddess Asherah. The female head is made in a mold.

High Places

"Green trees on high hills," the classic expression originating with Hosea (4:13), designated cultic installations known as "high places" (*bamot*) where fertility rites were practiced and possibly cult prostitution. The Israelites imitated their Canaanite neighbors by constructing comparable sanctuaries.

In addition to his condemnation of "the high place of Topheth" (Jer 7:31; also 19:5; 32:35), Jeremiah denounced frequently the cult of Baal at high places:

> For long ago you broke your yoke and burst your bonds, and you said, "I will not serve!" On every high hill and under every green tree you sprawled and played the whore. (Jer 2:20; also 3:6; 17:2)

"Played the whore" is probably figurative, not literal, cult prostitution.

Understanding *bamot* simply as high places can be somewhat misleading. Not all *bamot* were situated on hills. Although usually located outside towns,

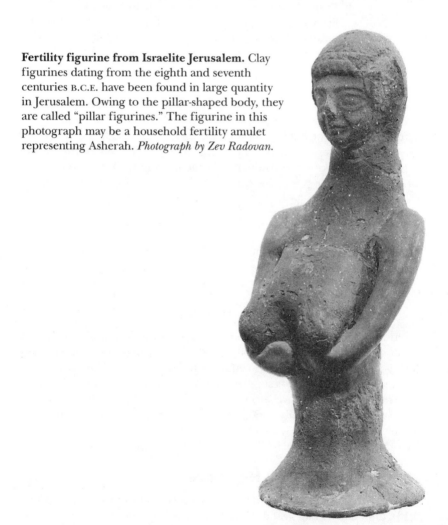

Fertility figurine from Israelite Jerusalem. Clay figurines dating from the eighth and seventh centuries B.C.E. have been found in large quantity in Jerusalem. Owing to the pillar-shaped body, they are called "pillar figurines." The figurine in this photograph may be a household fertility amulet representing Asherah. *Photograph by Zev Radovan.*

some were within towns. *Bamot* were really artificial mounds or platforms for the purpose of cultic worship. Verdant trees were characteristic of these sanctuaries that were ordinarily open-air, although some were roofed. In the ancient Near East, trees had religious associations and sometimes were venerated as sacred.

Among the cultic furnishings at high places were an altar for sacrifice, *maṣṣebot* (standing stones serving as commemorative stelae), and Asherahs (wooden cult poles symbolic of female fertility). The stone pillars may have represented Baal, just as the wooden poles symbolized Asherah. Jeremiah alluded to both on two occasions in a polemic against these nature cults:

> As a thief is shamed when caught, so the house of Israel shall be shamed—they, their kings, their officials, their priests, and their prophets, who say to a tree, "You are my father," and to a stone, "You gave me birth." (Jer 2:26–27)

In this passage Jeremiah reversed the sexual imagery of the cult objects, apparently out of derision.

> Because she [Israel] took her whoredom so lightly, she polluted the land, committing adultery with stone and tree. (Jer 3:9)

That Israel was not alone in worshiping at high places is evident from the LORD's judgment against Moab:

> And I will bring to an end in Moab, says the LORD, those who offer sacrifice at a high place (*bamah*) and make offerings to their gods. (Jer 48:35)

Earlier, the high places appear to have been endorsed by the religion of Israel. For example, the shrine at Dan, with its *bet bamot* ("house on the high places," 1 Kings 12:31) and its bull-calf, were perfectly legitimate in northern Israel. Later, the prophets vehemently opposed them because of the syncretistic worship practiced at the high places. More important still, the attempt to centralize worship in Jerusalem caused a change in attitude toward these rustic sanctuaries.

Incense

Incense is a mixture of spices emitting a fragrance when burned. The offering of incense was broadly practiced in ancient religions and was also an integral part of Israelite ritual as early as the First Temple period (1000–586 B.C.E.). Outside of ritual, incense was used as a perfume, deodorant or fumigant. In ancient Israelite ritual, incense was used in the following circumstances: as a supplement to a sacrifice (as in the vegetable offering [*minḥah*], consisting of flour mixed with oil, and accompanied by an offering of incense); in offering spices as a separate sacrifice; and placing incense on the altar of gold (Ex 30:1–10).[14]

The detailed formula for mixing incense is described in Ex 30:34–38. Incense was burned twice daily, in the morning and in the evening, on the altar of incense that stood before the veil of the Holy of Holies. Only the high priest was permitted to offer incense on the incense altar.

Incense (from Latin *incendere*, "to burn") is the English word often used to translate two Hebrew words—*qetoret* and *lebonah*. *Qetoret* is the term for any type of burnt sacrifice. The (Pi'el) verb form *qitter* means "to burn incense," hence, to offer a sacrifice, as in the following verse:

> Will you [people of Judah] steal, murder, commit adultery, swear false-ly, make offerings (*qatter*) to Baal, and go after other gods that you have not known . . . ? (Jer 7:9; also 1:16; 11:13)

Lebonah, translated "frankincense," is one of the principal ingredients of incense and perfume used in worship. *Lebonah* may be so named from its white (*laban*) color. Frankincense, the symbol of wealth and holiness, is the authentic incense. This luxury item is a fragrant, white gum resin from *Boswellia* trees, native to Somaliland and South Arabia. Michael Zohary described the trees that were a major source of the aromatic resin for frankincense as "medium-sized shrubs with pinnate leaves and small greenish or whitish flowers."[15] The resin is obtained from the trees by tapping.

Jeremiah refers to *lebonah* three times:

> Of what use to me [the LORD] is frankincense (*lebonah*) that comes from Sheba, or sweet cane (*qaneh hattob*) from a distant land? Your burnt offerings (*'olot*) are not acceptable, nor are your sacrifices (*zebahim*) pleasing to me. (Jer 6:20; also 17:26; 41:5)

Sheba (Saba, in South Arabia) designates the Sabean state situated in the southwestern corner of the Arabian Peninsula (modern Yemen). This was the homeland of the famous queen who traveled to Jerusalem to test the wisdom of Solomon (1 Kings 10:1–2). The Sabeans were a nomadic group, well known as traders in metals, jewelry, spices, and resins. Sweet cane (literally, reed) is an aromatic grass-like plant. It was used as a perfume as well as a sacrificial offering.

"Sweet cane," paralleled here to "incense from Sheba," designates aromatic spice cane. Exodus 30:23 mentions *qaneh* among the ingredients of the anointing oil. *Hattob* means more than simply "good"; here it means "precious."

In antiquity the purpose of sacrifice was to maintain communion with the deity. In Israel, offerings were given to the Lord by being burned on the altar. The types of Israelite sacrifices were numerous, which makes it difficult to be precise in the use of technical terms. *'Olot* (whole burnt offerings) designate those sacrifices in which the animal was totally consumed on the altar. *Zebahim* (partly burnt offerings) signify sacrifices in general. With respect to partly burnt offerings, certain portions of the animal were burned upon the altar; the remainder were eaten by the priests and the participants together, or by the priests alone. Whereas meat and vegetable sacrifices were presented as food for the deity, it appears that the deities, including Yahweh, were often happiest with sweet odors emanating from incense.

Sarcastically, Jeremiah suggested that the Israelites wipe out the distinction among the various kinds of burnt offerings: "Thus says the LORD of hosts, the God of Israel: Add your burnt offerings (*'olot*) to your sacrifices (*zebaḥim*), and eat the flesh" (Jer 7:21).

Like his prophetic predecessors, Jeremiah condemned merely external observance in worship. Worship was meaningful only when performed with sincere interior dispositions.

Excavations have produced a large variety of horned and unhorned incense altars in Israel, Judah, and Philistia. At the Arad temple two altars for burning incense flanked the entrance to the shrine and served to separate the Holy of Holies from the main room. The Tel Miqne-Ekron excavation has added considerably to current knowledge about incense altars. This eighty-acre Philistine site, ten miles inland from the Mediterranean coast, has yielded ten horned incense altars dating from the late seventh century B.C.E. According to Seymour Gitin,[16] these altars were of two kinds: freestanding (finished on all sides) and engaged (unfinished on one or more sides).

Perfumes and Spices

Perfumes and spices, both luxury items, were in great demand in the ancient Near East, including Israel.[17] In addition to their importance in worship, perfumes had cosmetic, mortuary, and medicinal uses. The blossoms, leaves, fruits, bark, and resin of certain plants produced the perfumes. Some of those plants are indigenous to Palestine, including henna, saffron, balm, and labdanum. Both archaeological evidence and literary sources (including a document from one of the Judean Desert Caves, the "Cave of the Letters" in Naḥal Ḥever) confirm that En-gedi, an oasis on the west shore of the Dead Sea, was a center for the cultivation of perfume-producing plants. En-gedi was considered to be one of the most important places for the cultivation of balm.

In antiquity, perfume was made in an oil base, olive oil serving the purpose in Palestine. Three steps were required to produce perfume from the chopped plants: pressing (as with olives or grapes), cold steeping, and hot steeping. Stone vessels made ideal perfume containers. Pottery vessels were less desirable because the scent of the liquid would evaporate through the porous clay.

Most of the spice-producing plants and resins had to be obtained from South Arabia and the Far East, the centers of trade for perfumes and incense. Myrrh and frankincense were the main commodities of the spice trade. Myrrh was used mainly for perfumes and cosmetics, whereas frankincense, as noted, was one of the four ingredients of ritual incense. Caravans brought the perfumes and spices along the desert routes to Palestine. Similarly, certain spices native to Palestine were exported to Egypt and Syria. An intricate network of trade routes connected the east and the west, Arabia and Palestine.

Solomon's Temple

The biblical text of 1 Kings 6–8; 2 Chronicles 2–4; and Ezekiel 41, supplemented by recent archaeological discoveries, including both artifacts and iconography, furnishes valuable guidelines for reconstructing the Solomonic Temple in Jerusalem, which took seven years to complete. Comparative material from neighboring peoples is also exceedingly useful.

In preparation for building the Temple, Solomon extended the borders of the City of David northward to include the present-day Temple Mount or Haram esh-Sharif ("the Noble Sanctuary"), as it is known in Islam. The Temple, according to Asher Kaufman,[18] may have been located about 330 feet to the northwest of the Dome of the Rock, the Islamic sanctuary situated atop the Temple Mount since the seventh century C.E. Leen Ritmeyer,[19] defending the traditional view, maintains that both the Solomonic Temple and the Herodian Temple were built on the same spot as the Dome of the Rock. Solomon undertook the actual construction of the Temple in the fourth year of his reign (956 B.C.E.).

Hiram, king of Tyre, furnished the Phoenician architects, masons, and other skilled workers, as well as the building materials, while Solomon provided unskilled local laborers. The foreign artisans left their mark on the Jerusalem Temple by building it in Phoenician architectural style.

Modest by modern standards, the Temple was set on a platform and consisted of three rooms: the *ulam*, or vestibule (fifteen feet by thirty feet); the *hekal* or main room (thirty feet by sixty feet); and the cella or inner shrine, also called the *debir*, or Holy of Holies (a cube thirty feet square). The vestibule was roofed but not enclosed in front. The main hall (*hekal*) of the sanctuary was forty-five feet high, had windows, was floored with cypress, and paneled with cedar which in turn was decorated with palm trees, cherubim (winged celestial figures) and other Phoenician motifs, inlaid with gold leaf. The *hekal* had a flat roof supported by cedar beams. The Holy of Holies, windowless and lined with cedar, contained two large pine[20] cherubim (sphinxes or griffins, since both are found on Phoenician ivories) standing fifteen feet high. The Ark of the Covenant reposed under the outstretched wings of the cherubim. Cherubim were popular in Phoenician, Canaanite, and Syrian art. The Canaanite (Late Bronze Age) temple at Lachish and the Philistine temple at Tel Qasile (on the north bank of the

Cherubim guarding a sacred tree. Two large wooden cherubim (winged sphinxes), standing fifteen feet high and overlaid with gold leaf, overshadowed the Holy of Holies. Figures of cherubim also decorated the Solomonic Temple. *Reconstruction by Emily Wright from motifs in Phoenician art. Courtesy of the American Schools of Oriental Research.*

The Solomonic Temple. Two massive pillars flanked the east door of the Temple. This is the Stevens reconstruction of the Solomonic Temple based on specifications prepared by William F. Albright and G. Ernest Wright, 1955. *Courtesy of the American Schools of Oriental Research.*

Yarkon River, near Tel Aviv) were also paneled in cedarwood. On either side of the Temple were three-storied chambers used for storage and as residential rooms for the Temple priests.

The entrance of the Temple was flanked by two freestanding, ornamental bronze columns, named Jachin ("he will establish") and Boaz ("in strength"), perhaps the initial words of longer inscriptions. These huge pillars, cast in bronze, measured thirty-seven feet high (including bases and capitals), and eighteen feet in circumference. Similar (but certainly not of bronze) columns were associated with the Late Bronze Age temple at Hazor. The capitals of the Jerusalem Temple columns were elaborately decorated, as Jeremiah attested:

> Upon it [the column] was a capital of bronze; the height of the one capital was five cubits [more than eight feet]; latticework and pomegranates, all of bronze, encircled the top of the capital. And the second pillar had the same, with pomegranates. There were ninety-six pomegranates on the sides; all the pomegranates encircling the latticework numbered one hundred. (Jer 52:22–23)

Although no archaeological remains from the Solomonic Temple have been recovered, comparison with other extant temples in the ancient Near East makes reconstruction plausible. Archaeologists trace the origin of the Temple architecture to northern Syria, where comparable temples have been discovered. In 1930, the Oriental Institute of the University of Chicago excavated a small temple at Tell Tainat (ancient Hattina) in the Amuq Valley of Syria. Although dating only from the eighth century B.C.E., this temple shared a plan similar to the Temple in Jerusalem. Divided into three sections, both were long-axis temples, that is, they were oriented with the entrance on the short side, with the Holy of Holies at the opposite end of the building. Long-axis temples originated in northwest Syria in the second millennium B.C.E. In contrast, the Iron Age Arad temple in the eastern Negev was a broad-room temple, with the entrance on the long side and the building oriented by the long wall. Other second-millennium, long-axis temple prototypes exist, including the Middle Bronze Age temples at Shechem and Megiddo in Canaan and also a temple at Ebla in Syria.

The biblical writers describe the Temple furnishings in detail. Hiram, the bronzeworker from Tyre in Phoenicia, cast all the Temple bronzes. Jeremiah mentions several of the bronze furnishings:

> The pillars of bronze that were in the house of the LORD, and the stands (*mekonot*) and the bronze sea (*yam hannehošet*) that were in the house of the LORD, the Chaldeans [Babylonians] broke in pieces, and carried all the bronze to Babylon. (Jer 52:17)

The stands (*mekonot*) refer to ten smaller bronze bowls, used for washing sacrificial animals. These bowls were supported by elaborately crafted stands mounted on four bronze wheels for moving them about. Each of these water basins had a capacity of two hundred gallons (1 Kings 7:27–37).

The bronze "Sea" (1 Kings 7:23–26) was a huge basin cast in bronze, measuring over fifteen feet in diameter and seven and a half feet in height. It rested on the backs of twelve bronze oxen, arranged in threes, each group facing in a different direction. This vessel, which held some 10,000 gallons of water, was used by the priests for ritual washing.

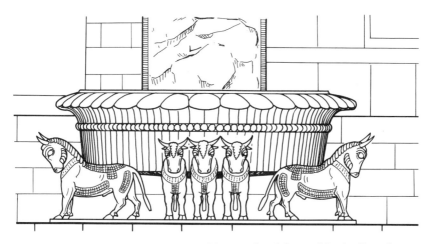

Reconstruction of the Bronze Sea. This great bowl, located in the Temple courtyard, measured over fifteen feet in diameter and stood more than seven feet high. Cast in bronze, it held 10,000 gallons of water for ritual washing. *Drawing based on the reconstruction of William Morden. Photograph at the Oriental Institute Museum, University of Chicago.*

Inasmuch as scholars recognize the bronze sea as having cosmic significance, Albright stated:

> In function it [the bronze sea] cannot be separated from the Mesopotamian *apsû*, employed both as the name of the subterranean freshwater ocean from which all life and all fertility were derived and as the name of a basin of holy water erected in the Temple.[21]

Jeremiah observed:

> As for the two pillars, the one sea, the twelve bronze bulls that were under the sea, and the stands, which King Solomon had made for the house of the LORD, the bronze of all these vessels was beyond weighing. (Jer 52:20)

The Temple was essentially a state sanctuary forming part of the administrative center in Jerusalem. Called the "house of God," it symbolized the divine presence, serving primarily as the residence for the deity and not intended as the place for public worship. Worshipers were admitted only to the courts of the Temple.

As a consequence of the Deuteronomic reform instituted by King Josiah, the cult was centralized in the Jerusalem Temple. This fostered a superstitious trust in the Temple but had little effect on the daily lives of the people who reverted to their former pagan practices, completely oblivious of social obligations. Disillusioned with the reform of Josiah, Jeremiah delivered a classic sermon in the Temple court in which he repudiated external observance devoid of interior dispositions.

Two versions of this famous Temple sermon are recorded in the book of Jeremiah, the first being a complete account (Jer 7:1–15) and the latter (Jer 26:1–19) a summary contained in Baruch's memoirs, describing the consequences of the Temple sermon:

> The word that came to Jeremiah from the LORD: Stand in the gate of the LORD's house, and proclaim there this word, and say, Hear the word of the LORD, all you people of Judah, you that enter these gates to worship the LORD. Thus says the LORD of hosts, the God of Israel: Amend your ways and your doings, and let me dwell with you in this place. Do not trust in these deceptive words: "This is the temple of the LORD, the temple of the LORD, the temple of the LORD." (Jer 7:1–4)

Solomon's Royal Palace

The second of Solomon's building enterprises was the construction of the palace complex which required thirteen years to complete (1 Kings 7:1–12). Both the Temple and the palace were located on the royal acropolis, which was the administrative area. Just as at Tell Tainat in Syria, Solomon's palace adjoined the Jerusalem Temple. Both were *bit hilani* palaces, an architectural term describing their colonnaded entrances. In antiquity, *bit hilani* referred only to the lavish porticoed entrance of a building; later the term designated the whole building.

The House of the Forest of the Lebanon, a large detached building, perhaps the best-known building of the palace ensemble, may have served as the royal reception hall. Adorned with columns, beams, and paneling of cedarwood, it was built on four rows (three rows, in the Septuagint) of fifteen cedar columns crowned with cedar capitals, imported from Lebanon, the homeland of the Phoenicians (1 Kings 7:2–5).

The extensive use of cedar columns accounts for the name "House of the Forest of the Lebanon," which must have resembled a forest. A parallel to the "forest" of cedar columns is the temple of Astarte at Kition (Cyprus). In the book of Jeremiah, "forest" (*ya'ar*) is understood as an expression for the royal palace. This would appear to be the intent of Jeremiah when citing the Lord's threat:

> I will punish you according to the fruit of your doings, says the LORD; I will kindle a fire in its forest (*beya'rah*), and it shall devour all that is around it. (Jer 21:14)

Jeremiah 22, an exhortation to repent, has three further references to wood from the cedars of Lebanon:

> For thus says the LORD concerning the house of the king of Judah: You are like Gilead to me, like the summit of Lebanon. (Jer 22:6)

> I [the LORD] will prepare destroyers against you . . . ; they shall cut down your choicest cedars and cast them into the fire. (Jer 22:7)

> O inhabitant of Lebanon, nested among the cedars, how you will groan when pangs come upon you. (Jer 22:23)

Robert Carroll suggests that these references may be

> an allusion to the firing of the city's [Jerusalem] wooden palaces and houses. . . . Solomon built "the house of the forest of Lebanon" using wood from the great cedars of Lebanon. . . . Such buildings may be the object of the burning which devastates the city and would justify the references to Lebanon in 22.6–7, 23 as an allusion to the city of Jerusalem.[22]

The architectural style of royal residences in Iron Age II (1000–586 B.C.E.) is rather well known from examples elsewhere, especially in the use of motifs borrowed from Phoenicia, such as ashlar masonry, window balustrades, and Proto-Aeolic capitals.

Ashlar construction refers to building stones that have been squared smoothly on all sides. The classic example of Iron Age ashlar construction is Samaria, capital of the Northern Kingdom of Israel. Ashlar masonry was also utilized in building the palaces in Jerusalem and Ramat Raḥel as well as the temple platform at Dan.

The window balustrade, familiar from its depiction on ivory inlays showing "the woman at the window," "consists of a row of identical colonnettes, each carved in the round in several sections, which include a flat-bottomed shaft, a wreath of drooping petals with molded rings of varying width above and below, and a voluted capital."[23]

The Proto-Aeolic capital, so called because it may have inspired the style of later Greek architecture, is an aggrandized version of the balustrade. Proto-Aeolic capitals probably imitate the sedge plant in Egypt, a motif borrowed by Phoenician craftsmen. In addition to Jerusalem and Ramat Raḥel

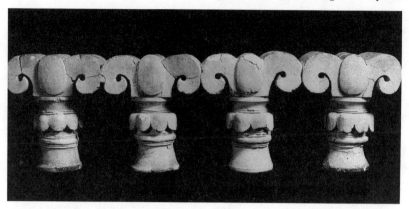

Restored palace window balustrade. Dating from the late eighth to the early seventh century B.C.E., these limestone balusters were found in the royal Judahite palace at Ramat Rahel. Similar architectural features were found at the City of David. *Courtesy of the Israel Department of Antiquities and Museums, Jerusalem.*

in the Southern Kingdom, Proto-Aeolic capitals have also been discovered in excavations at Samaria, Megiddo, and Hazor in the Northern Kingdom.

Also, Gabriel Barkay points out how the burial caves beneath the St. Stephen Convent (Ecole Biblique) in Jerusalem help to clarify the masonry and decoration of royal palaces:

> [The walls of the entrance chamber] reveal that they are decorated with shallow sunken panels, rectangular in shape, that were hewn into the rock faces of the walls. These rectangular panels are probably stone

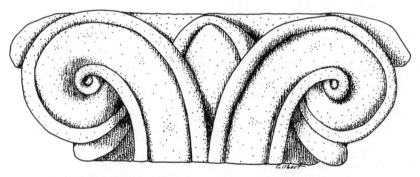

Proto-Aeolic stone capital. Dating from the ninth century B.C.E., this capital was found at Hazor in the Northern Kingdom. Capitals of this style have been recovered at Jerusalem, Megiddo, Samaria, Ramat Rahel, and elsewhere. *Drawing by Douglas Gilbert. Courtesy of the Israel Exploration Society.*

copies of wooden panels that typically covered walls of Judean palaces during the Israelite period.[24]

Jehoiakim's Royal Palace

Jeremiah spoke in a menacing manner of King Jehoiakim, who, having engaged workers to build his royal palace, defrauded them of their wages. The palace building is described in detail:

> Woe to him [Jehoiakim] who builds his house by unrighteousness, and his upper rooms (*'aliyyot*) by injustice; who makes his neighbors work for nothing, and does not give them their wages; who says, "I will build myself a spacious house (*bet middot*) with large upper rooms (*'aliyyot meruwwahim*)," and who cuts out windows (*hallonim*) for it, paneling it with cedar (*'erez*), and painting it with vermilion (*šašar*). (Jer 22:13–14)

Whether a "spacious house" (*bet middot*) refers to a new palace or the renovation of Solomon's palace is uncertain. B. Mazar suggests the prophet is describing Jehoiakim's summer palace located in the Mishneh, the residential area on Jerusalem's Western Hill.

Burial cave in the courtyard of the St. Stephen Convent. Between the two doors on the stonewall facing the entrance to Cave Complex One is a sunken panel. Door frames and ceiling cornices are also in evidence in these burial chambers. Each doorway leads to a burial chamber. *Photograph by Avraham Hay. Courtesy of Gabriel Barkay.*

Discussing the structure of pillared houses, Stager argues against the concept of an open central courtyard surrounded by three side rooms. He maintains that the houses were completely roofed. In the case of multistoried dwellings, "the ground floor had space allocated for food processing, small craft production, stabling, and storage; the second floor (*'aliyyah*) was suitable for dining, sleeping, and other activities."[25]

Paneling with cedar (*'erez*) was common in royal buildings. The durability of cedar made it especially suitable in the construction of pillars, ceilings, support beams, and paneling. Cedar, a cone-bearing evergreen tree associated with Lebanon, can attain a height of ninety feet and endure as long as two thousand years. Today, the cedar woods of Lebanon are quite sparse. In the Bible the cedar symbolizes dignity, strength, power, and beauty.

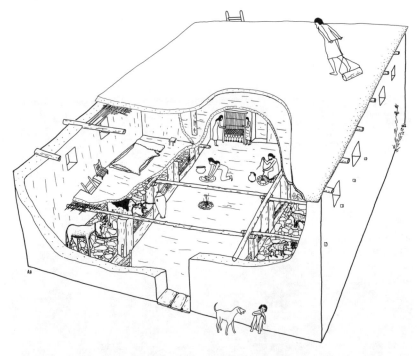

Iron Age pillared house. The typical house was a small rectangular building, incorporating two to four rooms that measured fifty feet long and thirty feet wide. The flat-roofed house consisted of one or two stories. The ground floor was composed of a broad room in the rear extending along the width of the house; also a central room for food preparation, flanked by side rooms serving as stables. Note the built-in troughs for animal feeding. The second floor was reserved for eating and sleeping. *Drawing by Abbas Alizadeh, as reconstructed by Lawrence Stager.*

People of the ancient Near East obviously liked bright colors, especially vermilion (*šašar*), which is a vivid, red pigment consisting of mercuric sulphide. The prophet Ezekiel mentioned this reddish-orange color when describing the images of Chaldeans (Babylonians) depicted in vermilion on a wall (Ezek 23:14). In a polemic against idols, the book of the Wisdom of Solomon, dating probably from the latter part of the first century B.C.E., refers to a woodcutter who daubs a wooden idol, "giving it a coat of red paint and coloring its surface red" (Wis 13:14). Smearing of vermilion on standing stones, as at the Arad temple, and on the capitals at Ramat Raḥel, was common in Palestine. The biblical writers' aversion to vermilion may have been due to its association with foreign cultures.

Ramat Raḥel

Ramat Raḥel, situated on a hill between Jerusalem and Bethlehem, is the site where for the first time a palace of a Judahite king was excavated systematically. The Israelite-Phoenician architecture of the palace at Ramat Raḥel sheds light on the style and plan of Jehoiakim's palace. When Aharoni excavated at Ramat Raḥel in the 1950s, he identified the site with Beth-haccherem; Barkay, continuing Aharoni's work in the 1980s, disagreed. Jeremiah mentions Beth-haccherem as a stronghold south of Jerusalem whence fire signals were sent to warn Jerusalem of imminent invasion (Jer 6:1).

None of the pottery at Ramat Raḥel dates before the eighth century B.C.E. In Stratum V A (600–586 B.C.E.), Aharoni uncovered the remains of a splendid Judahite royal palace, built by one of the last kings of Judah. Aharoni was inclined to identify the palace as the one built by Jehoiakim. More likely Jehoiakim's palace was situated in Jerusalem, not in suburban Ramat Raḥel. The palace, measuring 165 feet by 250 feet, was surrounded by an ashlar casemate wall (a double wall divided by cross walls into internal chambers).

Limestone balustrades in the form of colonnettes decorated with petals and voluted capitals served as railings in the palace windows at Ramat Raḥel. The well-known carved ivory plaques, referred to familiarly as the "woman at the window," have similar depictions and have been found at many sites in the Near East, including Nimrud (biblical Calah, twenty miles south of Nineveh) and Samaria.

Richard Barnett interpreted the "woman at the window," supposedly a sacred prostitute, as the goddess Astarte. He described the plaque from Nimrud as follows:

> This subject depicts a woman wearing an Egyptian sort of wig, looking fixedly in front, with a slight smile, over a window, consisting of a balustrade resting on three small columns with double palm-leaf capitals. The whole is enclosed in a triple-recessed embrasure.[26]

Reconstruction of a window frame. Found at Ramat Raḥel, it adorned a royal palace in the First Temple period. The stone balustrade, composed of four colonnettes, is similar in style to structures carved on Phoenician ivory plaques of the "woman at the window." Identical colonnettes were found in the City of David excavations. *Original drawing by Leen Ritmeyer. Courtesy of Simon & Schuster.*

Jeremiah may be alluding to the "woman at the window" in the following two passages:

> Therefore the showers have been withheld, and the spring rain has not come; yet you have the forehead of a whore, you refuse to be ashamed. (Jer 3:3)

Indicted for infidelity, Judah, the faithless spouse of the Lord, is compared to a harlot.

> And you, O desolate one, what do you mean that you dress in crimson, that you deck yourself with ornaments of gold, that you enlarge your eyes with paint? In vain you beautify yourself. Your lovers despise you; they seek your life. (Jer 4:30)

Jerusalem is personified here as a seductive woman, reminiscent of Queen Jezebel, who "painted her eyes, and adorned her head, and looked out of the window" when King Jehu (843–815 B.C.E.) came to Jezreel (2 Kings 9:30).

8

Funerary Customs
and Mourning

Burial was an ancient and almost universal practice in Palestine. The Bible attests to the necessity of a proper burial; it was a great dishonor for a corpse to remain unburied. One's burial place was considered to be a continuation of a person's dwelling in the land of the living. Burials customarily took place outside the city; only kings were allowed to be interred within the city walls. When a city expanded its walls, original burials were removed outside the new boundaries. Thousands of excavated tombs, especially those more recently examined in the vicinity of Jerusalem, are illuminating burial practices in ancient Israel. Israelite interment most often was in family tombs that accommodated successive generations. Burial in family tombs accorded with the biblical expression "to be buried with one's fathers" or "to sleep with one's fathers." In the First Temple period (1000–586 B.C.E.), tombs were ordinarily hewn into the rock.

Multiple burials took place in either natural caves or rock-cut tombs hewn out of the soft rock in a hillside. Rock-hewn caves date as early as the Early Bronze II Age (3050–2800 B.C.E.). These tombs were composed of multiple chambers, each equipped with elevated benches carved from the rock. These benches served as the resting place of the deceased. From early times, burials were divided into primary and secondary. In primary burials the corpse, once placed on a bench in a burial chamber, was not removed from its original position.

In secondary burials, when the space was required for a new burial, after a period of time the remains of the deceased were gathered in a pile on the floor or relegated to a repository or pit. In the postexilic period, especially in the first century B.C.E. and later, the bones were collected and deposited in limestone boxes called ossuaries (from the Latin word for "bones"), as a way of making room for additional burials in the same chamber.

Aharoni described a typical burial cave in use during the Iron II period (1000–586 B.C.E.):

> The entry was through a vertical shaft with a few steps at the end leading through a small rectangular entrance (stomium) to a rectangular vestibule (atrium). This opened onto several burial chambers with benches or arcosolia along the sides, the number of which may vary from one to four, with additions being made as needed.[1]

Cremation ordinarily was not practiced in ancient Israel. Burial was also the rule among the Canaanites, although some of the neighboring peoples did dispose of the deceased by cremation. A ritual with fire, quite different from cremation, was performed in the burials of prominent figures like kings.

Embalming was not practiced, nor were coffins used. Instead, the corpse was transported on a bier, with burial taking place on the day of death, as is the custom today in the Middle East. As part of the burial rite, the deceased was interred fully clothed, and some personal belongings were buried with the corpse.

Jeremiah

The book of Jeremiah has many references to burials as well as to the denial of burial which was considered a great curse. Herbert Brichto, commenting on the importance of a decent Israelite burial and the effect of lack of burial for the afterlife, states:

> Jeremiah stands out among the prophets in his penchant for invoking the punishment of exposure of the dead's physical remains in the form of initial privation of burial or of malicious disinterment. . . . Is this testimony enough to a belief, at least on the part of Jeremiah's contemporaries, that worse than death is the disturbance of a person's physical remains?[2]

In a menacing oracle of judgment, Jeremiah described how leading figures would be dishonored by the disinterment of their remains for having had recourse to astral cults:

> At that time, says the LORD, the bones of the kings of Judah, the bones of its officials, the bones of the priests, the bones of the prophets, and the bones of the inhabitants of Jerusalem shall be brought out of their tombs; and they shall be spread before the sun and the moon and all the host of heaven, which they have loved and served, which they have followed, and which they have inquired of and worshiped; and they shall not be gathered or buried; they shall be like dung (*domen*) on the surface of the ground. (Jer 8:1–2)

In a dirge over the land, Jeremiah issued comparable threats:

> Speak! Thus says the LORD: "Human corpses shall fall like dung (*domen*) upon the open field, like sheaves ["grain stalks"] behind the reaper, and no one shall gather them." (Jer 9:22 [Hebrew 9:21])

Jeremiah used the same, somewhat crude, language in his devastating prophecy about the future of the people of Judah:

> For thus says the LORD concerning the sons and daughters who are born in this place [Jerusalem?], and concerning the mothers who bear them and the fathers who beget them in this land: They shall die of deadly diseases. They shall not be lamented, nor shall they be buried; they shall become like dung (*domen*) on the surface of the ground. They shall perish by the sword and by famine, and their dead bodies shall become food for the birds of the air and for the wild animals of the earth. (Jer 16:3–4)

In addition to the curse of being left unburied, these victims were subjected to the added indignity of being unlamented.

In the Lord's controversy with the nations the same dreadful sentiments are expressed:

> Those slain by the LORD on that day shall extend from one end of the earth to the other. They shall not be lamented, or gathered, or buried; they shall become dung (*domen*) on the surface of the ground. (Jer 25:33)

In his denunciation of lying prophets Jeremiah prophesied not only that they would be punished but also that the people of Jerusalem who listened to false prophets would experience firsthand the tragedy of not being buried:

> And the people to whom they prophesy shall be thrown out into the streets of Jerusalem, victims of famine and sword. There shall be no one to bury them—themselves, their wives, their sons, and their daughters. For I [the LORD] will pour out their wickedness upon them. (Jer 14:16)

The punishment of King Jehoiakim included the incredible (for a king!) fate of being unmourned and unburied:

> Therefore thus says the LORD concerning King Jehoiakim son of Josiah of Judah: They shall not lament for him, saying, "Alas, my brother!" or "Alas, sister!" They shall not lament for him, saying, "Alas, lord!" or "Alas, his majesty!" With the burial of a donkey he shall be buried—dragged off and thrown out beyond the gates of Jerusalem. (Jer 22:18–19)

In a further judgment pronounced after King Jehoiakim burned the scroll of Jeremiah, the prophet predicted that the king, in addition to being denied proper burial, would have no successor:

> Therefore thus says the LORD concerning King Jehoiakim of Judah: He shall have no one to sit upon the throne of David, and his dead body shall be cast out to the heat by day and the frost by night. (Jer 36:30)

Whether this curse was fulfilled literally is open to question.

Because Uriah, otherwise unknown, proclaimed a threatening message similar to Jeremiah's, King Jehoiakim sought to kill him. Desperate to avoid that fate, Uriah fled to Egypt, but he was pursued and apprehended:

> Then King Jehoiakim sent Elnathan son of Achbor and men with him to Egypt, and they took Uriah from Egypt and brought him to King Jehoiakim, who struck him down with the sword and threw his dead body into the burial place of the common people (*qibre bene ha'am* [literally, "the graves of the sons of the people"]). (Jer 26:22–23)

"Common people" may not be the most accurate translation of *bene ha'am*, especially if *bet ha'am* refers to the Parliament of the gentry. The offspring of the landed gentry were not "common people." If the commoners' burial ground is intended, it may have been simply a trench where the ordinary people, in contrast to the upper classes, were buried. On the basis of a similar reference in 2 Kings 23:6 connecting "the Wadi Kidron" and "the graves of the common people," it may be that the commoners' grave was located in the Kidron Valley on the east side of Jerusalem, between the Temple Mount and the Mount of Olives.

Throughout its history Jerusalem has been a "city of the dead." In apocalyptic, the dead of Jerusalem will rise first on the day of resurrection.

Tombs North of Jerusalem

Tombs of the First Temple period (1000–586 B.C.E.) surrounded Jerusalem. More than a hundred and ten burial caves have been uncovered on the north, east, and west sides of the city. Since burials would have been located outside the walls of the city, they provide valuable evidence for determining the extent of the boundaries of the ancient city.

North of Jerusalem, two lavish and extensive burial-cave complexes have been uncovered on the grounds of the St. Stephen Convent (Ecole Biblique), located on Nablus Road just north of the Old City's Damascus Gate. These are the most elaborate and spacious tombs thus far discovered in modern Israel. Each complex, covering about 10,000 square feet, was part of a much larger necropolis situated north of Jerusalem.

The well-known but controversial Garden Tomb, dating from the First Temple period, was part of this complex. Considered by many to be the tomb of Jesus, the Garden Tomb was so identified in 1883 by General Charles Gordon, a British military officer. Some Protestants espoused the position of Gordon, while Roman Catholics continued to view the Church of the Holy Sepulchre as the site of Jesus' tomb, a tradition going back to the fourth century C.E. The difference of opinion soon deteriorated into a polemic. Meanwhile, archaeology has established that the Garden Tomb was not in use in the period between the end of Iron Age II and the beginning of the Byzantine period, from about 586 B.C.E. to 324 C.E., thus ruling it out as the site of Jesus' burial.

Although the cave tombs on the grounds of the Ecole Biblique were known for a long time, they had been mistakenly dated to the Roman period (63 B.C.E.–324 C.E.). Gabriel Barkay and Amos Kloner established beyond doubt that these elegant burial chambers dated from the First Temple period, eighth or seventh century B.C.E., on the basis of their plan and architecture.

The two Cave Complexes are similar, consisting basically of a central entrance chamber surrounded by burial chambers. With respect to Cave

Reconstruction of burial cave in the courtyard of the St. Stephen Convent.
Part of the necropolis in the northern section of Jerusalem. The central entrance chamber is surrounded by burial chambers. Most of the burial chambers have benches along three of the walls. *Original drawing by Leen Ritmeyer. Courtesy of Simon & Schuster.*

Complex One, the entrance is about six feet high, and the entrance chamber measures seventeen by fourteen feet and is ten feet high. Six burial chambers lead off the entrance chamber. Each of these tomb chambers contained three burial benches hewn from the rock and located along three of the walls. Each bench was fashioned with a headrest in the shape of a horseshoe, also hewn from the rock. The remains of the deceased were placed on these burial benches. Repositories or pits for collecting the bones of previous generations of deceased were also uncovered.

Burial benches were typical of the First Temple period, but the arrangement was quite different in the Second Temple period (515 B.C.E.–70 C.E.). In place of benches, burial niches (*kokhim*) carved into the rock were used to support the bodies of the deceased in the later time.

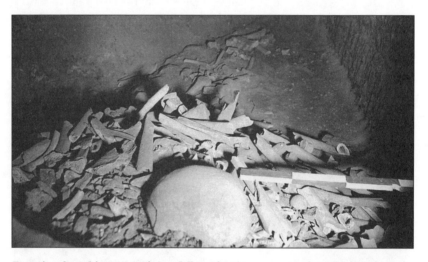

Remains found in a repository. When the time came to clear the benches of remains from initial burials, the bones of the deceased and the accompanying funerary offerings were relegated to a repository in the floor of the chamber. Evidence of this practice has been found in the Cave Complex at the St. Stephen Convent, at Ketef Hinnom, and elsewhere in the First Temple period. *Courtesy of Gabriel Barkay.*

Silwan Necropolis

Between 1968 and 1970 Ussishkin, assisted by Barkay, excavated the Silwan necropolis, situated on the steep east slope on the eastern side of the Kidron Valley, opposite the City of David. "The graves in Siloam [Silwan]," according to Dan Bahat, "are a particularly good example of the method of burial employed in Jerusalem during the First Temple period."[3]

Tomb entrances at Silwan. More than forty monumental tombs were cut in the cliffs at Silwan on the east slope of the Kidron Valley, opposite the City of David. These tombs were intended for prominent individuals, and not as family tombs. *Photograph by David Harris. Courtesy of David Ussishkin.*

"Tomb of Pharaoh's Daughter" at Silwan. This famous monolithic tomb, whose name is not to be taken literally, used to have a pyramid on the roof. Today it has a flat roof. It is cube-shaped and consists of a burial chamber with a gabled ceiling. There is but a single bench to accommodate one burial. *Photograph by David Harris. Courtesy of David Ussishkin.*

Dating from the eighth and seventh centuries B.C.E., the cemetery had its tomb entrances cut into the vertical Silwan cliffs, high above the surface. The necropolis included more than forty monumental rock-cut tombs. The nobles of Jerusalem, or at least rich and prominent citizens, may have been buried in these tombs. In contrast to the northern necropolis, some of the Silwan tombs were one-chamber structures. In common with the northern tombs, these were furnished with headrests.

Although all the Silwan tombs have much in common with respect to their plan and architectural features, the excavators distinguished three kinds of tombs.

First, there were tombs with a gabled ceiling. Their entrance, twenty to twenty-four inches square, led into a rectangular burial chamber with a gabled ceiling. This chamber measured approximately seven feet long, four feet wide, and seven feet high. The bench with its headrest was hewn in the long wall of the chamber.

Second, there were tombs with a straight ceiling and decorated with a cornice. Some of these tombs had two or three burial chambers, some chambers measuring ten feet square.

"Tomb of the Royal Steward." An aboveground monolithic tomb situated on the main street of the Silwan village. Note the sunken panels on the facade where two burial inscriptions were engraved before removal. The larger inscription referring to Shebna was located on the left side of the facade above the entrance of the tomb. *Courtesy of David Ussishkin.*

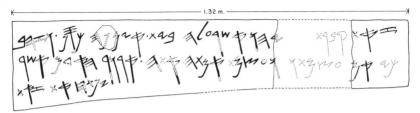

The Shebna tomb inscription. The four-foot-long inscription was discovered by Charles Clermont-Ganneau in 1870 at the village of Silwan. *Original drawing by Nahman Avigad. Courtesy of the Israel Exploration Society.*

Finally, three aboveground monolithic tombs were situated at the north end of the Silwan village. These cube-shaped tombs had Hebrew inscriptions on the facade.

One of the most elaborate tombs is an aboveground monolithic tomb called the "tomb of the Royal Steward" from the inscription that Charles Clermont-Ganneau discovered in 1870. Engraved on the facade above the tomb's entrance, the inscription, ingeniously deciphered by Avigad, reads:

> This is the tomb of [   ] Yahu who is over the house [an official of high rank at the court]. There is no silver and no gold here, only his bones and the bones of his slave wife [who is] with him. Cursed be the one who will open this.[4]

Clermont-Ganneau thought it might be the tomb of Shebna. Avigad suggested that "Yahu" composes the final letters of the name "Shebna" which appears in Isaiah:

> Thus says the Lord GOD of hosts: Come, go to this steward, to Shebna, who is master of the household, and say to him: What right do you have here? Who are your relatives here, that you have cut out a tomb here for yourself, cutting a tomb on the height, and carving a habitation for yourself in the rock? (Isa 22:15–16)

Isaiah accused Shebna, state secretary in the court of Hezekiah, of carving an elaborate tomb for himself in high rock (not the customary subterranean rock-chamber) for all to see. Avigad commented that this "Shebna inscription" is the first-known text of a Hebrew sepulchral inscription from preexilic times.

As with the Temple and the royal palace in Jerusalem, the architecture of these tombs reflects Phoenician influence. On the basis of comparative studies, Ussishkin attributes the origin of the Silwan monumental tomb architecture with its gabled ceilings and straight ceiling with cornices to a Phoenician prototype. Similar tombs have been discovered at the necropolis of Salamis, the ancient capital situated on the eastern coast of Cyprus. At

Salamis more than one hundred and fifty tombs, dating from the eighth and seventh centuries B.C.E., have been excavated, some under the direction of Vassos Karageorghis. From 1966, he excavated the famous Tomb 79, the richest tomb on Cyprus. Rock-cut tombs belonging to ordinary people at Salamis were hewn from the hard, surface rock and had rectangular chambers with a flat roof.

Comparable tombs belonging to the kings of Urartu in Van of Armenia (today, in Turkey) have also been unearthed. The Urartians, descendants of the Hurrians, lived on the plateau surrounding Lake Van. During the first half of the first millennium B.C.E. the kingdom of Urartu was one of the most powerful states in the Near East. Distinguished for their metalworking, the Urartians were also outstanding in rock architecture. Like the necropolis at Silwan, at Urartu the tombs, dating from the eighth century B.C.E., were cut into the cliffs. Their chambers have straight ceilings, decorated with a cornice. Ussishkin points out that the striking similarity between the burials at Silwan and Urartu illustrates the cultural connection between Urartu and Judah.

Excellent examples of Iron Age II Phoenician tombs carved out of the bedrock have been uncovered from the cemetery at Achzib on the Mediterranean coast. The excavators distinguished two kinds of burials at Achzib: rock-cut or ashlar-built burial chambers and cremation burials in amphora urns.

Ketef Hinnom

Ketef Hinnom—literally "shoulder of Hinnom"—accurately describes a series of rock-cut burial caves extending the length of the Hinnom Valley, which lies south and southwest of Jerusalem. Hewn into the hard limestone of the cliff, these caves, located on the grounds of the St. Andrew's Scottish Hospice, date from the end of the First Temple period, and perhaps even a little later. Serving as family tombs for successive generations, this vast necropolis yielded evidence of continuous settlement in Jerusalem, extending from the late monarchy into the early exilic period. That is to say, the Iron II period did not cease, as is commonly thought, with the conquest of Jerusalem in 586 B.C.E. but continued into the Persian period.

During three seasons of digging between 1975 and 1980, Barkay excavated nine of these burial caves. Most of the caves have only one chamber, measuring approximately nine feet square. According to the description of Barkay:

> A step led down from the entrance to the central passage, which has high burial benches on three sides. In two of the caves, a slightly raised cushion was carved out of the rock bench, with hollows to serve as head-rests for the deceased.[5]

Pottery assemblage from Ketef Hinnom. Archaeologists recovered almost 300 intact vessels from Ketef Hinnom, including oil lamps, perfume bottles, and small juglets. These vessels date mostly from the sixth century B.C.E. *Photograph by Avraham Hay. Courtesy of Gabriel Barkay.*

As in other burial caves in Jerusalem, repositories were dug under the burial benches as receptacles for the bones of the deceased and the accompanying funerary offerings after their removal to accommodate new burials.

Grave robbers had looted the repositories of many burial caves in this necropolis. But one cave (Number 25) at Ketef Hinnom remained undisturbed, and its contents have furnished important information about both life and death in Jerusalem during Jeremiah's era. The remains in that cave attest to the wealth of those interred in the tombs, in contrast to the "poor people," whom Jeremiah mentioned specifically:

> Nebuzaradan the captain of the guard left in the land of Judah some of the poor people who owned nothing, and gave them vineyards and fields at the same time. (Jer 39:10)

The chamber, measuring approximately ten feet by six feet, and seven feet high, held the remains of some ninety-five deceased. Among the artifacts in the repository of this chamber were pottery, iron arrowheads, and objects of bone and ivory. More important were the jewelry, including six gold items and ninety-five pieces of silver jewelry, and the semiprecious beads. These luxury items, worn by Jerusalem's wealthy women, attest to the opulence of the period. The foreign style of the art objects recovered at Ketef Hinnom indicates that the Judahites of Jeremiah's time had cultural contacts with neighboring nations, particularly Assyria, Babylonia, Syria, and Urartu.

This exquisite hoard recalls the words of the prophet Zephaniah, a contemporary of Jeremiah, speaking about the day of judgment:

> All who weigh out silver are cut off. . . . Neither their silver nor their gold will be able to save them on the day of the LORD's wrath. (Zeph 1:11, 18)

These verses are a reminder of the use of silver for payment in commercial transactions. In addition to the silver ingots used as weighed "coinage" at En-gedi, silver objects dating from the tenth century B.C.E. were discovered at Eshtemoa (es-Sammo'a) in the southern Hebron hills.

Tophet

The Hinnom Valley bounds Jerusalem on the west and south, whereas the Kidron Valley bounds the city on the east. The Hinnom, also known in the Bible as the Valley of Ben (the son of) Hinnom, and the Valley of Benei (the sons of) Hinnom, acquired a sinister reputation because of its association with the gruesome Tophet. Located south of the Old City of Jerusalem, near the junction of the Hinnom and the Kidron valleys, the Tophet was the name of the cultic installation where children were sacrificed to the god Molech.

The etymology of the word Tophet is disputed, but it may be of Aramaic origin with the meaning "hearth," "fireplace," or "roaster." The term is associated with the book of Jeremiah, although it does occur occasionally in other biblical books. As with high places and other cult centers in ancient Israel, much remains to be learned about the Tophet. The texts of Jeremiah help to clarify the nature and function of the Tophet, but they too are sometimes ambiguous.

The texts of 2 Kings 16:3; 21:6 and 2 Chr 28:3; 33:6 attest that two kings of Judah, Ahaz (735–715 B.C.E.) and Manasseh (687–642 B.C.E.), consigned their sons to the fires of the Tophet. Conversely, King Josiah (640–609 B.C.E.) dismantled the Tophet:

> He [Josiah] defiled Topheth, which is in the valley of Ben-hinnom, so that no one would make a son or a daughter pass through fire as an offering to Molech. (2 Kings 23:10)

When the Tophet was later rebuilt, Jeremiah pronounced harsh judgment upon it on at least two occasions:

> And they [the people of Judah] go on building the high place of Topheth, which is in the valley of the son of Hinnom, to burn their sons and their daughters in the fire (*lisrop ba'eš*)—which I did not command,

nor did it come into my mind. Therefore, the days are surely coming, says the LORD, when it will no more be called Topheth, or the valley of the son of Hinnom (*ge' ben-hinnom*), but the valley of Slaughter (*ge' haharegah*): for they will bury in Topheth until there is no more room. (Jer 7:31–32; also 19:5–6)

A further divine indictment of the people of Judah alluded to the Tophet:

They built the high places of Baal in the valley of the son of Hinnom, to offer up (*leha'abir*) [literally, "to pass through (the fire)"] their sons and daughters to Molech, though I did not command them, nor did it enter my mind that they should do this abomination, causing Judah to sin. (Jer 32:35; also 2 Kings 17:17)

Jeremiah 32:35 connected the Tophet with the worship of the god Baal. However, texts of the first millennium B.C.E. associated human sacrifice with the god El. The reference to Baal may be intended as a polemic against the cult of Baal.[6]

Molech in this verse is a deity of uncertain origin. Instead of Molech, the translation, according to Paul Mosca,[7] should read *mulk*, a technical term denoting a live sacrifice in fulfillment of a Tophet vow. While Mosca contends that *molek* is strictly a sacrificial term in the Bible, others like George Heider assert that *molek* represents a West Semitic deity in all uses.

Scholars dispute whether these texts refer literally to child sacrifice. Attempting to moderate the evidence for child sacrifice by burning in Israel and neighboring nations, Moshe Weinfeld[8] and others argue that expressions such as "to burn their sons and daughters in the fire" and "to offer up their sons and daughters" refer to an initiation rite, or are intended figuratively, or are to be understood as prophetic hyperboles. They maintain that children buried in the Tophet had died of natural causes and not as sacrificial victims. Other scholars, insisting that these foreboding expressions are to be taken literally, maintain that biblical texts mean what they say, especially when supported by nonbiblical texts and artifactual evidence.[9]

Nonbiblical texts and archaeological data that deal with child sacrifice at Carthage illuminate the Tophet of Jeremiah's time. The great Phoenician city of Carthage was founded on the northern coast of Africa (modern Tunisia) in 814 B.C.E. and fell to the Romans in 146 B.C.E. Between 1976 and 1979, as an American participant in the UNESCO-sponsored Save Carthage Project, Stager[10] reexcavated nine stratified levels of burials, dating from 750 to 146 B.C.E., at the open-air precinct of the goddess Tanit. She is identified by some with Astarte and Asherah, Canaanite and Phoenician goddesses of love and war.

As part of his excavation strategy, Stager undertook a systematic recovery of complete burial units, including urns, cremated remains, grave goods, and cippi (L-shaped monuments of sandstone). These artifacts, combined with the inscriptions on the stelae (commemorative stones) stating that the vows made to the deities by the offerants were being fulfilled, make it clear that child sacrifice took place at ancient Carthage. In addition, the charred remains of children, or sometimes of animals used as substitutes for children, were uncovered at Carthage.

In preparation for final publication, Stager and his team are conducting a systematic analysis of the data so as to clarify the question of child sacrifice at Carthage. This study may, in turn, cast light on the issue of infanticide in its various forms, as practiced both in biblical and in modern times.

Archaeological evidence from Carthage supports the thesis that children were sacrificed in the walled precinct (so-called Tophet) to the god Baal Hammon, identified with El, as well as to Tanit. Statuary at Carthage shows a bearded and seated Baal Hammon. Dating from the eighth to the second

Precinct of Tanit at Carthage. Looking west across the field of monuments erected over the urns filled with the charred remains of children sacrificed to Tanit and Baal Hammon, the patron deities of Carthage during the Punic (Phoenician) period (725–146 B.C.E.). In the foreground are Director Lawrence Stager, Douglas Esse (*right*), Joseph Greene (*center*), and Samuel Wolff (*rear*). *Photograph by James Whitred. Courtesy of the Punic Project.*

century B.C.E., the precinct of Tanit has the dubious distinction of being the most extensive cemetery of sacrificed humans ever uncovered.

Archaeology of the Tophet at Carthage, according to Stager, provides strong evidence against those scholars who consider Jeremiah as being tendentious in his condemnation of the Tophet in Jerusalem. If Jeremiah had been incorrect about "burning" children in the Tophet, his opponents could easily have proved him wrong. Nor can Jeremiah be accused of being an "outsider" disparaging his own people, as was the case with Greek-Roman writ-

Urns from the Sanctuary of Tanit at Carthage. These burial urns date to Tanit II (600–300 B.C.E.). Each was filled with the charred remains of a child and then placed in a pit. *Photograph by James Whitred. Courtesy of the Punic Project.*

ers who have been dismissed for accusing the Phoenicians/Carthaginians of practicing child sacrifice. Jeremiah was very much an "insider" who knew firsthand that the shameful practice existed in Jerusalem itself.

The sad fact is that with the passage of time infant sacrifice at Carthage increased, not decreased, especially in the fourth and third centuries B.C.E. Even sadder, archaeologists have discovered other Tophets in Sicily, Sardinia, Cyprus, and Tyre.

Mourning Rites

Mourning as an expression of sorrow for the dead went hand in hand with burial rites. Mourning rituals were observed for deceased family members and national figures as well as on the occasion of public calamities. Mourning generally lasted seven days, but in the case of important people it was extended to seventy days. Mourning practices included weeping, wailing, rending garments, donning sackcloth, shaving the hair, and cutting the body. The origin of these tokens of mourning is not always clear; some were adopted from the Canaanites. Although the laws of Leviticus expressly forbade some of these expressions of mourning (e.g., shaving the hair and cutting the body), nonetheless they were practiced. Brichto thinks that some of these rites "in all likelihood derive from the belief in the powers (possibly malevolent) of the spirits of the dead."[11]

References in Jeremiah to mourning are so extensive, especially those dealing with the national disaster, that only key verses can be cited:

Describing the coming of Judah's enemy "from the north" as a national calamity (Jer 6:22), Jeremiah advised:

> O my poor people, put on sackcloth, and roll in ashes; make mourning as for an only child, most bitter lamentation: for suddenly the destroyer will come upon us. (Jer 6:26; also 4:8; 47:5; 48:37)

Sackcloth (*saq*, English "sack"), a symbol of mourning, denoted a garment woven from goat's hair or camel's hair. This coarse cloth was the same material used for making grain bags. It was dark in color and uncomfortable when worn next to the skin.

The pilgrims from the north came prepared to mourn the destruction of the Temple and the fall of Jerusalem:

> Eighty men arrived from Shechem and Shiloh and Samaria, with their beards shaved and their clothes torn, and their bodies gashed, bringing grain offerings and incense to present at the temple of the LORD. (Jer 41:5)

Whereas women ordinarily sang laments, professional mourners were often hired. Jeremiah referred to professional women mourners in the midst of impending disaster:

> Thus says the LORD of hosts: Consider, and call for the mourning women to come; send for the skilled women to come; let them quickly raise a dirge over us, so that our eyes may run down with tears, and our eyelids flow with water. (Jer 9:17–18 [Hebrew 9:16–17])

Marzeaḥ

The word *marzeaḥ*[12] occurs only twice in the Old Testament: in Amos 6:4–7 (vocalized *mirzaḥ*), depicting a sumptuous banquet accompanied by sensuous excesses; and in Jer 16:5–9, describing a mourning rite that consisted of eating and drinking. Although the *marzeaḥ* has a long history, dating from the fourteenth century B.C.E., much is still unknown about it. The *marzeaḥ*, both a religious and a social institution, denoted the association or guild sponsoring the banquet or designated the place where the banquet was held. The concept of celebration appears to be at the center of the *marzeaḥ*, although the occasion could be either joyful or sorrowful.

The Lord forbade Jeremiah to marry and have children, and at the same time prohibited him from entering the *bet marzeaḥ* (house of mourning) to participate in memorial meals connected with mourning the dead and consoling the mourners. In view of the imminent disaster to befall the nation, Jeremiah was instructed to distance himself from the community. Thereby he was deprived of the consolation associated with ordinary human discourse:

> For thus says the LORD: Do not enter the house of mourning (*bet marzeah*), or go to lament, or bemoan them; for I have taken away my peace from this people, says the LORD, my steadfast love and mercy. Both great and small shall die in this land; they shall not be buried, and no one shall lament for them; there shall be no gashing, no shaving of the head for them. No one shall break bread for the mourner, to offer comfort for the dead; nor shall anyone give them the cup of consolation to drink for their fathers or their mothers. You shall not go into the house of feasting (*bet mišteh*) to sit with them, to eat and drink. For thus says the LORD of hosts, the God of Israel: I am going to banish from this place, in your days and before your eyes, the voice of mirth and the voice of gladness, the voice of the bridegroom and the voice of the bride. (Jer 16:5–9)

The *bet marzeah* was the site of the funerary cult that included mourning, eating, and drinking. From the context, the "house of mourning" and the "house of feasting" in this passage are virtually parallel. Partaking of food and drink, an integral part of the *marzeah*, was also a way of offering consolation to the bereaved. The *marzeah* described by Amos had no funerary implications, whereas the funerary ritual was at the heart of the *marzeah* described in Jeremiah.

Tumuli West of Jerusalem

A tumulus is an artificial mound over a grave. Consisting ordinarily of earth and rubble, it may cover a single burial or multiple burials. A cairn, as distinct from a tumulus, is constructed of stone; such piles of stones functioned as memorials or landmarks. Amihai Mazar indicates that tumuli fields are found on the heights of mountain ridges in the Negev.

In 1953, Ruth Amiran surveyed and excavated some of the nineteen tumuli situated on summits and ridges west of Jerusalem. She excavated Tumulus Number 5 totally; it measured twenty feet in height and one hundred and five feet in diameter. She noted, "Most of the tumuli are built, or rather heaped, on ridges well above the level of their surroundings and overlook far distances."[13]

These tumuli, shaped like truncated cones with a flat top and steep slopes, were utilized from the second half of the eighth and the seventh century B.C.E.

They were equipped with platforms, pits, and a place for burning, all suitable for ritual acts. It seemed to the excavator that burning took place at these sites in conjunction with either cooking or sacrifice. After surveying, mapping, and excavating, Amiran was still uncertain about the meaning and purpose of the tumuli.

Barkay suggested that inasmuch as tombs were not found connected with the tumuli west of Jerusalem, "they [the tumuli] were associated with impressive ceremonies of burning for the dead conducted in behalf of the Jerusalem aristocracy."[14] That is, incense and perfumes would have been burned near the body as a ritual accompanying the interment. This ceremony was quite different from cremation—it was a burning for, not of, the deceased.

Barkay's explanation may clarify some puzzling biblical texts, especially Jeremiah:

> Yet hear the word of the LORD, O King Zedekiah of Judah! Thus says the LORD concerning you: You shall not die by the sword; you shall die in peace. And as spices were burned for your ancestors, the earlier kings who preceded you, so they shall burn spices for you and lament for you, saying, "Alas, lord!" For I have spoken the word, says the LORD. (Jer 34:4–5)

Holladay comments on the same passage:

> The Hebrew text simply says "were burned" (*misrepot*) and "burn" (*yisrepu*), without an explicit statement of what is burned; but the phraseology of 2 Chr 16:14 and 21:19 makes it clear that it is spices that were burned.[15]

In Jeremiah's oracle against Babylon, the Lord pronounced doom:

> I am against you, O destroying mountain, says the LORD, that destroys the whole earth; I will stretch out my hand against you, and roll you down from the crags, and make you a burned-out mountain (*har serepah*). No stone shall be taken from you for a corner and no stone for a foundation, but you shall be a perpetual waste, says the LORD. (Jer 51:25–26)

The significance of "burned-out mountain" has been a problem for commentators. Bright's explanation adds some clarity to the verse:

> Yahweh burns the mountain to a cinder so that [Jer 51:26] even its stones are useless. Once again, one sees the ambiguity of the figure: Babylon both *is* the mountain, and is seized and rolled down from it.[16]

Jeremiah certainly expected the overthrow of Babylon.

9

Agriculture

In biblical times Israelite society was primarily agricultural. Every aspect of life, including the domestic, economic, cultural, and religious, was affected by agriculture. Agriculture was the basis of biblical metaphors, as it was the inspiration of art, architecture, and poetry. Owing to their familiarity with the land, the trees, and the plants, the prophets, especially Jeremiah, often expressed their ideas poetically in the language of nature.

Despite the importance of agriculture in the Bible, the study of ancient agriculture has been somewhat neglected. As Near Eastern archaeology is becoming more interdisciplinary, it has been taking a greater interest in reconstructing the environment and ecology of past cultures. The archaeological evidence of ancient agriculture, including plant remains, can be retrieved today through the techniques of flotation and sieving. In the flotation process when ancient soil and sediments are mixed with water, organic fragments such as carbonized seeds float to the surface and then can be retrieved and analyzed. Both wet and dry sieving improve the retrieval rate of smaller artifacts, such as seeds, shells, and bones, that may have gone undetected during the digging.

C. H. J. de Geus has summarized the importance of the study of agriculture:

> It goes without saying that a better knowledge of ancient agriculture and of the natural conditions in antiquity is a great help in understanding texts which are full of the terminology and expressions derived from the daily life of the Hebrew farmer.[1]

Agriculture is dependent upon many factors, especially the climate which in Palestine is subtropical. There are only two seasons: the summer which is hot and dry, and the winter which is mild and wet. Rainfall is critical in a land dependent upon natural farming (farming without irrigation). The rainy season extends from the end of October to the end of April. In the intervening summer months when there is no rain, the dew provides beneficial moisture to the crops. The early rain (*yoreh*), coming in the autumn (October-November), prepares the ground for planting. Until the ground is softened by this rain, plowing cannot begin. The heavy winter rain (*gešem*) soaks the ground and fills the cisterns. The later rain (*malqoš*) comes in March-April.

Jeremiah, vitally aware of the rainy season as an act of God, indicts the people's obtuseness for not recognizing it:

> They do not say in their hearts, "Let us fear the LORD our God, who gives the rain (*gešem*) in its season, the autumn rain (*yoreh*) and the spring rain (*malqoš*), and keeps for us the weeks appointed for the harvest." (Jer 5:24)

The sirocco, known in modern Arabic as the khamsin, was a hazard for the crops. It is the "east wind" of the Bible. Occurring between April-June and September-November, this is the oppressive, dust-laden wind from the eastern desert. Jeremiah used the sirocco as a symbol of the coming judgment:

> At that time it will be said to this people and to Jerusalem: A hot wind (*ruaḥ ṣaḥ*) comes from me [the LORD] out of the bare heights in the desert toward my poor people, not to winnow or cleanse—a wind too strong for that. Now it is I [the LORD] who speak in judgment against them. (Jer 4:11–12)

Flora

Plants play a significant role in the Bible. Like agriculture in general, they illuminate many phases of life in Palestine. Despite the prominence of biblical flora, their precise identification is a perennial problem. Evidence for this statement is readily found by consulting various translations of the Bible. English translations often do not agree on the identification of a plant, partly because of the inadequate description given in the biblical text and partly because translators apply names of plants known from their own homeland, although the plants may never have been cultivated in Palestine.

On the problem of identification of biblical plants, Zohary observed:

> Despite the numerous efforts made by many scholars, among them experts in Semitic languages, and the already great achievements in botanical research, a fair number of biblical plant names have not so far been identified, and some have perhaps no prospect of ever being fully cleared up.[2]

A concrete illustration of the problem of identifying plants is found in a series of wisdom sayings where Jeremiah contrasts the righteous and the wicked. The similarity between this text and the opening psalm of the Psalter is striking. The righteous are compared to "a tree planted by water, sending out its roots by the stream" (Jer 17:8), and the unrighteous to "a shrub (*'ar'ar*) in the desert, and shall not see when relief comes" (Jer 17:6).

Comparison of several English translations shows the differences in rendering "a shrub (*'ar'ar*) in the desert." One commentator referred to this example as "a biblical botanical puzzle."[3] Zohary speculated that *'ar'ar* should be identified with the Phoenician juniper, on the basis of the Arab practice of calling the juniper *'ar'ar*. He described the Phoenician juniper as "a tree or shrub, usually less than 5 m. [fifteen feet] tall, which attains an age of several hundred years."[4] Botanist Nogah Hareuveni identified *'ar'ar* with the "apple of Sodom," a small tree attaining a height of about ten feet. Since both these trees are associated with the wilderness, they would fit Jeremiah's description.

Jeremiah's frequent references to flora illustrate that the prophet lived close to nature. In the famous description of the Promised Land, Deuteronomy lists the "seven species" symbolizing the bounty of the land. Jeremiah included all of these, and many more, in his vivid oracles: "A land of wheat and barley, of vines and fig trees and pomegranates, a land of olive trees and honey" (Deut 8:8). Cereals and fruit trees, as Deuteronomy attests, were the principal agricultural crops in biblical times.

Wheat

Wheat (*ḥiṭṭah*), a member of the grass family, has been known in Palestine since at least the Early Bronze Age (3500–2000 B.C.E.). Two species of wheat were cultivated in Palestine, one is durum wheat (*Triticum durum*), the other emmer (*Triticum dicoccum*). Zohary maintained that biblical wheats were from the emmer class, a wild-growing wheat with dense ears and a brittle rachis. Emmer, a translation of the Hebrew *kussemet*, is inferior to durum wheat.

Whereas the Hebrew word *ḥiṭṭah* distinguishes wheat from other cereals, Hebrew also uses other words for wheat. Among them, *dagan* is a generic term for cereal grains (Jer 31:12), and *bar* denotes the final product of winnowing. Wheat and barley were the principal field crops and among the main cereal grasses of biblical times. Planted in the valleys during autumn at the beginning of the rainy season, wheat was harvested during May or June. The wheat and barley harvest extended over seven weeks. Wheat was converted into flour only after the processes of threshing, winnowing, parching, and grinding had taken place. In addition to its use as a food staple, wheat was offered in sacrifice and was exported, especially to Tyre.

Oded Borowski[5] lists several sites in modern Israel that have yielded samples of wheat in an Iron Age context. These sites include Afula, Lachish, Tel Qiri, Beer-sheba, Arad, and Shiloh.

To distinguish God's authentic word from the word of the false prophet, Jeremiah contrasted wheat and straw, which are worlds apart:

> Let the prophet who has a dream tell the dream, but let the one who has my word speak my word faithfully. What has straw (*teben*) in common with wheat (*habbar*)? says the LORD. (Jer 23:28)

Straw, the refuse from winnowing, was used for hay; it was also mixed with clay in preparing unbaked bricks.

Barley

Second in importance to wheat, barley (*se'orim*, usually plural) is often described as the bread of the poor because of its inferiority to wheat. Cheaper to produce, it was also used for feeding animals. Barley is more common in marginal zones because it withstands drier and saltier soil conditions. It requires only minimal rainfall and is sown in October and November. The barley harvest begins in late April or early May, about two weeks earlier than the wheat harvest. Barley, an important grain in biblical times, not only was used as food and as a cereal offering in worship but also was exported.

Vine

The wild vine (*gepen*) was probably first cultivated in Anatolia (modern Turkey).[6] The grapevine was one of the most important plants in biblical times, especially for the economy of Palestine. Grape cultivation and wine production began in Early Bronze Age I (late fourth millennium B.C.E.). Grapes were cultivated in several ways. The vines could be draped over a trellis; they could be trained to climb trees; or the stems could trail along the ground, with the branches bearing clusters of grapes propped up on poles to keep them off the ground; or they could be cultivated in vineyards. Vineyards were planted on mountains or hillsides in biblical times, as they are today: "Again you shall plant vineyards (*keramim*) on the mountains of Samaria; the planters shall plant, and shall enjoy the fruit" (Jer 31:5).

The Hebrew word for vineyard, *kerem*, appears in biblical place-names denoting local produce, as *Beth-haccherem* ("house of the vineyard," Jer 6:1), situated two miles south of Jerusalem and identified with Ramat Raḥel. Such occurrences in names indicate the importance of vineyards in biblical times.

The planting of vineyards was a sign of permanent settlement, as Jeremiah demonstrated when expressing confidence in the return of his people to their homeland after the Babylonian exile: "For thus says the LORD of hosts, the God of Israel: Houses and fields and vineyards (*keramim*) shall again be bought in this land" (Jer 32:15).

Using a negative example, Jeremiah made the same point when commending the fidelity of the Rechabites in contrast to the unfaithful Judahites.

The Rechabites, who traced their origin to northern Sinai, did not settle permanently in the land; instead, they deliberately embraced the nomadic way of life as tent dwellers:

> Nor shall you [Rechabites] ever build a house, or sow seed; nor shall you plant a vineyard (*kerem*), or even own one; but you shall live in tents all your days, that you may live many days in the land where you reside. (Jer 35:7)

The grapes ripened in June or July, and the vintage began in September. During the harvest the people erected booths in the vineyards, both for lodging and to protect the harvest. Traditionally the vintage was the season for great rejoicing as the people treaded the grapes.

In the manufacture of wine, after the treading process which took place on a flat rock where the grapes were spread out, the juice of the grapes was collected in a bell-shaped vat. Then the grape pulps were pressed again under the weight of a beam to extract the remaining juice. This latter process resembled the pressing of olives. Hundreds of winepresses have been discovered throughout Palestine.

In his judgment on Moab, Jeremiah spoke negatively about the vintage:

> Gladness and joy have been taken away from the fruitful land of Moab; I [the LORD] have stopped the wine from the wine presses; no one treads them with shouts of joy; the shouting is not the shout of joy. (Jer 48:33)

In the Bible the grapevine is frequently associated with the fig tree. Jeremiah used this dual imagery negatively in an indictment of both the religious leaders and the people of Judah. As harvester, the Lord was unsuccessful in picking grapes and figs, owing to the sterility of the grapevines and fig trees:

> When I wanted to gather them, says the LORD, there are no grapes on the vine (*'anabim baggepen*), nor figs on the fig tree (*te'enim batte'enah*); even the leaves are withered, and what I gave them has passed away from them. (Jer 8:13)

Utilizing the common figure of Judah as a vine, Jeremiah continued his indictment of Judah for its ongoing degeneracy:

> Yet I planted you as a choice vine (*soreq*), from the purest stock. How then did you turn degenerate and become a wild vine (*haggepen nokriyyah*)? (Jer 2:21)

Soreq (*surik* in Arabic) refers to an especially choice grape, specifically the dark-red grapes with soft seeds or seedless from the Sorek valley (Wadi es-Sarar), southwest of Jerusalem. This large valley, lying between Jerusalem and the Mediterranean Sea, is the route of the modern railway from Jaffa to Jerusalem. The valley may have been named from the *soreq* vines on its slopes.

The Hebrew Bible has several words for wine, the commonest being *yayin*, which may trace its origin to a Hittite cognate *wiyanas*. In his condemnation of certain professional prophets Jeremiah described his disillusionment:

> Concerning the prophets: My heart is crushed within me, all my bones shake; I have become like a drunkard, like one overcome by wine (*yayin*), because of the LORD and because of his holy words. (Jer 23:9)

Tiroš is synonymous with *yayin*, as in the expression "the grain, the wine, and the oil," describing the joyful return from Babylonian exile:

> They shall come and sing aloud on the height of Zion, and they shall be radiant over the goodness of the LORD, over the grain, the wine (*tiroš*), and the oil. (Jer 31:12)

Fig

Evidence of fig remains (*te'enah*, fig tree; *te'enim*, figs) in Palestine can be traced to 5000 B.C.E., during the Neolithic period. In the biblical period, figs played a crucial role in the economy. For that reason, the destruction of fig trees was one of the signs of pending economic catastrophe:

> They [the invading Babylonian army] shall eat up your flocks and your herds; they shall eat up your vines and your fig trees; they shall destroy with the sword your fortified cities in which you trust. (Jer 5:17)

The fig tree may attain a height of fifteen feet and is famous for its shade. Its branches with their broad leaves form a circle with a diameter as extensive as twenty-five feet. Fig trees and trellised vines were often planted together near houses to provide maximum shade as well as fruit.

The fig tree yields two annual crops: one in June and the other in August-September. The first crop is known as *bakkurot* (from the root *bakker*, "to bear early fruit"). The second crop of figs may be classified under *qayiṣ*, "summer fruits," mentioned in Jeremiah (40:10, 12; 48:32) and elsewhere in the Bible.

Jeremiah's vision of two baskets of figs placed before the Temple (24:1–10) is well known:

> One basket had very good figs (*te'enim ṭobot me'od*), like first-ripe (*habbakkurot*) figs, but the other basket had very bad figs (*te'enim ra'ot me'od*), so bad that they could not be eaten. (Jer 24:2)

The good figs symbolize those Judahites exiled to Babylon in 597 B.C.E., who would turn to the Lord in repentance and would be returned to Judah. The bad figs represent those, including King Zedekiah and the nobles, remaining in Jerusalem in 597 B.C.E., who resisted Nebuchadrezzar and were unrepentant; they in turn would be rejected.

Figs, with their high sugar content, were vital for nutrition in the daily diet. They were eaten fresh or dried, pressed into cakes, or preserved. Cakes of dried figs (*debelah*) were a favorite and convenient food for a journey.

Pomegranate

The pomegranate (*rimmon*) is mentioned frequently in the Hebrew Bible, including place-names compounded with *rimmon* (e.g., Rimmono, En-rimmon, Gath-rimmon). This beautiful, symmetrical fruit is the size of an apple and red-scarlet in color. The shrublike pomegranate tree may grow to a height of ten to fifteen feet. When the fruit ripens in summer it is filled with small seeds surrounded by a juicy pulp. Wine is made from the juice of the fruit. Owing to its juicy fruit and innumerable seeds, the pomegranate is a popular symbol of fertility.

The pomegranate was also a decorative motif in art throughout the ancient Near East, used for ornamentation of the Temple furnishings as well as for embellishment on the high priest's vestments.

In describing the Jerusalem Temple, Jeremiah referred to the profusion of pomegranates adorning the capitals of the two bronze columns in front of the Temple entrance:

Pomegranate (*rimmon*). Found in 1977 at Tel Halif in southern Judah, fourteen miles north of Beer-sheba. This red-burnished ceramic bowl measures seven inches in diameter and dates between the tenth and eighth centuries B.C.E. It is decorated with a single raised pomegranate (*rimmon*), which suggests that Tel Halif may be the site of ancient Rimmon, a town in southern Judah. *Photograph by Patricia O'Connor-Seger. Courtesy of the Lahav Research Project.*

Upon it [the bronze pillar] was a capital of bronze; the height of the one capital was five cubits [about eight feet]; latticework and pomegranates, all of bronze, encircled the top of the capital. And the second pillar had the same, with pomegranates. There were ninety-six pomegranates on the sides; all the pomegranates encircling the latticework numbered one hundred. (Jer 52:22–23)

In 1988, the Israel Museum in Jerusalem acquired a prized object—a small, inscribed, ivory pomegranate scepter head, which may have been used by the priests in Solomon's Temple. This "thumb-sized" pomegranate, carved in ivory with a Hebrew inscription, dates from the mid-eighth century B.C.E., although its provenience is unknown. The dedicatory inscription reads: "Sacred donation for the priests of [or "in"] the Temple [literally, "House"] of Yahweh [the Lord]." This interpretation of the inscription is Avigad's, but not everyone would agree.[7]

Olive

The olive tree (*zayit*) is an evergreen with a gnarled, hollow trunk. Found mostly on mountain slopes, the olive tree may grow as high as twenty-one feet. The olives begin to fall in September and are gathered in November with the help of a long pole for beating the trees. Olive pits have appeared at Bethel, Gezer, Beer-sheba, Arad, Lachish, and several other sites.

In an oracle of impending disaster Jeremiah, using the imagery of Israel and Judah as a luxuriant olive tree, described the covenant people as they had been in the past, before the conflagration:

> The LORD once called you [Israel and Judah], "A green olive tree, fair with goodly fruit"; but with the roar of a great tempest he will set fire to it, and its branches will be consumed. (Jer 11:16)

Olive oil (*šemen*) was one of the most valuable products of Palestine. Besides serving as an offering in the cultic life of the people and being used in anointing ceremonies of kings, priests, and prophets, olive oil furnished lighting for the homes, was a staple food, and functioned as a medicine and an unguent. Olives and olive oil were the chief sources of fat for people in antiquity. In the hierarchy of "fruits and vegetables," olive oil was paramount. In addition to domestic and religious uses, oil played a vital role in the economy as a principal export. Syria-Palestine was the chief supplier of olives and olive oil to Egypt, a land unable to cultivate olives.

Recent excavations at two important archaeological sites—Ekron (Tel Miqne) and Timnah (Tel Batash)—cast light on the production of olive oil in Iron Age II (1000–586 B.C.E.). Both were engaged in the olive oil industry during the seventh century B.C.E., the time of Jeremiah. In naming the cities to be destroyed by the Babylonians, Jeremiah included Ekron (Jer 25:20), which was ravaged in 603 B.C.E. when Nebuchadrezzar campaigned against Philistia. Of Ekron and Timnah, the Philistine city-state of Ekron, situated on the frontier between Philistia and Judah, was the more important industrial center and perhaps the greatest producer of olive oil in the ancient Near East. The Philistine border site of Ekron had more than a hundred olive oil installations. They were used for extracting the oil, first by crushing and then by pressing the olives. Timnah, situated on the border between Judah and Philistia, was at various times under the dominion of Israel, Philistia, and Judah. It fell to Babylon about 600 B.C.E.

The olive oil industry accounts for the great economic prosperity of the region in the seventh century B.C.E. The excess olive oil was exported, in addition to Egypt, to Phoenicia and perhaps even to Greece.

Date Honey

Three kinds of honey can be distinguished: date honey (*debaš*), called *dibs* in Arabic, made by boiling the fruit of the date palm (*tamar*); wild honey (*debaš*), as found in the lion's carcass of the Samson saga (Judg 14:8); and true honey (*debaš*) collected by domesticated bees. Owing to the fact that Canaan is often referred to as the "land of milk and honey," bees were plentiful. The honey listed among the "seven species" of Deut 8:8 was probably the product of the date palm (*tamar*), not the true honey collected by bees.

Jeremiah mentioned this same date honey (*debaš*) in connection with the ten mourning pilgrims who bribed Ishmael to spare their lives in exchange for products hidden in the field:

> But there were ten men among them [pilgrims from the north] who said to Ishmael, "Do not kill us, for we have stores of wheat, barley, oil, and honey (*debaš*) hidden in the fields." So he refrained, and did not kill them along with their companions. (Jer 41:8)

The fruit-bearing palm tree, attaining a height ranging between thirty and sixty feet, symbolizes righteousness. The date palm tree and its leaves provided motifs for many of the decorations carved in the Temple.

Honey was used as a substitute for sugar in the preparation of food. The juice extracted from the dates and boiled into a syrup is still used as a sweetener. Honey was also exported to Tyre. According to Lev 2:11, honey could not be used in burnt offerings because it is liable to ferment.

Cedar

The cedar (*'erez*), mentioned more than seventy times in the Bible, is a stately evergreen associated especially with the mountains of Lebanon. This majestic tree, which may attain a height of one hundred and thirty feet and live for hundreds of years, is a symbol of strength and dignity.

Cedarwood, an expensive import known for its durability, was used as a luxury item in building. It is well suited for ceilings and paneling. Solomon utilized cedarwood extensively in constructing the Temple and especially the House of the Forest of Lebanon (1 Kings 7).

Jeremiah referred to the cedar four times in an exhortation to the kings of Judah about the ideals of kingship. The prophet was particularly critical of Jehoiakim who fell far short of the virtues of his father Josiah. Jeremiah was especially disturbed by the lavish construction of Jehoiakim's palace, including cedar paneling, built by exploitation of the workers:

> Who [Jehoiakim] says, "I will build myself a spacious house with large upper rooms [upper story]," and who [Jehoiakim] cuts out windows for it, paneling [ceiling] it with cedar (*sapun ba'arez*), and painting it with vermilion. Are you a king because you compete in cedar? (Jer 22:14–15)

"Paneling it with cedar" (*sapun ba'arez*) is the same phrase used to describe the construction of the House of the Forest of Lebanon (1 Kings 7:3). A vermilion-painted ceiling was known as a "Syrian ceiling."[8]

Almond

The almond (*šaqed*), the herald of spring, is a beautiful tree and the first to bloom, as early as late January or early February. It attains a height measuring between fifteen and thirty feet. The almond flowers, which appear before the leaves, are white and tinted with pink. About ten weeks after the flowers appear, the almond fruit begins to ripen. *Luz*, the Arabic name for the almond tree, also occurs in Genesis where Jacob outwits Laban by recourse to streaked rods:

> Then Jacob took fresh rods of poplar and almond (*luz*) and plane, and peeled white streaks in them, exposing the white of the rods. (Gen 30:37)

Luz was also the Canaanite name of Bethel ("house of God"), north of Jerusalem, before being renamed by Jacob (Gen 28:11–22).

Jeremiah's reference to the almond tree appears in his well-known vision utilizing a wordplay (paronomasia) on the Hebrew root *šqd*, "to watch, wake":

> The word of the LORD came to me, saying, "Jeremiah, what do you see?" And I said, "I see a branch of an almond tree (*šaqed*)." Then the LORD said to me, "You have seen well, for I am watching (*šoqed*) over my word to perform it." (Jer 1:11–12)

In this vision Jeremiah was told that the Lord was "watching over" the fulfillment of the divine word. Despite the vision's straightforwardness, it is somewhat ambiguous. As often happens in puns, meaning is sacrificed for wordplay.

Elsewhere in Jeremiah the verb *šaqad* is used with the connotation of threat:

> Therefore a lion from the forest shall kill them, a wolf from the desert shall destroy them. A leopard is watching (*šoqed*) against their cities; everyone who goes out of them shall be torn in pieces—because their transgressions are many, their apostasies are great. (Jer 5:6; also 31:28; 44:27)

Balm

Balm (*ṣori*) occurs in the Bible six times; three are found in Jeremiah. In the popular mind as well as in the Bible, balm is automatically associated with Gilead, despite the fact that there is no evidence for a balm-producing tree or shrub having grown in Gilead, and certainly not today. The region of Gilead is not well defined geographically, its boundaries changing at various times in history. In general, Gilead in Transjordan lies between Bashan and Moab and extends from the Arnon to the Yarmuk river. The principal trade route, the King's Highway, passed through Gilead, and that may account for the presence of balm in the region as an item of commerce. The fact is that spice caravans from the east followed that route, as an early reference in Genesis attests:

> Then they [Joseph's brothers] sat down to eat; and looking up they saw a caravan of Ishmaelites coming from Gilead, with their camels carrying gum, balm (*ṣori*), and resin, on their way to carry it down to Egypt. (Gen 37:25)

Gilead is hilly, and a heavily forested area, as Jeremiah attested when paralleling Gilead and Lebanon:

> For thus says the LORD concerning the house of the king of Judah: You are like Gilead to me, like the summit of Lebanon; but I swear that I will make you a desert, an uninhabited city. (Jer 22:6)

Ṣori, probably the resin of the storax tree, is obtained through an incision on the bark of the tree. The storax grows between eighteen and thirty feet high. Zohary[9] suggested that the Greek name "storax" derived from the Hebrew *ṣori*.

Beginning in 1961, B. Mazar excavated at Tel Goren, the principal site in the oasis at En-gedi on the west shore of the Dead Sea. En-gedi was a flourishing settlement, perhaps a royal estate, in the time of Jeremiah. In Stratum V, dating from 630 to 582 B.C.E., Mazar discovered an installation, complete with furnaces and pottery vessels (jars, juglets, decanters), used for the production of perfume, which is identified as balm. As noted, this find concurs with the document from the "Cave of the Letters" in Naḥal Hever mentioning En-gedi as one of the centers for the cultivation of perfume-producing plants. Other written sources, including those of the historian Josephus, make the same observation.

Although the identity of biblical balm is difficult to determine because ancient writers used various names in their description, the reference appears to be to an aromatic gum or spice with medicinal qualities. It would have been used as a perfume or a restorative.

In a lamentation over Jerusalem, Jeremiah asked rhetorically why the wounded people of Judah had refused the balm of Gilead:

> Is there no balm in Gilead? Is there no physician there? Why then has the health of my poor people not been restored? (Jer 8:22)

The following two texts from Jeremiah support the popular belief that balm alleviated pain:

> Go up to Gilead, and take balm, O virgin daughter Egypt! In vain you have used many medicines; there is no healing for you. (Jer 46:11)

> Suddenly Babylon has fallen and is shattered; wail for her! Bring balm for her wound; perhaps she may be healed. (Jer 51:8)

In 1988, Israeli archaeologists[10] discovered a juglet from the Roman period containing a viscous plant oil in a cave near Qumran in the En-gedi region. They describe the juglet, which was wrapped in palm fibers, as a globular Herodian juglet with a flat base and a cup rim. The remnant of oil in the juglet may be the same precious balsam (*opobalsamum*, balsam sap) produced in the Jericho valley and the En-gedi region.

Cisterns

In agricultural societies, cisterns (*bor, borot*; *bo'r, bo'rot*) are important for several reasons. A principal use of these underground chambers is as storage for rainwater collected through drains as it accumulated on flat roofs or in courtyards. This rainwater is then stored for use in the dry season (from May through September). Cisterns were of various sizes and shapes in antiquity. Many were bottle-shaped, approximately ten feet wide and sixteen feet deep, with a stone-covering over the small opening at the top. The neck was the narrow shaft through which vessels were lowered into the cistern by rope. Other cisterns were bell-shaped, approximately eight feet wide and twelve feet deep. Some cisterns had steps—for example, the cisterns at Qumran where the Dead Sea Scrolls were discovered. Cisterns were hollowed out of natural rock or converted from natural cave formations.

The assumption was that cisterns had to be lined with lime plaster (a waterproofing cement) to make them watertight. However, that would depend upon the geological conditions of the region. In the hill country of

Palestine, for example, the bedrock (Cenomanian limestone) is impermeable, so lining is superfluous.

Cisterns may also be used for the storage of grain. Borowski, in his treat-
ment of grain and food storage, has provided a serviceable table of the various kinds of storage facilities. He divides them into convenient categories:
public and private, underground and aboveground.

Another useful grain-storage project has been completed by John Currid and Jeffrey Gregg at Tel Halif (Lahav), twelve miles north of Beer-sheba.
They constructed a series of pits and then stored wheat in them for a period from four to six months to test their ability to reserve grain. Despite a
problem created by insects penetrating the pits, the archaeologists concluded that these pits were an efficient means of storing grain.

The ten mourners from the north, as mentioned, were able to bribe Ishmael to spare their lives by offering him the food they had in storage:

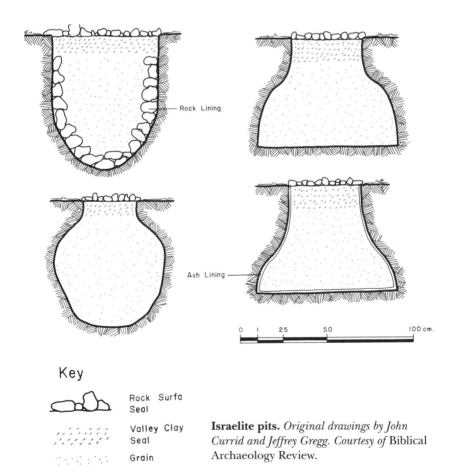

Key

Rock Surfa
Seal

Valley Clay
Seal

Grain

Israelite pits. *Original drawings by John
Currid and Jeffrey Gregg. Courtesy of* Biblical
Archaeology Review.

But there were ten men among them who said to Ishmael, "Do not kill us, for we have stores (*maṭmonim*) of wheat, barley, oil, and honey hidden in the fields." So he refrained, and did not kill them along with their companions. (Jer 41:8.)

Maṭmonim is from the verb *ṭaman*, "to hide (in the earth)." A specific description of this storage facility is not possible without additional details. Both dry and liquid produce, placed in pottery storage jars, could be buried in the field.

In addition to their use for water and grain storage, subterranean pits sometimes functioned as prisons, as Jeremiah learned from bitter experience:

Yet they have dug a pit (*šuḥah*) for my life. . . . For they have dug a pit (*šiḥah*) to catch me, and laid snares for my feet. (Jer 18:20, 22; also Gen 37:24)

The cistern (*habbor*) motif is prominent in Jeremiah, as the following texts illustrate:

The [administrative] officials were enraged at Jeremiah, and they beat him and imprisoned him in the house of the secretary Jonathan, for it had been made a prison. Thus Jeremiah was put in the cistern house (*bet habbor*, [dungeon]), in the cells (*haḥanuyot*), and remained there many days. (Jer 37:15–16)

"Cistern house" would be like a well house, that is, a small building that covers the actual cistern/well shaft or pit. It protects the water from contamination and intrusions from without.

So they took Jeremiah and threw him into the cistern (*habbor*) of Malchiah, the king's son, which was in the court of the guard, letting Jeremiah down by ropes. Now there was no water in the cistern (*babbor*), but only mud, and Jeremiah sank in the mud. (Jer 38:6)

Had the cistern been filled with water, Jeremiah would have drowned. The bottle shape of the cistern would have prevented him from climbing out on his own. Had he not been rescued, he would have perished inside.

In fact, it required four men to extricate Jeremiah from the cistern:

So Ebed-melech took the [three] men with him and went to the house of the king, to a wardrobe of the storehouse, and took from there old rags and worn-out clothes, which he let down to Jeremiah in the cistern by ropes. Then Ebed-melech the Ethiopian said to Jeremiah, "Just put the rags and clothes between your armpits and the ropes" [to protect the prophet from injury]. Jeremiah did so. Then they drew Jeremiah up by the ropes and pulled him out of the cistern. (Jer 38:11–13)

Sometimes corpses were thrown into cisterns, as with the seventy ill-fated pilgrims from the north whom Ishmael, the assassin of Gedaliah, slaughtered:

When they [the pilgrims] reached the middle of the city [Mizpah], Ishmael son of Nethaniah and the men with him slaughtered them, and threw them into a cistern (*habbor*). . . . Now the cistern (*habbor*) into which Ishmael had thrown all the bodies of the men whom he had struck down was the large cistern that King Asa had made for defense against King Baasha of Israel; Ishmael son of Nethaniah filled that cistern with those whom he had killed. (Jer 41:7, 9)

Regarding the cistern hewn by King Asa (913–873 B.C.E.) of Judah for the defense of Mizpah, there is no specific information in the Bible. However, 1 Kings 15:16–22 chronicles the conflict between Asa and Baasha (900–877 B.C.E.), king of Israel, and how Asa made an alliance with Benhadad of Syria in his border warfare against Israel.

Mizpah is usually identified with Tell en-Nasbeh, eight miles north of Jerusalem. Excavators uncovered and cleared fifty-three small (domestic) cisterns at this site. It is not uncommon to find large cisterns at Palestinian town sites.

Jeremiah often uses the cistern motif in a metaphorical sense:

For my people [the LORD's] have committed two evils: they have forsaken me, the fountain of living water [running water of a spring], and dug out cisterns (*bo'rot*) for themselves, cracked cisterns that can hold no water. (Jer 2:13)

Apparently these cisterns were hewn from porous rock that had not been made watertight by lime-plaster lining. Cisterns hewn from the impermeable Cenomanian limestone of the Judean hill country were naturally waterproofed.

Terraces

Throughout the biblical period rural settlers in Palestine used agricultural terraces; in fact, ancient terraces are still evident on the slopes west of Jerusalem. Terracing is the ideal way of utilizing all available land. Without terracing, cultivation of the central highlands would not have been possible. Figs, olives, almonds, and grapes are among the crops grown on terraces.

Terraces have been the subject of investigation in Palestine for at least the past thirty years. In the 1960s, Joseph Callaway excavated Iron Age I terraces at 'Ai (et-Tell), a mile southeast of Beitin. From 1972, as part of his study of ancient irrigation agriculture in the northeastern part of the Judean Desert (the Buqe'ah Valley), Stager surveyed terraces in the region.[11] In 1975, de Geus wrote about Palestinian agricultural terraces.[12]

Since 1977, Gershon Edelstein, Shimon Gibson, and other archaeologists, in their study of agriculture, have been concentrating on terraces, some dating from the eighth to the sixth century B.C.E. These terraces are associated with ancient agricultural settlements in the Judean hills, not far from Jerusalem. Describing the terracing in that vicinity, they state that the terraces "transformed hillsides into stepped flat fields supported by retaining walls."[13]

The construction of terraces involves the following basic steps. On each natural terrace, a stone retaining wall is built at the front edge of the successive limestone terraces; gravel fill is placed behind the terrace wall; alternating layers of gravel and soil fill are then added; and finally, organic soil is spread on the top. Constructing artificial agricultural terraces requires a large labor force as well as careful organization. Maintenance and repair are also time-consuming.

Jeremiah's following verses, providing insight into the economic life of Judah after the Babylonian conquest of 586 B.C.E., may bear some relationship to terraces:

> Nebuzaradan the captain of the guard left in the land of Judah some of the poor people who owned nothing, and gave them vineyards (*keramim*) and fields (*wigebim*) at the same time. (Jer 39:10)

> But Nebuzaradan the captain of the guard left some of the poorest people of the land to be vinedressers (*lekormim*) and tillers of the soil (*uleyogebim*). (Jer 52:16)

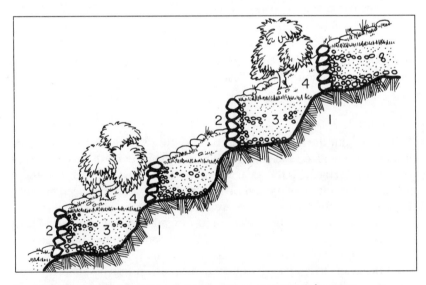

Schematic drawing of ancient terrace construction. (1) Stepped-limestone forming the bedrock; (2) battered stone terrace wall; (3) stone fill and terra rosa subsoil; (4) partly decomposed organic litter. *Original drawing by Gershon Edelstein and Shimon Gibson. Courtesy of* Biblical Archaeology Review.

The Hebrew word *gbi* has occasioned much speculation on the part of both philologists and agriculturalists. De Geus[14] suggests that *yogebim* are the workers/owners of irrigated terraces. Stager ventures that *gebim* can mean "vats," as the "salt pans" are called in Ezek 47:11. Perhaps these vineyards had *gebim* near them, that is, vats and pressing floors. This root would then link up with *gebi'im* ("pitchers") in Jer 35:5: "Then I [Jeremiah] set before the Rechabites pitchers (*gebi'im*) full of wine, and cups; and I said to them, 'Have some wine.' "

In sum, the Hebrew words for "fields" and "tillers of the soil" in the two preceding verses (Jer 39:10; 52:16) are uncertain. On the assumption that they derive from the verb *yagab*, "to plough," commentators understand them as referring to terrace farming on former royal estates. After the deportation of the aristocrats and artisans to Babylon, the royal property was distributed among the remaining peasants to be cultivated. In accordance with the Babylonian policy, conquered states were to be self-supporting.

In the counterclockwise survey of Jerusalem's boundaries, the book of Jeremiah mentions the agricultural "terraces of the Kidron" (*šadmot qidron*) situated on the southeast side of Jerusalem and running between the Temple Mount and the Mount of Olives. In biblical times, as today, the terraces on the west side of the Kidron Valley were cultivated:

> The whole valley of the dead bodies and the ashes, and all the fields ["terraces" (*haššedemot*), instead of *haššeremot*] as far as the Wadi Kidron, to the corner of the Horse Gate toward the east, shall be sacred to the LORD. (Jer 31:40)

King Josiah commanded the high priest to rid the Temple of the articles of foreign worship and to burn them "outside Jerusalem in the fields of the Kidron (*šadmot qidron*)" (2 Kings 23:4). On the basis of this text, Stager reads *šadmot qidron* in Jer 31:40, translating the phrase as the "agricultural terraces of the Kidron valley," situated on the steep eastern slope of the City of David where vineyards, as well as orchards of figs and olives, were cultivated.

Yoke

The plow (*maharešah, maharešet*) was an outgrowth of the hoe. Of very simple construction, the plow was used for breaking up the ground. Exhorting the people to change completely the direction of their lives and to embark upon a new beginning, Jeremiah used the image of plowing:

> For thus says the LORD to the people of Judah and to the inhabitants of Jerusalem: Break up your fallow ground (*niru lakem nir*), and do not sow among thorns. (Jer 4:3)

"Break up your fallow ground" is a quotation from Hos 10:12. *Nir* refers to land tilled for the first time, or land lain fallow for a long time.

Metal plowhead. Dating from the seventh century B.C.E., this two-headed iron plow was found at Tel Miqne-Ekron. *Photograph by Douglas Guthrie. Courtesy of the Tel Miqne-Ekron Excavations.*

In the Bible the yoke (*moṭah*, *'ol*) is associated with the plow and signifies in its simple form a wooden crossbar fastened to the necks of the two draft oxen. The yoke was secured to the animals' necks by means of yoke pegs (*moṭot*) and ropes (*moserot*). The plowpoint was attached by a socket to a simple shaft which, in turn, was connected to the middle of the crossbar. The plow was fashioned from wood; the plowpoint (plowshare), between eight and twelve inches long, was made of iron in Jeremiah's time. The plow was also equipped with a handle for applying pressure on the iron blade. Contrary to the practice in rural areas of the Middle East, Deuteronomic law forbade plowing with mixed teams, such as an ox and a donkey (Deut 22:10).

Jeremiah has numerous references to the yoke, some to be understood literally and others figuratively, signifying hardship and servitude.

> For long ago you broke your yoke (*'ol*) and burst your bonds (*moserot*), and you said, "I will not serve!" (Jer 2:20; also 5:5; 30:8)

Most of Jeremiah's references to the yoke are found in chs. 27–28, describing events set in 594 B.C.E., the fourth year of King Zedekiah's reign. This section highlights the polemical encounter between Jeremiah and the prophet Hananiah. Jeremiah prophesied that Judah would be restored only after a very long time (seventy years); the prophet counsels the people meanwhile to submit to Nebuchadrezzar. To make his point more dramatically,

Jeremiah wore a yoke (or perhaps only the collar formed by cords and yoke pegs), symbolizing subjection to Nebuchadrezzar:

> Thus the LORD said to me [Jeremiah]: Make yourself a yoke of straps and bars (*moserot umoṭot*), and put them on your neck. (Jer 27:2)

> But if any nation or kingdom will not serve this king, Nebuchadnezzar of Babylon, and put its neck under the yoke (*'ol*) of the king of Babylon, then I [the LORD] will punish that nation with the sword. (Jer 27:8; also 27:11–12)

The prophet Hananiah contradicted Jeremiah in the Temple, predicting instead the downfall of Nebuchadrezzar and the return of the exiles in a

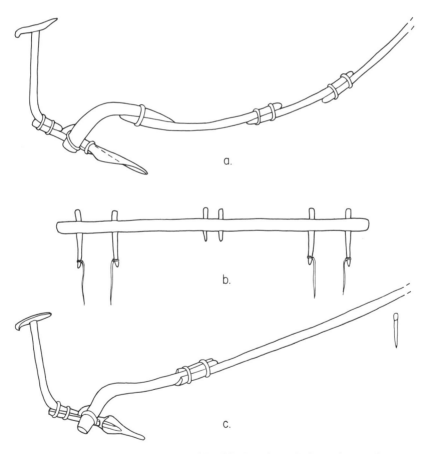

a.

b.

c.

Peasant agriculture in the Judean hills. (a) Plow from Hebron (town nineteen miles south of Jerusalem); (b) yoke from Beit Jala (village west of Bethlehem); (c) plow from Beit Jala. *Original drawings by Lucian Turkowski. Courtesy of* Palestine Exploration Quarterly.

short two years. To accentuate his point, Hananiah went so far as to break the wooden yoke that Jeremiah was wearing:

> In that same year, at the beginning of the reign of King Zedekiah of Judah, in the fifth month of the fourth year, the prophet Hananiah son of Azzur, from Gibeon, spoke to me [Jeremiah] in the house of the LORD, . . . saying, "Thus says the LORD of hosts, the God of Israel: I have broken the yoke (*'ol*) of the king of Babylon." (Jer 28:1-2)

> Then the prophet Hananiah took the yoke (*motah*) from the neck of the prophet Jeremiah, and broke it. And Hananiah spoke in the presence of all the people, saying, "Thus says the LORD: This is how I will break the yoke (*'ol*) of King Nebuchadnezzar of Babylon from the neck of all the nations within two years." At this, the prophet Jeremiah went his way. (Jer 28:10-11)

Jeremiah alluded figuratively to the imposition of an iron yoke (*'ol barzel*) in order to suggest even more onerous servitude. Understood literally, an iron yoke, because of its weight, would have rendered such a device impractical for plowing:

> The word of the LORD came to Jeremiah: Go, tell Hananiah, Thus says the LORD: You have broken wooden bars (*motot 'eṣ*) only to forge iron bars (*motot barzel*) in place of them! For thus says the LORD of hosts, the God of Israel: I have put an iron yoke (*'ol barzel*) on the neck of all these nations so that they may serve King Nebuchadnezzar of Babylon. (Jer 28:12-14)

10

Crafts

In paying grateful tribute to the skilled workers of antiquity, the book of Sirach (Ecclesiasticus), written about 180 B.C.E., included the farmer, engraver, smith, and potter:

> All these rely on their hands, and all are skillful in their own work. Without them no city can be inhabited, and wherever they live, they will not go hungry. . . . But they maintain the fabric of the world, and their concern is for the exercise of their trade. (Sir 38:31–32, 34)

Although ancient Israel was an agricultural society, not all workers were farmers. To satisfy the daily needs of the community, a large number of skilled workers, called artisans, made a significant contribution. Both men and women were counted among them. Included among the artisans were carpenters, carvers in ivory, smiths, weavers, tanners, leather workers, basket weavers, woodworkers, metallurgists, and potters. The Hebrew word for potter is *yoṣer;* not only does it designate one who fashions in clay but it may also refer to one who works with wood or metal.

Some of the crafts were executed at home, usually out of doors. The workers of other crafts had their own shops. As today, in the souk (marketplace) of Jerusalem's Old City and in cities throughout the Middle East, certain streets and quarters were set aside for specific crafts, as the book of Jeremiah relates:

> So King Zedekiah gave orders, and they committed Jeremiah to the court of the guard; and a loaf of bread [round, flat bread] was given him daily from the bakers' street (*ḥuṣ ha'opim*), until all the bread of the city was gone. So Jeremiah remained in the court of the guard. (Jer 37:21)

Pottery

Owing to the need for earthenware vessels for daily life, pottery making was one of the earliest and most widespread of the crafts. Pottery includes all objects modeled from clay and hardened by fire. Pottery (*ḥeres*) is defined as "a synthetic stone produced by firing clay to a sufficiently high temperature to change its physical characteristics and its chemical composition."[1]

Sun-dried brick (mudbrick), made from inferior clay, is not pottery. Clay (*ḥomer*), already in use before pottery vessels were ever manufactured, has two characteristics that make it suitable for ceramic ware: it is plastic, that is, when mixed with water it can be formed into a permanent shape; second, it becomes hard when fired. Firing preserves the fixed shape of the vessel.

The invention of pottery was a very important development in the cultural history of the ancient Near East. A. Mazar speculates:

> Its [pottery's] invention most probably resulted from the earlier uses of clay for plastering floors and sunken basins; a chance or intentional fire in such a basin would have transformed the clay into hard and durable material. Once human beings learned to add tempering materials such as straw or pieces of stone to the clay, they could produce portable containers.[2]

In the ancient Near East, handmade pottery dates from the Neolithic period (8500–4300 B.C.E.), as early as 6500 B.C.E. The pottery of this period was simple and coarse. Sometimes powdered straw or crushed rock was added to the clay to enhance the strength and plasticity of the vessels. The pottery of the Chalcolithic period (*chalkos*, "copper"; *lithos*, "stone," 4300–3500 B.C.E.) is more refined, and sometimes it is painted. Vessels made of pottery replaced those constructed previously of stone, wood, skin, and reeds.

Archaeologists divide the Neolithic period into Prepottery Neolithic (PPN) and Pottery Neolithic (PN), with further subdivisions into phases: PPNA (8500–7500 B.C.E.), PPNB (7500–6000 B.C.E.), PNA (6000–5000 B.C.E.), and PNB (5000–4300 B.C.E.). Jericho (Tell es-Sultan) in the Jordan Valley is the key site for the study of the Neolithic period. Although Jericho had been the object of three earlier excavations, Kathleen Kenyon was responsible for clarifying the complex stratigraphy of the site. Excavating at Jericho in the 1950s, she established its chronology, which extended from 8000 to 1200 B.C.E. She uncovered evidence demonstrating that the oldest permanent occupation at Jericho began in the Prepottery Neolithic period (about 7000 B.C.E.), although indications were present of earlier beginnings about 8000 B.C.E. In the Prepottery Neolithic period, Jericho was surrounded by a stone wall, conferring the distinction of "the oldest walled town in the world."

The largest known PPNB site is 'Ain Ghazal ("spring of the gazelle"). Nearly thirty acres in size, it is situated north of Amman (Jordan). There its occupants experimented with making crude pottery in the PPNB period. 'Ain Ghazal, excavated in the 1980s by Gary Rollefson and others, is best known today for the groups of plaster, human statuary (statues and busts) found there, similar to statuary found at Jericho. These statues were made of lime plaster formed around a reed core.

A pottery vessel is composed of a body—which is its principal part—a base or foot, neck, rim, and handles. The earliest vessels—namely, bowls and jars—were fashioned by hand and were sun-dried. The potter's wheel, invented late in the fourth millennium, facilitated the turning of the vessels. Before the invention of the wheel, all pots were made by hand.

Associated with the potter's workshop were the potter's wheel, a space for treading, a kiln, a field for storing vessels, a dump for the discards, and a source of water, either a cistern or a stream. As Henk Franken comments: "The potters were living and working near the clay sources and where water was available. They needed a lot of space."[3]

Pivot of a potter's wheel. Dating from the seventh century B.C.E., this wheel was found in the industrial zone at Tel Miqne-Ekron. *Photograph by Ilan Sztulman. Courtesy of the Tel Miqne-Ekron Excavations.*

The book of Jeremiah contains the only specific reference in the Hebrew Bible to the potter's wheel. It is mentioned in the prophet's classic passage on the potter and the clay (18:1–11), which teaches that the Lord is supreme over Israel, Judah, and all the nations:

> The word that came to Jeremiah from the LORD: "Come, go down to the potter's house (*bet hayyoṣer*), and there I will let you hear my words." So I went down to the potter's house, and there he was working at his wheel (*'al-ha'obnayim*). The vessel he was making of clay was spoiled in the potter's hand, and he reworked it into another vessel, as seemed good to him. (Jer 18:1–4)

Just as the potter was able to rework a vessel, the possibility for the people of Judah to be redeemed was still very real.

Ha'obnayim, "the wheel," a word most likely derived from the same root as *'eben*, "stone," is a Hebrew dual form, appropriate for describing the fast wheel. Inasmuch as the process for producing pottery in antiquity varied among cultures, terminology sometimes differs. The potter's wheel is of two kinds: the slow, or hand-turned wheel, also called a tournette; and the fast, or kick wheel rotated by foot, considered the true potter's wheel.

The slow wheel or tournette, introduced into Syria-Palestine about 2000 B.C.E., during the Middle Bronze Age, was used for finishing vessels. Technically, it was not a wheel but a simple turntable allowing the potter to rotate (not spin) a vessel under preparation. The slow wheel was probably made of stone or wood. Excavators at Hazor (in Upper Galilee) discovered a potter's wheel dating between 1500 and 1200 B.C.E. It consists of two basalt stones, one pivoted above the other. The upper cone-shaped stone was socketed into the recess cut in the lower stone.

The fast wheel, which appeared about 1650–1550 B.C.E., during the Middle Bronze Age II, consisted of two disks or stones, one pivoted upon the other. The potter shaped the clay vessel by hand on the smaller, revolving stone located on top; it was socketed into the lower disk, which, being larger and heavier, provided the momentum and accelerated the turning. The potter, ordinarily seated at the edge of a shallow pit where the wheel was located, rotated the lower disk with the foot, whence the name kick wheel.

Pot-throwing relies on the centrifugal force of the fast wheel, with the potter simply shaping the vessel with the hands. However, not all vessels were made on the fast wheel from that time on; some continued to be made by hand. The method of making pottery on the fast wheel has changed little since pottery was first invented.

Sirach (preserved in Greek) describes the work of the potter in graphic terms:

> So too is the potter sitting at his work and turning the wheel (*trochos*) with his feet; he is always deeply concerned over his products, and he

produces them in quantity. He moulds the clay with his arm and makes it pliable with his feet; he sets his heart to finish the glazing, and he takes care in firing the kiln. (Sir 38:29–30)

In the Late Bronze Age (1550–1200 B.C.E.) and through the Iron Age I period (1200–1000 B.C.E.), the technology of pottery making declined. But in Iron Age II (1000–586 B.C.E.), especially in the eighth and seventh centuries B.C.E., the pottery was of very good quality. Elegant pottery of this period was the so-called "Samaria Ware," the name applied to "thin, delicate bowls with a red slip and concentric burnished red and yellowish stripes."[4] The pottery of Jeremiah's time undoubtedly was made on the fast wheel and is characterized by an orange-red slip, or clay decoration.

Potter's stone wheel. Found at Hazor in Galilee, and dating from the Late Bronze Age. The simplest form consisted of an indented stone set in the ground, with a pivot revolving in the indented stone.

James Kelso[5] listed three methods that Israelite potters used for shaping their pottery: throwing it on the wheel, modeling it freehand, and pressing it into a mold. The potter threw the ball of clay onto the rotating disk and then shaped it into the desired form by using both hands. When this process was completed, the vessels had to dry thoroughly before being fired. Then the potter would put the vessel back on the wheel for more refined modeling.

Next, the vessels were placed in the kiln to be fired. The firing welds the clay particles together. Early kilns were merely holes in the ground, over which a fire was ignited. Later, ovens fired by coal or wood were introduced. Sometimes dung was used for fuel. It is estimated that firing would take two or three days. Pottery usually fired in about 800 degrees C (1472 degrees F).

Between 1969 and 1974 James Pritchard excavated in Lebanon at modern Sarafand. It is identified with biblical Zarephath, a Phoenician port city situated between Tyre and Sidon. The excavator unearthed over twenty Iron Age kilns for firing pottery. This site, no doubt, was a center for the manufacture of Phoenician pottery.

The potter refined the clay by treading it out in water by foot, as Isaiah remarked: "He [Cyrus] shall trample on rulers as on mortar, as the potter treads clay (*yoṣer yirmas ṭiṭ*)" (Isa 41:25). Treading designates the process of mixing water with washed clay (*ṭiṭ*) until the water is evenly distributed and the air removed.[6] Potters ordinarily treaded their own clay, to be certain it was prepared properly for throwing and firing.

The vessels were sometimes embellished with decoration in the following ways. Before firing the pot, the potter would apply a slip, defined as a liquid (wash) composed of fine clay suspended in water. This accounts for the orange-red slip characteristic of eighth to seventh century B.C.E. pottery vessels in Judah. Israelite pottery, however, was not glazed. Burnishing was the smoothing or polishing of the pot's surface with a hard, smooth tool (stone, shell, or bone) before and/or after the vessel was fired. Franken estimates that finishing (polishing) a bowl required at least a whole day. Wheel-burnishing was introduced in Iron Age II.

Pottery in the Age of Jeremiah

In Jeremiah's time many types of pottery vessels were mass-produced, and wheel-burnished bowls were common. The pottery used in Jerusalem and Judah was of good quality. In his study of Jerusalem's Iron Age II pottery, found in the part of the City of David outside the city wall north of the Gihon spring, Franken lists the following classes of vessels: bowls (small, medium, and large), lamps, saucers, cooking pots, large storage jars, small bottles with narrow rims, hole-mouth jars (for transporting water from springs), and widemouthed jars (sunk in floor for storage of drinking water).

Pottery vessels had multiple uses. In addition to storage of food and liquids, large pottery jars were used to preserve documents, as in the case of Jeremiah's deeds for the field he purchased at Anathoth:

> Thus says the LORD of hosts, the God of Israel: Take these deeds, both this sealed deed of purchase and this open deed, and put them in an earthenware jar (*keli ḥares*), in order that they may last for a long time. (Jer 32:14)

In addition to household vessels, other objects manufactured in clay included the following: mudbricks, figurines, jewelry, lids, toys, lamps, cult objects, pottery stands, construction tiles, ovens, loom weights (used for textile production), spindle whorls, and writing materials (seals, ostraca, and cuneiform tablets). In the case of cuneiform tablets, only the more important documents were fired; others were sun-dried. Ironically, when a city was demolished by burning, the fire preserved the clay tablets by baking them, instead of destroying them. Some of the objects mentioned above were also crafted in stone or in metal.

Assemblage of Iron Age II pottery. Included in the assemblage are storage jars, hole-mouth jars, a chalice, pot, saucer, elongated dipper juglets, and angle-walled bowls. *Photograph by Douglas Guthrie. Courtesy of the Tel Miqne-Ekron Excavations.*

Ceramic Chronology

In addition to pottery's practical value in the everyday life of ancient Israel, pottery by its very nature is ideally suited as a chronological indicator for archaeological sites for the following reasons. In the first place, potsherds (broken pieces of pottery) are strewn everywhere in Palestine. It is impossible to excavate a site without unearthing countless sherds as well as whole vessels. Second, fired clay being practically indestructible does not disintegrate, nor is it easily pulverized. The vessels retain their original shape and form. On the other hand, as everyone knows from experience, pottery is fragile and breaks easily, causing the vessels to be short-lived. Ordinarily, discarded earthenware was replaced by vessels of different styles and shapes, as happens in households today.

Petrie is credited with developing a ceramic chronology for dating sites in Palestine. After excavating in Egypt for ten years, in 1890 he went to Palestine and dug at Tell el-Hesi situated on the northern edge of the Negev. Petrie's archaeological experience in Egypt qualified him to date Palestinian sites by comparing artifacts recovered from Egyptian cemeteries with those at Tell el-Hesi. The method of comparing artifacts from different cultures is known as cross-dating.

Understanding that Palestine's tells (artificial mounds) were formed by a sequence of occupational strata (layers), Petrie applied the principles of sequence dating to establish a relative ceramic chronology for Palestine. Excavators determine sequence dating by observing changes in style and form of pottery vessels in successive strata of a tell and then placing the pottery forms in chronological order. By correlating the soil layers and the pottery forms therein, Petrie was able to date the layers. Later, Albright brought greater precision to Petrie's chronology, and it continues to be refined today.

As well as providing chronological information, pottery vessels furnish insights into social and economic activities, such as cultural ties among neighboring peoples, trade routes and commerce, economic structures in ancient societies, and the level of technological advances among the peoples of the ancient Near East. Also, the quantity of pottery associated with a site indicates population density.

Pottery and Science

Modern science, including nuclear physics, is making a significant contribution to chronology and other aspects of archaeology by examining the physical and chemical properties of the clay. Among the newer techniques in pottery study is neutron activation analysis which measures a wide variety of chemical elements present in pottery. It is effective in establishing the provenience of the pottery which, in turn, indicates cultural influences and patterns of trade.

Certain radioactive tests assist in assigning dates to artifacts. Potassium-argon dating is a useful technique in testing geological samples, including pottery, rocks, and minerals, that are more than 50,000 years old. Thermoluminescence is another method of dating pottery and other fired clay objects; it determines the date when the pottery was fired.

Petrological analysis is concerned with the study of rocks and minerals. With regard to pottery, it can help to determine the source of the materials used. Spectographic analysis is used in the investigation of the composition of the clay, indicating the source of the clay beds.

Pottery in the Book of Jeremiah

Matching pottery vessels named in the Bible with the various types found in excavations cannot always be done with assurance. The book of Jeremiah refers by name to several pottery vessels.

Jeremiah's call to be a prophet provides an example. Two well-known visions form part of this call (1:11–16). The first, concerning the almond tree, is hopeful; the second, concerning the boiling pot, is ominous:

The word of the LORD came to me [Jeremiah] a second time, saying, "What do you see?" And I said, "I see a boiling pot (*sir napuah*), tilted away from the north." (Jer 1:13)

Despite the obscurity of this vision, it appears that the angle of the pot boiling on the fire portends an invasion "from the north" that will devastate Judah.

It is difficult to know whether this reference is to ceramic or metal ware, since the same vocabulary is often used for both; also, the vessels, whether ceramic or metal, served the same purpose. On the assumption that the "boiling pot" is a ceramic vessel, it probably was a widemouthed, round-based cooking pot, described as broad and shallow. Because this vessel was also used as a wash basin, it would have had a wide mouth. In Iron Age I, such vessels had no handles; in Iron Age II, they were two-handled.

Another of Jeremiah's allusions to specific pottery vessels involved the symbolic action of breaking an earthenware jug:

Thus said the LORD: Go and buy a potter's earthenware jug (*baqbuq yoṣer ḥares*). Take with you some of the elders of the people and some of the senior priests, and go out to the valley of the son of Hinnom at the entry of the Potsherd Gate, and proclaim there the words that I tell you. . . . And in this place [Tophet] I will make void (*baqqoti*) the plans of Judah and Jerusalem, and will make them fall by the sword before their enemies, and by the hand of those who seek their life. . . . Then you shall break the jug (*habbaqbuq*) in the sight of those who go with you, and shall say to them: Thus says the LORD of hosts: So will I break this people and this city, as one breaks a potter's vessel (*keli hayyoṣer*), so that it can never be mended. (Jer 19:1–2, 7, 10–11)

Ceramicists describe with some certainty the earthenware jug (*baqbuq*) mentioned in this passage as an expensive, ring-burnished decanter that functioned as a carafe. "It had a heavy body and a narrow neck with a handle attached to neck and rim."[7] Its distinctive narrow neck emits a gurgling sound when water is poured. On the basis of onomatopoeia (the use of a word whose sound suggests the sense), the Hebrew name *baqbuq* appears to be derived from the gurgling sound discharged when water was dispensed. The Potsherd Gate, mentioned only in Jeremiah, refers to one of the city gates leading to the Hinnom Valley and located in the southeastern section of Jerusalem. The potters discarded unused potsherds at the Potsherd Gate, identified by some scholars as the present-day Dung Gate.

Baqqoti, "I will make void," is thought to be a play on *baqbuq*, the name of the vessel. In Jeremiah's prophecy this costly decanter typified Jerusalem, and the breaking of the vessel symbolized the Lord's destruction of the city

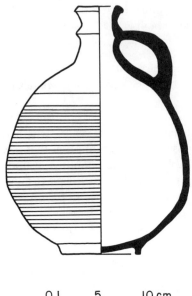

0 | 5   10 cm.

A decanter (*baqbuq*). This ceramic vessel varies in height from four to ten inches. *Baqbuq,* meaning "the gurgling vessel," is appropriately named. Since the neck of the vessel is too narrow to be mended, it is a fitting metaphor in Jeremiah 19. *Original drawing by T. M. Taylor. Courtesy of the American Schools of Oriental Research.*

A pitcher (*gabi'a*). This ceramic pitcher, eight to ten inches high, held either wine or water. *Original drawing by T. M. Taylor. Courtesy of the American Schools of Oriental Research.*

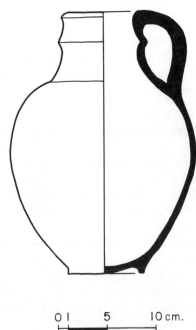

0 | 5   10 cm.

and its people. The vessel, once valued by the potter, was then smashed; unlike more sturdy vessels, it was too delicate to be mended.

Breaking pottery vessels symbolized the destruction of nations or individuals. Warning the eighteen-year-old King Jehoiachin of impending exile, Jeremiah prophesied he would become useless, like a broken pot:

> Is this man Coniah [Jehoiachin] a despised broken pot, a vessel no one wants? Why are he and his offspring hurled out and cast away in a land that they do not know? (Jer 22:28)

After only a three-month rule, Jehoiachin, his family, and servants were exiled to Babylon in 597 B.C.E.

God as Potter

The basis of the imagery of God as potter appeared in Jeremiah's classic passage, stating that the fate of the people was in the hands of God:

> Then the word of the LORD came to me [Jeremiah]: Can I not do with you, O house of Israel, just as this potter (*yoser*) has done? says the LORD. Just like the clay (*homer*) in the potter's (*yoser*) hand, so are you in my hand, O house of Israel. . . . Now, therefore, say to the people of Judah and the inhabitants of Jerusalem: Thus says the LORD: Look, I am a potter (*yoser*) shaping evil against you and devising a plan against you. Turn now, all of you from your evil way, and amend your ways and your doings. (Jer 18:5-6, 11)

The Lord's relation to Israel is the same as the potter to the clay.

Elsewhere in the Bible the God of Israel is compared to a potter (*yoser*); in some of these cases "potter" and "creator" are synonyms. Inasmuch as the Yahwist (J) creation account in Genesis pictures God as a potter (*yoser*), the verb *yasar* assumes the technical meaning "to create":

> Then the LORD God formed (*wayyiser*) man (*ha'adam*) from the dust (*'apar*) of the ground (*ha'adamah*), and breathed into his nostrils the breath of life; and the man became a living being. And the LORD God planted a garden in Eden, in the east; and there he put the man (*ha'adam*) whom he had formed (*yasar*). . . . So out of the ground (*ha'adamah*) the LORD God formed (*yiser*) every animal of the field and every bird of the air. (Gen 2:7-8, 19)

The verb "to form" (*yasar*) is the technical term to describe the potter (*yoser*) forming the clay into an earthen vessel. The play on "man" (*'adam*) and "ground" (*'adamah*), words that are almost alike in Hebrew, underscores the close relationship between humankind and the earth. The word for "dust" (*'apar*) designates a dry native clay. As Kelso observes, "The only kind of 'dust' out of which a figurine can be made is clay."[8]

The equation of God as potter and creator occurs again in the famous account of Jeremiah's conception, call, and commission:

> Now the word of the LORD came to me [Jeremiah] saying, "Before I formed ('*eṣṣareka*) you in the womb I knew you, and before you were born I consecrated you; I appointed you a prophet to the nations." (Jer 1:4–5)

The divine potter molded Jeremiah, the earthen vessel. "Formed" used here as in Gen 2:7 is understood as meaning "created."

In a satire on idolatry (Jer 10:1–16), Jeremiah alluded to God's creative activity with reference to the covenant people, with whom the Lord had a unique relationship:

> Not like these [idols] is the LORD, the portion of Jacob, for he is the one who formed (*yoṣer*) all things, and Israel is the tribe of his inheritance; the LORD of hosts is his name. (Jer 10:16; doublet, Jer 51:19)

The prophet emphasized the sharp contrast between the Lord and idols. The "portion of Jacob" is the Lord, so Israel had nothing to fear.

In a heartening passage about the restoration of Jerusalem and Judah, Jeremiah spoke of the Lord as creator:

> Thus says the LORD who made ('*osah*) the earth, the LORD who formed (*yoṣer*) it to establish it—the LORD is his name. (Jer 33:2)

Just as *yaṣar*, "to form," is a verb denoting creation in the Yahwist (J) account (Gen 2:4–25), so '*asah*, "to make," serves the same purpose in the Priestly (P) account of creation (Gen 1:1–2:4).

Wine and Wine Making

Another specific reference to a pottery vessel appears in the Lord's commendation of the Rechabites:

> The word that came to Jeremiah from the LORD in the days of King Jehoiakim son of Josiah of Judah: Go to the house of the Rechabites, and speak with them, and bring them to the house of the LORD, into one of the chambers; then offer them wine to drink. . . . Then I set before the Rechabites pitchers (*gebi'im*) full of wine, and cups (*kosot*); and I said to them, "Have some wine." But they answered, "We will drink no wine, for our ancestor Jonadab son of Rechab commanded us, 'You shall never drink wine, neither you nor your children.' " (Jer 35:1–2, 5–6).

This is the only description of the Rechabites in the Bible. Fervent in their loyalty to the Lord and to their own austere tradition, the Rechabites were an example of fidelity for the Judahites who, by contrast, were indifferent to their covenant obligations. The ultraconservative Rechabites, a nomadic tribe in the wilderness of Judah, rejected settled life, thereby shunning both agriculture and viticulture. They, like the Nazirites, abstained from drinking wine.

The Hebrew word *gabia'* (*gebi'im*, plural) designates a pitcher, not unlike modern types, that held either water or wine. It stood about eight to ten inches high. "The most plausible identification is with the one-handled jug with pinched spout found in Early Iron I and later."[9]

The Hebrew word *kos* (*kosot*, plural) denotes a drinking vessel, either a cup or a bowl. Unlike a modern-day cup, it would have been shaped more like a shallow bowl in a variety of sizes, with or without handles. Assyrian reliefs often depict scenes with the king drinking from such a bowl. One of the more famous is of Ashurbanipal (668–627 B.C.E.) and his queen, with cups in their hands, feasting in a garden.[10]

Jeremiah also uses the word *kos* in a figurative sense:

> For thus the LORD, the God of Israel, said to me [Jeremiah]: Take from my hand this cup (*kos*) of the wine of wrath, and make all the nations to whom I send you drink it. They shall drink and stagger and go out of their minds because of the sword that I am sending among them. (Jer 25:15–16)

The cup as a symbol of God's wrath, occurring frequently in the Bible, is used additionally in Jer 49:12; 51:7.

Jeremiah, borrowing images from wine making, pronounced judgment against Moab, a hostile land east of the Dead Sea with a reputation for the quality of its wine:

> Moab has been at ease from his youth, settled like wine on its dregs; he has not been emptied from vessel (*keli*) to vessel (*keli*), nor has he gone into exile; therefore his flavor has remained and his aroma is unspoiled. Therefore, the time is surely coming, says the LORD, when I shall send to him decanters to decant him, and empty his vessels (*keli*), and break his jars (*nebel*) in pieces. (Jer 48:11–12)

To enhance the strength and flavor of the wine, it was left undisturbed in the lees (sediment during fermentation). Like the undisturbed wine, Moab became nonchalant after being spared attack. But just as wine is tipped into bottles, so too Moab's tranquillity would be destroyed by the Babylonian conquerors.

The word *keli* is a generic term for a pottery vessel, although it may also refer to metalware. In this passage it is a synonym for *nebel*. The term *nebel* may describe a stringed instrument, a leather bottle, or a large storage jar. Apparently the earthen vessel (*nebel*) was shaped like an animal-skin bottle, whence the connection between the two. The musical instrument, too, may have been shaped like a skin bottle.

The *nebel* is a large storage jar, used especially for wine, oil, or grain. Measuring twenty-five inches high and sixteen inches in diameter, this pear-shaped vessel could hold from five to twelve gallons. The larger version had four handles for carrying, whereas the smaller jar had two handles.

Jeremiah 13:12–14, an independent unit expressing divine judgment on the nations, is somewhat ambiguous. Using the symbol of wine jars, Jeremiah utters a self-evident proverb (*mašal*), comparing the people of Judah to broken wine jars. The mention of "drunkenness" suggests destruction:

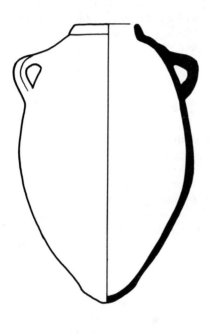

A storage jar (*nebel*). This large ceramic vessel, twenty-five inches high and sixteen inches in diameter, was used for wine, oil, or grain. *Original drawing by T. M. Taylor. Courtesy of the American Schools of Oriental Research.*

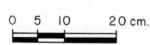

0   5   10   20 cm.

You [Jeremiah] shall speak to them this word: Thus says the LORD, the God of Israel: Every wine-jar (*nebel*) should be filled with wine. And they will say to you, "Do you think we do not know that every wine-jar (*nebel*) should be filled with wine?" Then you shall say to them: Thus says the LORD: I am about to fill all the inhabitants of this land . . . with drunkenness. (Jer 13:12–13)

Owing to the common use of wine, it is not surprising that the Bible contains so many references to practically all the steps in wine making, including harvesting, vintaging, treading, pressing, fermenting, and storing.

The grapes were brought in baskets from the vineyard to the winepress. Archaeologists have found several varieties of winepresses. Some consisted merely of two depressions, rectangular or circular in shape, cut in the bedrock. The larger of the vats or pits, called *gat*, was set higher, while the smaller and deeper one, called *yeqeb*, was set lower. The grape juice flowed through a channel connecting these two pits. Treading took place in the first pit; collecting the juice, in the second.

As in the case of olives, treading the grapes was sometimes done by foot. Crushing the grapes was done by stone rollers or wooden beam presses weighted with stones and anchored in a wall niche. The wine, after settling overnight, was collected in jars and transported to a cave or cistern, serving as a wine cellar, for fermentation.

Jeremiah alluded to these processes in three passages:

> Thus says the LORD of hosts: Glean thoroughly as a vine the remnant of Israel; like a grape-gatherer [vintager], pass your hand again over its branches. (Jer 6:9)

Uncertainty surrounds this verse, but the wrath of God is quite evident. Using among other metaphors the figure of harvesting grapes in the vineyard, the prophet spoke of the coming judgment as the complete destruction of Judah.

> You [Jeremiah], therefore, shall prophesy against them all these words, and say to them: The LORD will roar from on high, and from his holy habitation utter his voice; he will roar mightily against his fold, and shout, like those who tread (*dorkim*) grapes, against all the inhabitants of the earth. (Jer 25:30)

The Lord's universal judgment would be in the form of destruction of the nations, their leaders, and all their people. The Lord's roar is like that of a lion (Jer 2:15), and the shout like that of the vintage treaders. "The roar of those who trample the grapes and stain their garments red easily becomes a metaphor for the appalling slaughter of war (Isa 63:1-3)."[11]

> Gladness and joy have been taken away from the fruitful land of Moab; I have stopped the wine from the wine presses; no one treads (*yidrok*) them with shouts of joy; the shouting is not the shout of joy. (Jer 48:33)

This is part of the judgment against Moab, noted for its wine production. The vintage ordinarily is a season for great rejoicing, when large numbers of people gather the grapes. The "gladness and joy" ordinarily associated with the vintage have ceased.

One of the principal centers for the production and export of wine in the eighth and seventh centuries B.C.E. was Gibeon, the modern village of el-Jib, situated five miles northwest of Jerusalem. Pritchard's excavations at the site, between 1956 and 1962, uncovered rock-cut winepresses, rock-cut wine cellars (bottle-shaped cisterns) for storage, and storage jars whose handles were inscribed with the name *gb'n*, "Gibeon." He estimated that the sixty-three storage cellars had space for enough jars to hold 25,000 gallons of wine.

Oil Lamps

Foretelling the Babylonian captivity, Jeremiah described the sufferings the Judahites would experience by being deprived of the activities associated with daily life:

> And I [the LORD] will banish from them [Judah and neighboring nations] the sound of mirth and the sound of gladness, the voice of the bridegroom and the voice of the bride, the sound of the millstones and the light of the lamp (*'or ner*). (Jer 25:10)

The earliest lamps made their appearance in the Neolithic period (8500–4300 B.C.E.), perhaps in the sixth millennium, in the form of simple stone containers supplying oil to fuel the wick of twisted flax. The earliest lamps are described as simple bowls with smudges where the wicks were afire. Pottery lamps date from the fourth millennium when they were burnished to prevent the oil from leaking. The potter, according to Kelso, molded the lamp in the same way as a small bowl; and while the clay was still soft, the potter pinched in the rim at one point to hold the wick. The first appearance of lamp-bowls coincides with the domestication of the olive which was the primary fuel from the Chalcolithic period (4300–3500 B.C.E.) onward.

The evolution of lamps is easy to trace because they maintained their basic composition: a shallow clay saucer containing oil with a wick set in the oil, although the forms did change often. Since they were an important part of daily life, lamps are among the most common artifacts recovered on excavations in Palestine. For these reasons, they make excellent dating tools. Like pottery vessels, lamps too are valuable for the information they furnish about the development of cultural history, cross-cultural influences, ceramic techniques, art forms, and cult practices.

Characteristic of the Iron Age lamp is the flange (rim) surrounding the oil reserve, formed by folding the rim. During the Divided Kingdom (920–586 B.C.E.), lamps developed somewhat differently in the Northern Kingdom of Israel and in the Southern Kingdom of Judah, although each utilized the pinched spout and the flared rim. For the most part, northern lamps followed the traditional pattern but were shallower and had thinner walls. In contrast to the low, flat base of the northern lamps, the southern lamps had a flat, high disk base, described as "a rather heavy and somewhat clumsy disc base."[12] Ceramicists refer to this lamp as heavy-footed. These southern lamps also had a pinched spout and flared rim. Whereas the northern lamps appear also in Judah, the southern lamps are not found north of Megiddo.

The Hebrew word for "lamp" is *ner* (*nerot*, plural). In Palestine, olives provided the oil for the lamps, keeping them lighted from two to four hours. Wicks were ordinarily made of flax. The lamps were always kept burning and were usually placed in niches on the walls of dwellings or on lampstands.

In addition to their household functions, lamps were often used in the context of cultic rituals and especially of burials. The Bible has countless references to lamps, in both the literal and the figurative sense.

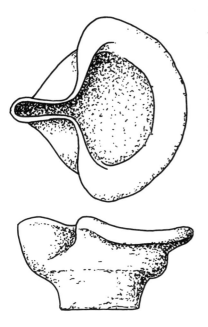

Iron Age II lamp from Kingdom of Judah. The pinched spout, flared rim, and flat, high disk base differentiate the Iron Age II lamps of the Southern Kingdom from the lamps of the Northern Kingdom which have low, flat bases. *Credit to Varda Sussman. Courtesy of* Biblical Archaeology Review.

Metallurgy

Sirach describes the work of the smith:

> So too is the smith, sitting by the anvil, intent on his iron-work; the breath of the fire melts his flesh, and he struggles with the heat of the furnace; the sound of the hammer deafens his ears, and his eyes are on the pattern of the object. He sets his heart on finishing his handiwork, and he is careful to complete its decoration. (Sir 38:28)

The metals used in ancient Palestine included gold, silver, copper, lead, tin, and iron; practically all are mentioned in Jeremiah either literally or figuratively. In the ancient Near East the predominant metals were bronze (an alloy of copper and tin) and iron. The use of these two metals as the principal materials for making tools defines, respectively, the Bronze and Iron ages.

The Bronze Age, extending from 3500 to 1200 B.C.E., is subdivided into Early Bronze (3500–2300 B.C.E.), Middle Bronze (2300–1550 B.C.E.), and Late Bronze (1550–1200 B.C.E.). The Iron Age, extending from 1200 to 330 B.C.E., is subdivided into Iron I (1200–1000 B.C.E.), Iron II (1000–586 B.C.E.), and Iron III (539–332 B.C.E.), although the latter is better known as the Persian period (539–332 B.C.E.). These dates are only approximate and are subject to change. In the light of new evidence, archaeologists continue to refine and revise chronology.

The era between 1200 and 900 B.C.E. was a transitional period, when the use of bronze was waning and the use of iron was increasing. No definitive break between the Bronze and Iron ages is evident; rather, continuity between the two cultures is clear. Archaeologists have discovered some iron weapons dating from the twelfth and eleventh centuries B.C.E. at Israelite sites, but it was only in the tenth century B.C.E. that iron came into common use, as Jane Waldbaum[13] has shown. Through the twelfth and eleventh centuries B.C.E., tools and weapons of bronze actually outnumbered those of iron, which were not of high quality.

Scholars offer several explanations for the introduction of iron into Palestine as well as the replacement of bronze by iron. It is often stated that the Philistines enjoyed a monopoly on iron, on the assumption that iron technology came about through the migration of the Philistines and other Sea Peoples from the Aegean into Palestine. Despite 1 Sam 13:19–21, recounting that the Israelites went down to the Philistines to sharpen their tools, although iron is not mentioned, archaeological evidence does not confirm Philistine superiority owing to their possession of iron.

As well as this explanation, James Muhly[14] and others propose that the disruption of the international trade routes in 1200 B.C.E. made copper and tin unavailable, causing a scarcity of bronze and, at the same time, hastening the development of iron.

A third theory, proffered by Theodore Wertime and Stager,[15] is ecological and relates to deforestation in the Mediterranean region. They point to a correlation between deforestation and the introduction of iron. Deforestation was the inevitable result of the influx of a burgeoning population who had to settle and cultivate the land, as well as of pyrotechnologies and other human activities. Commenting on pyrotechnologies, Stager observes:

> Wood charcoal was in ever-increasing demand for various pyrotechnologies used to produce ceramics, glass, plaster, and metals. Although more labor intensive, iron production is much more fuel-efficient than copper smelting and processing. Copper requires two to four times as much wood charcoal as iron.[16]

Copper

Copper (*nehošet*) was the first metal to be extracted from its ores. It was the predominant metal in the Chalcolithc period when the first copper implements made an appearance. Pessah Bar-Adon, exploring in 1961 the Naḥal Mishmar Caves in the Judean Desert, made one of the greatest discoveries relating to this period. In the Cave of the Treasure a hoard of over four hundred vessels came to light. Included were assorted copper chisels and axes as well as copper mace-heads.

Bronze

Since the native copper was not a sufficiently strong metal, it was replaced by bronze (*nehošet*), an alloy of 90 percent copper and 10 percent tin. Bronze is harder than copper, so smiths smelted copper and tin ores into bronze.

Iron

Barzel meaning "iron" is a foreign word, thought to be of Hittite origin. The art of smelting (separating metal from ore) and working iron is often associated with the Hittites about the middle of the second millennium in the mountainous country to the south of the Black Sea. That they had a monopoly on iron in the Late Bronze Age is seriously questioned today.

Wrought iron is softer than bronze, but it has the ability to hold an edge and a point. It was used especially for smaller objects, such as axes, chisels, plowshares, and swords.

During the process of heating iron with charcoal, carbon is absorbed, and the soft iron becomes hard. Wrought iron to which carbon has been added is known as carburized iron or steel. Steel is more malleable than cast iron. Cast iron, an alloy of iron, carbon, and silicon, is cast in a mold and is non-malleable.

Iron containing carbon can be made even harder by quenching, that is, cooling off the red-hot steel by sudden immersion in a vat of cold water. Quenching is effective only with carburized iron, not with wrought iron. Quenching renders carburized iron hard but brittle. Tempering (heating in a hearth) overcomes the brittleness. The processes of carburization, quenching, and tempering render iron superior to bronze.

Iron occurs only in ores that are close to the surface of the ground; hence it is more easily extracted than copper, whose ores are embedded deep in the ground. The melting point of iron is 1535 degrees C (2795 degrees F), whereas copper melts at 1083 degrees C (1981 degrees F). Bellows or blowers are used to provide the forced draft of air by alternate expansion and contraction, drawing air in and expelling it.

In the Bible, iron is often associated with violence, oppression, and devastation. The following are examples of Jeremiah's literary metaphors on iron:

And I [the Lᴏʀᴅ] for my part have made you [Jeremiah] today a fortified city, and iron pillar (*'ammud barzel*), and a bronze wall, against the
whole land—against the kings of Judah, its princes, its priests, and the
people of the land. (Jer 1:18)

Accordingly, Jeremiah would be unbelievably strong, and like an invinci-
ble city he would be able to resist attack.

You [Jeremiah] shall say to them [the people of Judah], Thus says the
Lᴏʀᴅ, the God of Israel: Cursed be anyone who does not heed the
words of this covenant, which I commanded your ancestors when I
brought them out of the land of Egypt, from the iron-smelter (*mikkur
habbarzel*), saying, Listen to my voice, and do all that I command you.
So shall you be my people, and I will be your God. (Jer 11:3–4)

Since iron can be smelted only at a very high temperature, the furnace
had to be red-hot.

The sin of Judah is written with an iron pen (*'et barzel*); with a diamond
point it is engraved on the tablet of their hearts, and on the horns of
their altars. (Jer 17:1)

An iron stylus with a hard point was used to engrave an inscription on
rock, thus making the inscription indelible.

Go, tell Hananiah [who prophesied falsely against Jeremiah], Thus says
the Lᴏʀᴅ: You have broken wooden bars (*motot 'es*) only to forge iron
bars (*motot barzel*) in place of them! For thus says the Lᴏʀᴅ of hosts,
the God of Israel: I have put an iron yoke (*'ol barzel*) on the neck of all
these nations so that they may serve King Nebuchadnezzar of Babylon, and they shall indeed serve him; I have even given him the wild
animals. (Jer 28:13–14)

The wooden bars worn by Jeremiah signified enslavement to Babylonia.
In place of these wooden yoke-bars that Hananiah had deliberately broken,
the Lord forged iron bars, symbolizing an even harsher divine judgment
against Judah.

Lead

Lead (*'operet*) is present in several minerals. Silver is found associated with
lead ore. Galena, often mined as a source of silver, constitutes the principal
ore of lead. Refining (*sarap*) is the removal of impurities from metal ore, so
as to produce the desired metal in pure form. Lead served as an oxidizing
agent to remove the dross in refining silver.

Silver is extracted by cupellation, a refining process that takes place in a
cupel (a shallow, porous cup, especially of bone ash), used to separate the
silver from the lead. Bone ash is defined as the white residue, principally of

tribasic calcium phosphate, from bones calcinated in air. A blast of hot air
directed on the molten mass in a furnace oxidizes the lead.

Silver

Silver (*kesep*), mentioned over three hundred times in the Bible, was
known as early as 3000 B.C.E. One of the so-called precious metals, it is very
malleable. Silver, seldom found in the pure state, is extracted from a sulphide ore of lead. Owing to its malleable nature, silver is used for ornaments,
amulets, jewelry, decorations, cult vessels, and images. Silver also served as
a medium of monetary exchange before the introduction of coinage.

As noted already, at Eshtemoa (es-Sammo'a), twelve miles south of
Hebron, archaeologists found, in 1968, a sixty-two-pound silver hoard, the
largest ever discovered in Palestine. It consisted of five jugs, dating from the
First Temple period, each filled with broken pieces of silver and silver jewelry. The silver was used as payment in commercial transactions.

A remarkable example of silver ornamentation is a recently discovered
statuette of a silver calf at the coastal city of Ashkelon, dating from about
1550 B.C.E. According to Stager, the excavator:

> Less than 4.5 inches long and 4 inches high, the calf . . . is a superb
> example of Canaanite metalwork. . . . The body is made of bronze;
> only 2 to 5 percent is tin, the rest, copper. . . . The calf was once com-
> pletely covered with a thick overleaf of pure silver.[17]

In a satire on idolatry, Jeremiah described the adorning of idols with silver and gold:

> People deck it [the idol] with silver and gold; they fasten it with ham-
> mer and nails so that it cannot move. . . . Beaten silver is brought from
> Tarshish, and gold from Uphaz. (Jer 10:4, 9; also, 10:14 and parallel
> 51:17 concerning goldsmiths)

Tarshish cannot be identified with certainty. Associated with maritime
trade, it may be situated in the vicinity of Spain.[18] The location of Uphaz is
likewise unknown. Some suggest the text should read "Ophir," a place
famous for gold; but its location is also uncertain.

The key text on metallurgy in Jeremiah depicts the Lord casting the
prophet in the role of "a tester [assayer] and a refiner among my [the
LORD's] people":

> I [the LORD] have made you [Jeremiah] a tester and a refiner among
> my people so that you may know and test their ways. They are all stub-
> bornly rebellious, going about with slanders; they are bronze (*nehošet*)
> and iron (*barzel*), all of them act corruptly. The bellows (*mappuah*) blow
> fiercely, the lead (*'operet*) is consumed by the fire; in vain the refining

goes on (*sarap sarop*), for the wicked are not removed. They [the people of Judah] are called "rejected silver (*kesep*)," for the LORD has rejected them. (Jer 6:27–30)

In this case, the process of refining impure silver from crude lead by cupellation proved futile. Consequently, the people failed the test and were "rejected" (discarded), just as "rejected silver" is scrapped.

In a comparable passage the Lord, not Jeremiah, is the refiner and assayer:

> Therefore thus says the LORD of hosts: I will now refine (*sorpam*) and test them [the people], for what else can I do with my sinful people? (Jer 9:7 [Hebrew 9:6])

Gold

Because gold (*zahab*) is found in the relatively pure state in nature, it is perhaps the oldest precious metal known to humankind. The Bible has hundreds of references to gold, often in conjunction with silver. Silver is frequently mentioned first. *Zahab* is the common biblical word for gold, but several others are used to differentiate the various qualities of the precious metal.

Gold had many uses in ancient Israel, including the ornamentation of the Temple:

> The captain of the guard took away the small bowls also, the firepans, the basins, the pots, the lampstands, the ladles, and the bowls for libation, both those of gold and those of silver. (Jer 52:19)

As today, gold ornamented jewelry in antiquity. In a well-known passage from Jeremiah, the Lord mockingly addressed Jerusalem as a prostitute adorning herself with elegant clothes and jewelry to seduce her lover:

> And you, O desolate one [Jerusalem], what do you mean that you dress in crimson, that you deck yourself with ornaments of gold, that you enlarge your eyes with paint? In vain you beautify yourself. Your lovers despise you; they seek your life. (Jer 4:30; also 2:32)

Cave Number 25 at Ketef Hinnom, facing Jerusalem's walls, held a rich collection of women's jewelry, including six gold items and ninety-five silver items. Among the gold items, the excavator called attention especially to the "boat-shaped earrings."

In conclusion, ongoing cooperation between archaeologists and metallurgists is providing valuable insights into ancient technology as well as giving a greater understanding of the effect of metallurgy on the economy, trade, and other activities in the biblical world.

Notes

Introduction: Archaeology and Biblical Studies

1. C. de Geus, "The Development of Palestinian Archaeology and Its Significance for Biblical Studies," in *The World of the Bible*, ed. A. S. Van der Woude (Grand Rapids: Wm. B. Eerdmans Publishing Co., 1986), p. 64.

Chapter 1: Jeremiah: The Prophet and the Book

1. On the basis of a lower chronology, W. Holladay maintains that 627 B.C.E. denotes the birth of Jeremiah, with his mission beginning only in 609 B.C.E.

2. L. Stager, "The Archaeology of the Family in Ancient Israel," *BASOR* 260 (1985): 25.

3. N. Avigad, "The Contribution of Hebrew Seals to an Understanding of Israelite Religion and Society, in *Ancient Israelite Religion: Essays in Honor of Frank Moore Cross*, ed. P. Miller, Jr., P. Hanson, and S. D. McBride (Philadelphia: Fortress Press, 1987), p. 205.

4. The text of Jeremiah is not straightforwardly autobiographical. The parallel between Moses and Jeremiah is close and may indicate a literary device rather than an actual event.

5. "Nebuchadrezzar," the correct spelling, is closer to the original Akkadian form of the name. "Nebuchadnezzar," the incorrect variant, is more common in the Bible. Recent biblical commentaries and dictionaries use the first spelling.

6. J. Bright, "A Prophet's Lament and Its Answer: Jeremiah 15:10–21," *Interpretation* 28 (1974): 59.

7. H. Kuist, *The Book of Jeremiah*, Layman's Bible Commentary (Richmond: John Knox Press, 1960), p. 24.

8. J. Muilenburg, "Baruch the Scribe," in *Proclamation and Presence: Old Testament Essays in Honour of Gwynne Henton Davies*, ed. J. Durham and J. R. Porter (Richmond: John Knox Press, 1970), pp. 215–238.

Chapter 2: Historical Background

1. A. Malamat, "The Last Kings of Judah and the Fall of Jerusalem," *IEJ* 18 (1968): 137–156; idem, "Josiah's Bid for Armageddon: The Background of the Judean-Egyptian Encounter in 609 B.C.," *JANESCU* 5 (1973): 267–278; and idem, "The Twilight of Judah: In the Egyptian-Babylonian Maelstrom," in *Supplements to Vetus Testamentum*, no. 28, ed. G. Anderson et al. (Leiden: E. J. Brill, 1975), pp. 123–145.

2. M. Cogan, *Imperialism and Religion: Assyria, Judah and Israel in the Eighth and Seventh Centuries B.C.E.* (Missoula, Mont.: Scholars Press, 1974), p. 60. Cogan maintains that Assyria did not impose cultic obligations upon vassal states; rather, foreign, local cults were allowed to flourish.

3. N. Na'aman, "The Kingdom of Judah Under Josiah," *TA* 18 (1991): 3–71.

4. M. Cogan and H. Tadmor, *II Kings*, Anchor Bible (Garden City, N.Y.: Doubleday & Co., 1988), p. 301: "If one follows the laconic passage in 2 Kgs 23:29, which is the only contemporary evidence, there was no battle or military move."

5. D. W. Thomas, ed., *Documents from Old Testament Times* (New York: Harper & Brothers, Harper Torchbooks, 1958), pp. 78–79.

6. Ibid., p. 80.

Chapter 3: Geographical Setting

1. E. Oren, "Migdol: A New Fortress on the Edge of the Eastern Nile Delta," *BASOR* 256 (1984): 32.

2. J. M. Miller, ed., *Archaeological Survey of the Kerak Plateau* (Atlanta: Scholars Press, 1991).

3. J. A. Dearman, ed., *Studies in the Mesha Inscription and Moab* (Atlanta: Scholars Press, 1989).

4. J. A. Dearman, "The Location of Jahaz," *ZDPV* 100 (1984): 124.

Chapter 4: Edom and Judah

1. J. Bartlett, *Edom and the Edomites*, JSOT/PEF Monograph Series (Sheffield: Sheffield Academic Press, 1989), p. 157.

2. B. Rothenberg, "Ancient Copper Industries in the Western Arabah," *PEQ* 94 (1962): 44–56.

3. M. Kochavi, "Rescue in the Biblical Negev," *BAR* 6/1 (1980): 27.

4. D. Ussishkin, "The Date of the Judaean Shrine at Arad," *IEJ* 38 (1988): 156.

5. Y. Aharoni, ed., *Arad Inscriptions* (Jerusalem: Israel Exploration Society, 1981), p. 12.

6. Ibid., p. 46.

7. I. Beit-Arieh and B. Cresson, "An Edomite Ostracon from Ḥorvat 'Uza," *TA* 12 (1985): 97.

8. Ibid., p. 100.

9. I. Beit-Arieh, "The Ostracon of Ahiqam from Ḥorvat 'Uza," *TA* 13–14 (1986–1987): 37.

10. I. Beit-Arieh, "New Light on the Edomites," *BAR* 14/2 (1988): 31.

Chapter 5: Cities of Judah

1. D. Wiseman, *Nebuchadrezzar and Babylon* (Oxford: Oxford University Press, 1985), p. 42.

2. D. Gill, "Subterranean Waterworks of Biblical Jerusalem: Adaptation of a Karst System," *Science* 254 (1991): 1467–1471.

3. J. Waldbaum, *Metalwork from Sardis: The Finds Through 1974*, Archaeological Exploration of Sardis 8 (Cambridge: Harvard University Press, 1983). Instead of the ethnic designation "Scythian" arrowheads, Waldbaum prefers "trilobate socketed arrowheads."

4. D. Bahat, "The Wall of Manasseh in Jerusalem," *IEJ* 31 (1981): 235–236.

5. B. Mazar, "Jerusalem: From Isaiah to Jeremiah," in *Supplements to Vetus Testamentum*, no. 40, ed. J. Emerton (Leiden: E. J. Brill, 1988), pp. 1–6.

6. Y. Yadin, "The Lachish Letters—Originals or Copies and Drafts?" in *Recent Archaeology in the Land of Israel*, ed. H. Shanks and B. Mazar (Washington, D.C.: Biblical Archaeology Society, 1981), pp. 179–186.

7. Thomas, *Documents from Old Testament Times*, p. 216.

8. F. M. Cross, "A Literate Soldier: Lachish Letter III," in *Biblical and Related Studies Presented to Samuel Iwry*, ed. A. Kort and S. Morscauser (Winona Lake, Ind.: Eisenbrauns, 1985), pp. 41–47. Cross does not treat Yadin's position specifically; his comment is based on an oral communication.

9. Thomas, *Documents from Old Testament Times*, p. 214.

Chapter 6: Inscriptions and Literacy

1. R. L. Hicks, "Delet and *megillah*, A Fresh Approach to Jeremiah XXXVI, *VT* 33 (1983): 46–66.

2. J. P. Hyatt, "The Writing of an Old Testament Book," *BA* 6 (1943): 71–80.

3. J. Hoftijzer and G. van der Kooij, eds., *Aramaic Texts from Deir 'Alla* (Leiden: E. J. Brill, 1976). This is vol. 19 of the *editio princeps*.

4. Avigad, "Contribution of Hebrew Seals," p. 202.

5. N. Avigad, *Hebrew Bullae from the Time of Jeremiah* (Jerusalem: IES, 1986), p. 129 n. 164.

6. S. Layton, "The Steward in Ancient Israel: A Study of Hebrew *('ašer) 'al-habbayit* in Its Near Eastern Setting," *JBL* 109 (1990): 649.

7. G. Barkay, "A Bulla of Ishmael the King's Son," *BASOR* (forthcoming, 1993).

8. N. Avigad, "Baruch the Scribe and Jerahmeel the King's Son," *IEJ* 28 (1978): 56.

9. A. Yardeni, "Remarks on the Priestly Blessing on Two Ancient Amulets from Jerusalem," *VT* 41 (1991): 180.

Chapter 7: Worship and Architecture

1. R. de Vaux, *Ancient Israel: Its Life and Institutions* (New York: McGraw-Hill Book Co., 1961), p. 271.

2. W. Rast, "Cakes for the Queen of Heaven," in *Scripture in History and Theology: Essays in Honor of J. Coert Rylaarsdam*, ed. A. Merrill and T. Overholt (Pittsburgh: Pickwick Press, 1977), pp. 167–180.

3. S. Ackerman, " 'And the Women Knead Dough': The Worship of the Queen of Heaven in Sixth-Century Judah," in *Gender and Difference in Ancient Israel*, ed. P. Day (Minneapolis: Fortress Press, 1989), pp. 109–124.

4. M. Pope, *Song of Songs*, Anchor Bible (Garden City, N.Y.: Doubleday & Co., 1977), p. 379.

5. Rast, "Cakes for the Queen of Heaven," p. 172.

6. M. Smith, *The Early History of God: Yahweh and the Other Deities in Ancient Israel* (San Francisco: Harper & Row, 1990), p. 90.

7. F. M. Cross, "The Old Phoenician Inscription from Spain Dedicated to Hurrian Astarte," *HTR* 64 (1971): 189–195.

8. S. Olyan, "Some Observations Concerning the Identity of the Queen of Heaven," *UF* 19 (1987): 174.

9. R. Hestrin, "The Lachish Ewer and the 'Asherah," *IEJ* 37 (1987): 212–223. Michael Coogan, William Dever, and others would disagree with Hestrin. Combining the crude drawings and the religious inscriptions at Kuntillet 'Ajrud, they identify Asherah as the female deity. For a convenient summary of positions, see P. King, "The Contribution of Archaeology to Biblical Studies," *CBQ* 45 (1983): 12–14.

10. *KAI*, 37.

11. B. Peckham, "Phoenicia and the Religion of Israel: The Epigraphic Evidence," in *Ancient Israelite Religion: Essays in Honor of Frank Moore Cross*, pp. 84–85.

12. G. Dalman, *Brot, Öl und Wein*, vol. 4 of *Arbeit und Sitte in Palästina* (Gütersloh: C. Bertelsmann, 1935).

13. D. Ussishkin, "King Solomon's Palaces," *BA* 36 (1973): 90.

14. M. Haran, "The Uses of Incense in the Ancient Israelite Ritual," *VT* 10 (1960): 113–129.

15. M. Zohary, *Plants of the Bible* (Cambridge: Cambridge University Press, 1982), p. 197.

16. S. Gitin, "Incense Altars from Ekron, Israel and Judah: Context and Typology," in *Eretz-Israel: Yigael Yadin Memorial Volume*, ed. A. Ben-Tor, J. Greenfield, A. Malamat, vol. 20 (Jerusalem: IES, 1989), pp. 52*–67*.

17. M. Dayagi-Mendels, *Perfumes and Cosmetics in the Ancient World* (Jerusalem: Israel Museum, 1989).

18. A. Kaufman, "Where the Ancient Temple of Jerusalem Stood," *BAR* 9/2 (1983): 40–59.

19. L. Ritmeyer, "Locating the Original Temple Mount," *BAR* 18/2 (1992): 24–45, 64–65.

20. L. Stager, "The Archaeology of the Family in Ancient Israel," *BASOR* 260 (1985): 28 n. 1.

21. W. F. Albright, *Archaeology and the Religion of Israel*, Anchor Books (Garden City, N.Y.: Doubleday & Co., 1969), p. 144.

22. R. Carroll, *Jeremiah*, Old Testament Library (Philadelphia: Westminster Press, 1986), p. 415.

23. M. Dayagi-Mendels, in *Treasures of the Holy Land: Ancient Art from the Israel Museum* (New York: Metropolitan Museum of Art, 1986), p. 170.

24. G. Barkay and A. Kloner, "Jerusalem Tombs from the Days of the First Temple," *BAR* 12/2 (1986): 27.

25. Stager, "The Archaeology of the Family in Ancient Israel," 17.

26. R. Barnett, *A Catalogue of the Nimrud Ivories* (London: British Museum, 1957), p. 145.

Chapter 8: Funerary Customs and Mourning

1. Y. Aharoni, *The Archaeology of the Land of Israel* (Philadelphia: Westminster Press, 1982), p. 238.

2. H. Brichto, "Kin, Cult, Land and Afterlife—A Biblical Complex," *HUCA* 44 (1973): 37–38.

3. D. Bahat, *The Illustrated Atlas of Jerusalem* (New York: Simon & Schuster, 1990), p. 33.

4. N. Avigad, "The Epitaph of a Royal Steward from Siloam Village," *IEJ* 3 (1953): 137–152.

5. G. Barkay, *Ketef Hinnom: A Treasure Facing Jerusalem's Walls* (Jerusalem: Israel Museum, 1986), p. 19.

6. S. Olyan, *Asherah and the Cult of Yahweh in Israel* (Atlanta: Scholars Press, 1988), p. 12.

7. P. Mosca, "Child Sacrifice in Canaanite and Israelite Religion: A Study in Mulk and Molech" (unpublished diss., Harvard University). Mosca develops the thesis of Otto Eissfeldt.

8. M. Weinfeld, "The Worship of Molech and of the Queen of Heaven and Its Background," *UF* 4 (1972): 133–154.

9. M. Smith, "A Note on Burning Babies," *JAOS* 95 (1975): 477–479.

10. L. Stager and S. Wolff, "Child Sacrifice at Carthage—Religious Rite or Population Control?" *BAR* 10/1 (1984): 30–51.

11. Brichto, "Kin, Cult, Land and Afterlife," p. 38 n. 59.

12. P. King, *Amos, Hosea, Micah—An Archaeological Commentary* (Philadelphia: Westminster Press, 1988), pp. 137–161.

13. R. Amiran, "The Tumuli West of Jerusalem: Survey and Excavations, 1953," *IEJ* 8 (1958): 207.

14. Aharoni, *Archaeology of the Land of Israel*, p. 239.

15. W. Holladay, *A Commentary on the Book of the Prophet Jeremiah, Chapters 26–52,* Hermeneia (Minneapolis: Fortress Press, 1989), p. 235.

16. J. Bright, *Jeremiah*, Anchor Bible (Garden City, N.Y.: Doubleday & Co., 1965), p. 357.

Chapter 9: Agriculture

1. C. de Geus, "The Importance of Archaeological Research Into the Palestinian Agricultural Terraces, with an Excursus on the Hebrew Word *gbi*," *PEQ* 107 (1975): 70.

2. M. Zohary, *Plants of the Bible* (Cambridge: Cambridge University Press, 1982), p. 15.

3. H. Frenkley, "The Search for Roots—Israel's Biblical Landscape Reserve," *BAR* 12/5 (1986): 42.

4. Zohary, *Plants of the Bible*, p. 117.

5. O. Borowski, *Agriculture in Iron Age Israel* (Winona Lake, Ind.: Eisenbrauns, 1987), p. 90.

6. L. Stager, "The Firstfruits of Civilization," in *Palestine in the Bronze and Iron Ages: Papers in Honour of Olga Tufnell*, ed. J. Tubb (London: Institute of Archaeology, 1985), pp. 172–188.

7. H. Shanks, "The Pomegranate Scepter Head—From the Temple of the Lord or from a Temple of Asherah?" *BAR* 18/3 (1992): 42–45.

8. Stager, "The Archaeology of the Family in Ancient Israel," p. 12.

9. Zohary, *Plants of the Bible*, p. 192.

10. J. Patrich and B. Arubas, "A Juglet Containing Balsam Oil (?) from a Cave Near Qumran," *IEJ* 39 (1989): 43–59.

11. L. Stager, "Ancient Agriculture in the Judean Desert: A Case Study of the Buqeʻah Valley in the Iron Age" (unpublished diss., Harvard University); and idem, "Agriculture," *IDB* Supplementary Volume, ed. K. Crim et al. (Nashville: Abingdon Press, 1976), pp. 11–13.

12. De Geus, "The Importance of Archaeological Research Into the Palestinian Agricultural Terraces," pp. 65–74.

13. G. Edelstein and S. Gibson, "Ancient Jerusalem's Rural Food Basket," *BAR* 8/4 (1982): 54.

14. De Geus, "The Importance of Archaeological Research Into the Palestinian Agricultural Terraces," pp. 72–74.

Chapter 10: Crafts

1. J. Kelso, "Pottery," *IDB*, ed. G. Buttrick et al. (New York: Abingdon Press, 1962), 3:846.

2. A. Mazar, *Archaeology of the Land of the Bible* (New York: Doubleday & Co., 1990), p. 49.

3. H. Franken and M. Steiner, *Excavations in Jerusalem 1961–1967* (Oxford: Oxford University Press, 1990), 2:91.

4. A. Mazar, *Archaeology of the Land of the Bible*, p. 538.

5. J. Kelso, *The Ceramic Vocabulary of the Old Testament*, *BASOR* Supplementary Studies, nos. 5–6 (New Haven: ASOR, 1948), p. 8.

6. Kelso, "Pottery," 3:847.

7. Ibid., 3:851.

8. Kelso, *The Ceramic Vocabulary of the Old Testament*, p. 5.

9. A. Honeyman, "The Pottery Vessels of the Old Testament," *PEQ* 71 (1939): 80.

10. King, *Amos, Hosea, Micah–An Archaeological Commentary*, pp. 148–149.

11. Carroll, *Jeremiah*, p. 507.

12. V. Sussman, "Lighting the Way Through History," *BAR* 11/2 (1985): 48.

13. J. Waldbaum, *From Bronze to Iron: The Transition from the Bronze Age to the Iron Age in the Eastern Mediterranean*, Studies in Mediterranean Archaeology 54 (Göteborg: Paul Aströms Förlag, 1978).

14. J. Muhly, "How Iron Technology Changed the Ancient World—And Gave the Philistines a Military Edge," *BAR* 8/6 (1982): 40-54.

15. Stager, "The Archaeology of the Family in Ancient Israel," p. 11.

16. Ibid.

17. L. Stager, "When Canaanites and Philistines Ruled Ashkelon," *BAR* 17/2 (1991): 26-27.

18. The identification of Tarshish is unsettled. Tarsus in Asia Minor, the birthplace of Paul, is a real possibility, especially since the discovery of silver mines in Asia Minor. This was Josephus' identification. Tartessus in southwestern Spain may have been a colony of, or at least named after, the original Tarshish.

Glossary

acropolis: Greek word for "upper city"; a citadel; a defensible hilltop; the upper fortified center of a city.

adytum: Innermost sanctuary of an ancient temple where only the priests entered to officiate; also the Holy of Holies, or *debir*, of the Jerusalem Temple.

amphora: Large, two-handled, open-mouthed pottery vessel with a narrow neck and an oval body. It was used for the storage of wine, oil, water, or grain.

amulet: Small object worn as a charm around the neck to ward off evil and harm. It was often inscribed with a magic incantation.

apocalyptic: From the Greek word meaning "revelation." It is a type of literature that flourished from 200 B.C.E. to 200 C.E. By means of strange symbols and mysterious revelations, it deals with the final period of world history.

apocrypha: Greek word meaning "hidden things." It designates those books found in the Greek Old Testament but omitted from the Jewish canon of the Hebrew Scriptures. Roman Catholics and Eastern churches consider these books as part of the canonical Old Testament. Catholic Christians designate them as "deuterocanonical."

ashlar: Square-cut or dressed stone used for facing a wall.

baluster: Upright support of a balustrade rail; a banister.

balustrade: Row of balusters topped by a rail.

bamah, bamot (plural): Hebrew word designating a place of worship in a natural setting; often an artificial mound or "high place" for the purpose of worship.

bulla: Seal impression on clay or other material, affixed to a document.

capital: Uppermost element of a column or pillar, sometimes elaborately decorated.

casemate: Designation of chambers formed by two parallel walls joined at intervals by cross walls. The outer wall is thicker; chambers are often filled with rubble; sometimes used for storage or as living space. This kind of fortification wall was used especially in Iron Age I and later (1200–928 B.C.E.).

cella: Inner sanctuary or principal chamber of a temple; contained cult image of the deity.

Chalcolithic: Copper-stone age, dating from 4300 to 3500 B.C.E., when copper and stone implements and weapons were used.

colonnade: Series of regularly spaced columns with capitals.

dendrochronology: Dating technique based on the analysis of growth rings in trees and aged wood.

epigraphy: Decipherment of ancient inscriptions; concerned with analysis, classification, dating, and interpretation of inscriptions.

Idumeans: Designation of the Edomites in Greco-Roman times. At the time of the Hasmoneans (142–63 B.C.E.) they became Judaized.

khirbet (Arabic), ***ḥorvah*** (Hebrew): Ruins of an ancient settlement.

krater, crater: Greek word for a two-handled ceramic bowl with large round body and wide mouth; used for mixing wine and water.

maṣṣebah, maṣṣebot (plural): Derived from the Hebrew root "to stand"; sacred pillars, usually monoliths, set up to commemorate religious events or covenants.

millo: From the Hebrew *male'*, "to fill." A topographical term designating an artificial platform of earth. The millo was part of the fortification of the City of David (Jerusalem).

necropolis: Greek word meaning "city of the dead"; burial ground or cemetery of an ancient city.

negev: Hebrew word often translated "south," although literally it means "dry." It designates the southern part of Judah, extending approximately from Beer-sheba to the Gulf of Aqaba.

offset-inset wall: Also known as "salients and recesses"; so called because the offsets project like sawteeth and provide greater security against the battering ram and other methods of siege warfare. It replaced the casemate wall.

ophel: Derived from the Hebrew root *'pl*, meaning "to climb," "to swell." It designated the upper city enclosed within a wall where the administrative center of the city was built.

ossuary, ossuaries (plural): Container (small stone box) for collecting human bones. This type of depository was used in the Chalcolithic period (4300–3500 B.C.E.), and again in the Herodian period (30 B.C.E.–70 C.E.).

ostracon, ostraca (plural): Greek word for inscribed fragments of pottery; the most common of ancient writing materials. So called because the inscribed potsherds were used as ballots in voting for ostracism.

paleography: Science of dating ancient written materials. It is an aspect of epigraphy.

Palestine: Derived from "Philistine," the traditional enemy of Israel. The term is traced back to the Greek historian Herodotus (about 484–420 B.C.E.). Canaan was the older name of the land; Phoenicia was the Greek name.

Pentapolis: Confederation or group of five cities, usually with reference to the five Philistine cities: Ashdod, Ashkelon, Gaza, Gath, and Ekron.

portico: Structure with a roof supported by columns.

potsherds: Pottery fragments; also **sherds** or **shards**.

Septuagint: Greek translation of the Hebrew Scriptures, traditionally completed in Alexandria (Egypt) in the third century B.C.E.; abbreviated LXX.

Shephelah: Literally, "lowland." It designates the limestone foothills in western Palestine that separate the coastal plain from the central mountain ridge.

stela, stelae (plural): From the Latin verb "to stand"; the Greek forms are **stele, stelai** (plural); freestanding stone slabs, usually inscribed or bearing designs; used for memorial or commemorative purposes.

stratigraphy: Study of soil layers, including the order of their deposition, and their chronological relationship to one another.

syncretism: Synthesis of conflicting religious beliefs or practices; e.g., Canaanite and Israelite religions.

tell (Arabic), **tel** (Hebrew): Artificial mound built up by the accumulation of occupational debris.

theophoric: A name bearing a divine element. It contains a divine name as its principal component.

tumulus, tumuli (plural): Artificial mound of earth covering an ancient tomb.

typology: Systematic classification of objects.

volute: Derived from the Latin root "to roll"; spiral or scroll-shaped form of an Ionic or Aeolic capital.

wadi (Arabic), **naḥal** (Hebrew): Streambed that is dry except in the rainy season.

Selected Bibliography

Chapter 1:   Jeremiah: The Prophet and the Book

Carroll, R. *Jeremiah, A Commentary*. Old Testament Library. Philadelphia: Westminster Press, 1986.

Holladay, W. *A Commentary on the Book of the Prophet Jeremiah, Chapters 1–25*.
Hermeneia. Philadelphia: Fortress Press, 1986; and idem, *Chapters 26–52*, Minneapolis: Fortress Press, 1989.

Chapter 2:   Historical Background

Kitchen, K. *The Third Intermediate Period in Egypt, 1100–650 B.C.* 2nd ed. Warmin-
ster, Eng.: Aris & Phillips, 1986.

Malamat, A. "The Twilight of Judah: In the Egyptian-Babylonian Maelstrom." In
Supplements to Vetus Testamentum, no. 28, edited by G. Anderson et al. Leiden:
E. J. Brill, 1975. Pp. 123–145.

Na'aman, N. "The Kingdom of Judah Under Josiah." *TA* 18/1 (1991): 3–71.

Wiseman, D. *Chronicles of the Chaldaean Kings (626–556 B.C.) in the British Museum*.
London: British Museum, 1956; and idem, *Nebuchadrezzar and Babylon*. Schweich
Lectures. Oxford: Oxford University Press, 1985.

Chapter 3:   Geographical Setting

Aharoni, Y. *The Land of the Bible: A Historical Geography*. Philadelphia: Westminster
Press, 1979.

Kallai, Z. *Historical Geography of the Bible*. Jerusalem: Magnes Press, 1986.

Miller, J. M., ed. *Archaeological Survey of the Kerak Plateau*. Atlanta: Scholars Press, 1991.

Sauer, J. "Transjordan in the Bronze and Iron Ages: A Critique of Glueck's Synthesis." *BASOR* 263 (1986): 1–26.

Chapter 4:   Edom and Judah

Bartlett, J. *Edom and the Edomites*. JSOT/PEF Monograph Series. Sheffield: Sheffield Academic Press, 1989.

Beit-Arieh, I. "New Data on the Relationship Between Judah and Edom Toward the End of the Iron Age." In *Recent Excavations in Israel: Studies in Iron Age Archaeology*, AASOR, vol. 49, edited by S. Gitin and W. Dever. Winona Lake, Ind.: Eisenbrauns, 1989. Pp. 125–131.

MacDonald, B., et al. *The Wadi el Hasa Archaeological Survey 1979–1983, West-Central Jordan*. Waterloo: Wilfrid Laurier University Press, 1988.

Mazar, E. "Edomite Pottery at the End of the Iron Age." *IEJ* 35 (1985): 253–269.

Pratico, G. "Nelson Glueck's 1938–1940 Excavations at Tell el-Kheleifeh: A Reappraisal." *BASOR* 259 (1985): 1–32.

Chapter 5:   Cities of Judah

Avigad, N. *Discovering Jerusalem: Recent Archaeological Excavations in the Upper City*. Nashville: Thomas Nelson, 1983.

Bahat, D. *The Illustrated Atlas of Jerusalem*. New York: Simon & Schuster, 1990.

Bliss, F., and R. A. S. Macalister. *Excavations in Palestine During the Years 1898–1900*. London: PEF, 1902.

Shiloh, Y. *Excavations at the City of David*. Qedem, no. 19. Jerusalem: Hebrew University, 1984.

Ussishkin, D. "Excavations at Tel Lachish 1973–1977: Preliminary Report." *TA* 5/1 and 2 (1978): 1–97; and idem, "Excavations at Tel Lachish 1978–1983: Second Preliminary Report." *TA* 10/2 (1983): 97–175.

Chapter 6:   Inscriptions and Literacy

Avigad, N. *Hebrew Bullae from the Time of Jeremiah*. Jerusalem: IES, 1986.

——. "The Contribution of Hebrew Seals to an Understanding of Israelite Religion and Society." In *Ancient Israelite Religion: Essays in Honor of Frank Moore Cross*, edited by P. Miller, Jr., P. Hanson, and S. D. McBride. Philadelphia: Fortress Press, 1987. Pp. 195–208.

Shiloh, Y. "A Group of Hebrew Bullae from the City of David." *IEJ* 36 (1986): 16–38.

Chapter 7:   Worship and Architecture

Aharoni, Y. "Excavations at Ramat Raḥel." *BA* 24 (1961): 98–118.

de Vaux, R. *Ancient Israel: Its Life and Institutions*. New York: McGraw-Hill Book Co., 1961.

Chapter 8:   Funerary Customs and Mourning

Barkay, G. *Ketef Hinnom. A Treasure Facing Jerusalem's Walls*, Catalogue No. 274. Jerusalem: Israel Museum, 1986.

Barkay, G., and A. Kloner. "Jerusalem Tombs from the Days of the First Temple." *BAR* 12/2 (1986): 22–39.

Stager, L., and S. Wolff. "Child Sacrifice at Carthage—Religious Rite or Population Control?" *BAR* 10/1 (1984): 30–51.
Ussishkin, D. "The Necropolis from the Time of the Kingdom of Judah at Silwan, Jerusalem." *BA* 33/2 (1970): 34–46.

Chapter 9: Agriculture

Borowski, O. *Agriculture in Iron Age Israel.* Winona Lake, Ind.: Eisenbrauns, 1987.
Zohary, M. *Plants of the Bible.* Cambridge: Cambridge University Press, 1982.

Chapter 10: Crafts

Johnston, R. "The Biblical Potter." *BA* 37/4 (1974): 86–106.
Kelso, J. "The Ceramic Vocabulary of the Old Testament." *BASOR* Supplementary Studies, nos. 5–6. New Haven: ASOR, 1948.
Stager, L. "The Archaeology of the Family in Ancient Israel." *BASOR* 260 (1985): 1–35.
Waldbaum, J. *From Bronze to Iron: The Transition from the Bronze Age to the Iron Age in the Eastern Mediterranean.* Studies in Mediterranean Archaeology, no. 54. Göteborg: Paul Aströms Förlag, 1978.

Index of Subjects and Names

Index of Authors